DEAD END:
THE AUTOMOBILE IN MASS TRANSPORTATION

DEAD END:

THE
AUTOMOBILE
IN
MASS
TRANSPORTATION

RONALD A. BUEL

PRENTICE-HALL, INC.
Englewood Cliffs, N. J.

Dead End: The Automobile in Mass Transportation
By Ronald A. Buel
Copyright © 1972 by Ronald A. Buel
All rights reserved. No part of this book may be
reproduced in any form or by any means, except for
the inclusion of brief quotations in a review, without
permission in writing from the publisher.
ISBN: 0-13-196980-3
Library of Congress Catalog Card Number: 75-175808
Printed in the United States of America *T*
Prentice-Hall International, Inc., London
Prentice-Hall of Australia, Pty. Ltd., North Sydney
Prentice-Hall of Canada, Ltd., Toronto
Prentice-Hall of India Private Ltd., New Delhi
Prentice-Hall of Japan, Inc., Tokyo

Acknowledgment is gratefully expressed for
permission to quote from the following:

"All Along the Watchtower," copyright © 1968
Dwarf Music. Used by permission of Dwarf Music.

Living-Room War by Michael J. Arlen, copyright
© 1967 by Michael J. Arlen. All rights reserved.
Reprinted by permission of The Viking Press, Inc.

Unsafe at Any Speed by Ralph Nader, copyright ©
1965 by Ralph Nader. All rights reserved.
Reprinted by permission of Grossman Publishers.

The View From the Road, by Donald Appleyard,
Kevin Lynch and John R. Meyer, M.I.T. Press,
copyright 1964.

CONTENTS

CHAPTER 1 INTRODUCTION AND OVERVIEW

In these times, social criticism that builds on an already existing base of analysis is badly needed. This book aims at no synthesis of a critique of the American society, at no new philosophy, at no new ideological stance. Instead, it aims to take a small but important part of America—its transportation system, and even more specifically, its urban transportation network—and to put this small piece in the political and social context of what ails us as a people. It aims to call to your attention some relevant information of political, social, and economic nature; to relate what has recently been happening to the U.S. urban transportation network to a broader social analysis; and thereby, to look at what everyone believes to be a problem—moving people and things about in urban areas—and to try to state exactly what the problem is and what remedies might exist, and further, how those remedies might be taken within the existing democratic framework.

> "There must be some way out of here,"
> Said the joker to the thief.
> "There's too much confusion,
> I can't get no relief.
> Businessmen they drink my wine.
> Plowmen dig my earth.
> None of them along the line
> Know what any of it is worth."

"No reason to get excited,"
  the thief he kindly spoke.
"There are many here among us
Who feel that life is but a joke.
But, you and I, we've been through that,
And this is not our fate.
So let us not talk falsely now,
The hour is getting late." [1]

Let's talk first about how falsely discussion of the "urban transportation problem" is carried on in the press, in college textbooks, in magazines, and trade journals. The most common description of "the problem" is congestion. Says George M. Smerk in his archetypical textbook, *Urban Transportation: The Federal Role*, "The urban transportation problem is universally understood to be congestion, or simply too many vehicles trying to pass through the same place at the same time."

Mr. Smerk adds, "The effects of this predicament are first suffered, of course, by the old central cities which lie at the heart of metropolitan areas. As crowded, slow, nerve-wracking, and expensive travel conditions add to the burdens of life, citizens endeavor to escape the congestion problem by seeking pleasanter business and living conditions in outlying areas." He later paraphrases Lewis Mumford, saying that, "Rapid industrialization and rapid urbanization has crowded cities and forced over-utilization of facilities, with the inevitable accompanying destruction or near sterilization of the amenities that normally tend to make concentrated urban living vital and attractive."

Talk of "congestion," "overcrowdedness," and "lack of amenities," and the choices people make to escape these conditions is factually inaccurate at its base. In reality, travel in most U.S. cities is speedier than ever (although there is more travel going on than ever because cities have spread out more). As John Meyer points out in an article in *The Metropolitan Enigma*,[2] the average time spent on freeways for the same trip (and 82 percent of U.S. urban commuting is done by auto) has been going down. What exists is a "failure of anticipations," Mr. Meyer points out; people drive urban freeways in off-peak hours and see how fast they can go and then expect freeways to work the same way at the rush hour.

It is just as inaccurate to say that "overcrowdedness" is the cause of the flight to the suburbs. Too high densities do occur in the ghettos, to be sure—but people are not escaping to the suburbs from our ghettos. In fact, as Jane Jacobs, the well-known urban anthropologist, has conclusively demonstrated, urban neighborhoods that disintegrate do so at least in part because *they are not dense enough* to provide the "street life," the variety, and intensity of use that gives neighborhoods vitality and zing and makes them places people want to stay in.

There are many more equally irrelevant descriptions of the urban transportation problem. Propagandists for the Automobile Manufacturers Association are always talking about how the private automobile is more flexible, more convenient, and a "superior" form of transportation to such "socialistic" forms of transportation as taxis, buses, streetcars, and rail rapid transit. Propagandists for transit point out how efficient rail rapid transit is because it moves thousands more people per hour than a freeway. But, in fact, each mode does what it is designed to do, and our technology is flexible.

Economists are prone to point out that their studies show mass transit (where it exists) is generally a less expensive way to commute than the automobile, but that most commuters now choose to travel by auto, even if it is more expensive, because it usually saves time or because they prefer its "luxury." Yet, it somehow seems to escape the people making these preference surveys that the answers they are getting are almost completely conditioned by what the larger social entity (consciously or unconsciously) decides is preferable. That is, if the government, be it federal, state, or local, decides to provide a magnificently all-encompassing road system, people will prefer the auto. Or, if the government puts its funds into a fine transit system that operates frequently and rapidly at low cost to the traveler, people will prefer transit to a higher degree.

The point is not simply that the common modes of talking about the so-called "urban transportation problem" are inaccurate and irrelevant. Our society refuses to recognize that its

nature is to divert attention away from the basic and fundamental problems by inventing a language and a one-dimensional
way of looking at subjects without touching upon the realities
of these fundamental problems. Public discussion consists of a
reflection of commonly held images, but little or no *dissection*
of what is really happening and why.

All of us should at least be able to describe what we see and
how we feel about what we see. It is not as if there is no
precedent for such description, and for some honest dissection
of the problems such description presents us with. It has been a
decade now since people like John Keats, Jane Jacobs, Lewis
Mumford, and Paul Goodman began demonstrating to us the
consequences of our transportation system and its inter-related-
ness to other problems of our society.

The importance of violence in American history is currently a
popular subject. We are a violent people. There is no doubt
about that. The war in Vietnam and our soaring crime rate are
only more recent examples of our society's inclination toward
violence. The auto falls solidly within this tradition. It keeps
people from treating other people as human beings. One thinks
of passing the car in front of you, or beating the other car to a
parking place, instead of passing the *person* in the car or
fighting the *person* for a parking place. The auto prevents casual
contact with others unlike oneself. And because we don't
understand the humanity of others, there are fewer limits to our
aggressive tendencies. Attitudes of persons behind the wheel of
an auto are closely related to other, more violent attitudes.

It is not enough to talk about the 50,000-plus people we kill
on our highways every year, or the hospitals which we fill up
with millions of injuries per year. We ought to think about our
individual attitudes when we are driving, the general lack of
courtesy (so evident when you want to make a left turn against
the flow of traffic, for example). The nervousness, the hurry-
hurry at all costs, the frustration with those not in quite as
much of a hurry. All these attitudes are closely related to
violence, I suspect. We ought to do some serious thinking about
why people stop, gawk, and gape at the scene of an accident.
An extremely common occurrence on Los Angeles freeways is

for an accident to have occurred, the wrecked auto or autos to be off on the side of the road, out of the way of traffic, and yet traffic is at an almost dead standstill at the site because of this "gawkers' knot" as the L.A. radio disc jockeys have come to call it.

And we ought to think not only about how callous Detroit has been in manufacturing unsafe automobiles, but about how poorly local governments have organized to help people injured in traffic accidents. We are, I repeat, a violent people, a people accustomed to violence as a way of life, and the automobile plays a part in keeping us that way.

The cult of the auto among American youth, with its pinstriping, souping-up, lowered and raked looks, so beautifully described by Tom Wolfe in his *Kandy-Kolored Tangerine-Flake Streamline Baby*, is not any weird aberration. It stems logically from the adult attitude toward autos. They position you and give you status with your peers. And they are symbols of sex, wealth, and power. Detroit understands this very well, of course. That is why we have style changes every year, a huge number of alternative models to choose from, and "hot" convertibles in showroom windows.

For the teen-ager, the auto can be more than a sex symbol, of course. It can enable sex. The drive-in movie theater and its role in the adolescent world can be seen as a statement about the importance of the auto in maintaining America's hypocrisy about sex. Without the automobile for teen-agers to escape in and hide in while investigating sex, America might have to confront sex in a much more open and healthy manner. This hypocrisy reaches its zenith in hassles over co-educational visiting privileges in our college dormitories. Administrators oppose such privileges while fully aware that college policies leave untouched what goes on in parked cars.

The other day I took a trip with a businessman in his expensive Lincoln. He proudly stated that he had worked all his life to own a car like that. And it did have a chronometer (clock), a stereo FM radio (which by the nature of FM works mostly when the car is parked), and a series of fancy dials on its dashboard. However, trying to speak objectively, the two-hour trip, which I had taken many times, differed very little from the times I had made it in my five-year-old Volkswagen. His back seat had little more room than mine did; the time it took was similar because of speed limits; and the auto did not magically transform the straight, dull freeway we were traversing into a pleasant place to be. Now, I know this man is not capable of repairing his Lincoln if it has trouble. He did not make the car himself, and he has a relationship to his auto similar to that of almost all car-owners. It "positions" him with those who know him. It is a device of emulation and imitation, an expression of his "standard of living," or his "life-style," in this way no different from Tom Wolfe's *Kandy-Kolored Tangerine-Flake Streamline Baby* is for the teen-ager who owns it.

We junk seven million of these automobiles a year, more automobiles than exist in all of Soviet Russia. We junk them because they are designed to be junked, styled to be obsolete, built to fall apart, advertised to be out of fashion. Let us imagine what would happen if people started to keep their cars longer, say seven or eight years instead of buying a new car every three years. Suddenly Detroit wouldn't be able to sell nine million automobiles a year and our economy would feel serious repercussions. On such principles as being "out of style" do we build the soundness of our economy. Meanwhile, derelict autos left by their owners on city streets are becoming a serious problem for local governments. And everywhere stacks of junked autos pollute the landscape. Recycling is insignificant at this date. The biggest product of our economy is sheer waste.

It seems clear enough that most people don't like their work these days. They seek shorter work days, longer vacations. They try to escape their work whenever possible. They live away from it, and do not bring it into their homes. This is generally as true of the white-collar executive as the unskilled laborer. It takes no magnificent powers of observation to see this all about you. Elinor Langer, in two articles on this subject in the *New York Review of Books*,[3] feels it necessary to mention "bureaucratization," "alienation," "exploitation," and the "false consciousness" of the workers in embracing their "oppressors." But whether or not you wish to deal in her terms, you cannot deny her observations. Consumerism, a high "standard of living," is the reason the women of New York Bell work, she states. She supports this statement, for example, by the simple fact of what the female clerks talk about. "Their leisure time is filled, first of all, with the discussion of objects. Talk of shopping is endless, as is the pursuit of it in lunch hours, after work, and on days off."

Miss Langer cites "the deadening nature of the work; the low pay ... the malfunctioning of the company; the pressure of supervision and observation," as problems the women face. But perhaps more important than any of these matters is the end product of the work and how the worker relates to it. Men and women have a basic need for work that is meaningful and of true worth. When less than one-tenth of our economy is needed to produce subsistence for all of our people, the use made of the non-subsistence goods our society produces becomes all-important. When so much of our work produces goods that have as their principal use the fulfillment of someone's desire to imitate and emulate others, men quickly understand that the work they are engaged in has little intrinsic worth or meaning.

The automobile has become the very symbol, the epitome of our leisure culture, our consumerism, our unnecessary affluence. Therefore, an article by Judson Gooding in the August, 1970, issue of *Fortune* magazine isn't too surprising when it states, "The deep dislike of the job and the desire to escape become terribly clear twice each day when shifts end and the men stampede out of the plant gates to the parking lots, where they sometimes actually endanger their lives in their desperate haste to be gone ... An average of 5 percent of GM's (General Motors') hourly workers are missing from work without explanation every day ... On some days, notably Mondays and Fridays, the figure goes as high as 10 percent. Tardiness has increased, making it even more difficult to start up the production line when a shift begins. ..."

How can men take pride or feel that there is any real worth in work in an auto plant? As Nicholas Von Hoffman wrote in an article for the Los Angeles *Times*-Washington *Post* News Service, "An automobile worker once had reason to be proud of what came off that assembly line; the car was the symbol of the American social genius. Now it's the sign of our idiocy. That car, even if it's well made, is a piece of polluting junk.

" 'Nothing works anymore; the country's falling apart,' people say as they push the buttons for the automated services and get nothing but smoking transistors. The reasons assigned are metaphysical—doomsday talk, radical activity, conspiracies, but the truth is probably far less grandiose. For a quarter of a century we've abused and used our social and economic systems while we've debauched ourselves in consumerism at home and adventurism abroad. Now we must stop, think and rebuild."

It is not simply the production-line job or that of a clerk with the telephone company that falls prey to judgments about its worth by the people doing it. Throughout the auto industry it is obvious that employees are not motivated by a sense that what they are doing is worthwhile or of value.

The American people are absolutely unique in their affluence. It is unparalleled since the beginning of man. We have developed our technology to a state never before equaled by any people. But to what end? As many social critics have pointed out, our modern technology baffles people and makes them afraid to innovate. As Paul Goodman has said, "Technology is a sacred cow left strictly to (unknown) experts, as if the form of the industrial machine did not profoundly affect every person; and people are remarkably superstitious about it. . . . They imagine, as an article of faith, that big factories must be more efficient than small ones; it does not occur to them, for instance, that it is cheaper to haul machined parts than to transport workmen.

"Indeed, they are outraged by the good-humored demonstrations of Borsodi that, in hours and minutes of labor, it is probably cheaper to grow and can your own tomatoes than to buy them at the supermarket, not to speak of the quality. Here once again we have the inevitable irony of history; industry, invention, scientific method have opened new opportunities but just at the moment of opportunity, people have become ignorant by specialization and superstitious of science and technology, so that they no longer know what they want, nor do they dare to command it . . . Where the user understands nothing and cannot evaluate his tools, you can sell him anything. It is the user, said Plato, who ought to be the judge of the chariot. Since he is not, he must abdicate to the values of engineers, who are craft-idiots, or—God save us!—to the values of salesmen. Insecure as to use and value, the buyer clings to the autistic security of conformity and emulation, and he can no longer dare to ask whether there is a relation between his Standard of Living and the satisfactoriness of life."[4]

Who is served by our auto-highway transport system? America, with all its affluence, continues to have a large minority of poverty-stricken peoples. And the automobile-highway system exacerbates their problems, because to a large degree, they are not served by it. More than half of all families with incomes under $4,000 and fully half of all Negro households own no autos. Some 55 percent of all black families have two or more wage earners, but only 10 percent have two cars. And our rapid transit, where it exists in large enough scale to complement the automobile, is more and more designed largely to serve trips from the suburbs to downtown, while, increasingly, the black man and other central city poor want to go in the other direction. And any meaningful discussion of the auto can't leave unmentioned the systematic victimizing of poor people that occurs at the hands of auto dealers, finance agencies, and collection agencies, to say nothing of the policies of auto insurance companies and the justice the poor get in court on these matters. In addition, designs for new rapid transit systems in this country—those that have recently been voted down, as well as those not yet to be proposed to the public for financing —call almost entirely for a reinforcement of suburb to downtown corridors. These plans are concerned largely with serving those who are already served, with improving the condition of the affluent, and seem little concerned about the infirm, the aged, the poor, who are not presently served.

There is also the question of environment. When it comes to the auto and mass transit, this question is often seen in quite narrow terms. Most public discussion touches on the fantastic air pollution caused by the auto, a serious enough problem all right. Often mentioned is the damage done to cityscape and countryside by massive freeways. One does not wish to deemphasize the importance of these problems, but they are only a small portion of the environmental difficulty that we reap from our current transport system. In terms of natural environment, we must ask about the simple loss of land, be it farmland or open space, or whatever. Each mile of four-lane freeway takes 17.4 acres of land. (There is, of course, an economic debate here. Those who favor highways state that the economic cost of taking land out of more productive economic use [and off the tax rolls, too] is offset by the increase in the value of the land that results from access provided by the highway. There is no doubt that our transportation system is what enables our economy to function at its current level. But land has historically been the primary basis for wealth, and there is sound reason for this—good land is in short supply. Thus, while our economy may "thrive" as a result of our extensive transportation system, what the economy produces is often unrelated to the satisfactoriness of life. And the land that goes out of use is sometimes irreplaceable. An example is the loss of 150,000 acres of prime farmland in San Jose, California, to suburban sprawl, almost directly as a result of highway construction. The ability of that land to produce fine pears, prunes, and other fruits is unduplicated anywhere in North America.)

Highways also provide access to areas that perhaps should not have such easy access—areas that have been damaged as wilderness areas because of the auto (one thinks immediately of Yosemite National Park, for example). It is not simply a matter of how many people use such areas, but also how the auto conditions the use.

The energy source of the automobile, the oil industry, also has its environmental problems. The offshore wells at Santa Barbara and in the Gulf Coast and their befouling of unique ocean life and areas of natural scenic beauty are but one example.

The loss of regional cultural diversity in the United States is another type of environmental loss we suffer from the auto system. It is now possible to drive from New York to Los Angeles eating entirely in franchised restaurant chains that serve exactly similar hamburgers. And we are all poorer for being able to do so.

Exactly what effect do highways and the automobile have on how people relate to one another in our cities? That is, do they affect the way our cities work as cities, the variety they have, how interesting or how civilized they are? Most architects and planners tend to pose the question of the auto's relation to the city in terms of loss of "amenity." There is much evidence, to be sure, that the aesthetic appearance of urban areas has some effect on the more fundamental urban problem of how people relate to one another. Whether or not cities are dominated by parks and pleasing vistas as opposed to ugly freeways and parking lots *must* have *some* effect. But there have also been very attractive urban settings which contained disastrously sick societies. And ugly urban settings that contained healthy and vital neighborhoods. It has been left to people like Jane Jacobs, not a professional planner or architect, to begin to describe how the form of cities affects their function. And she has given us some solid principles that have little to do with "amenity." She described what a vital urban neighborhood, one with variety and street life and many casual contacts among neighbors, is like; how such a neighborhood is not only a pleasant place to live, but helps in keeping streets "safe," in raising children, and in providing an education for its inhabitants. Then she analyzes the qualities of these vital neighborhoods as she finds them. The requirements she postulates are surprising indeed, but make eminently good sense. There must be, she tells us, a mix of primary uses of the neighborhood—commercial, residential, and industrial—so that people come and go at all hours and the streets are used actively. There must be enough old buildings so there can be a flexibility of use and a variety of economic activity, shops, and industries both big and small. There must be short blocks so that there can be a varied pattern of street usage, so that intermingling of neighbors is encouraged, so that the opportunity for wide casual contacts is increased. And there must be high residential density, a concentration of people (as opposed to overcrowding, which is not the same thing), so that there can be diversity and richness, so that cultural assets and small shops, which cannot flourish in sparsely populated areas, will have adequate patronage. She says that, "people gathered in concentrations of city size and density can be considered a positive good, in the faith that they are desirable because they are the source of immense vitality, and because they do represent, in small geographic compass, a great and exuberant richness of differences and possibilities, many of these differences unique and unpredictable and all the more valuable because they are."

It should be immediately obvious that heavy use of the automobile works against all four of these factors needed for a vital city neighborhood. Short blocks serve people, long blocks the auto. Mixes of primary neighborhood uses cause heavy auto congestion if most people drive. The auto is what encourages us to spread out so, decreasing residential densities. And the highway is a major destroyer of old buildings. In Mrs. Jacobs's book, *The Death and Life of Great American Cities*, she devotes an entire chapter to the destructive force of the automobile. Correctly, she does not blame it for the death of our cities, but merely points out that a series of wrong decisions about cities (see principles above) will be complicated and worsened by the automobile's presence. As she says, ". . . one of two processes occurs: erosion of cities by automobiles, or attrition of automobiles by cities." She described the process of erosion: ". . . a street is widened here, another is straightened there, a wide avenue is converted to one-way flow, staggered-signal systems are installed for faster movement, a bridge is double-decked as its capacity is reached, an expressway is cut through yonder, and finally whole webs of expressways." As she adds, no one step in this process is crucial, but a system of "positive feedback" is set up "in which each action produces a reaction which in turn intensifies the condition responsible for the first action," and so on, *ad infinitum*. This latter point is a very important one, for it is just because of this "positive feedback" that Jane Jacobs rightly calls for a strategy of attrition of autos. Such a strategy does not consist merely of building mass transit, for because of the "positive feedback" involved in the use of the auto, even new mass transit systems will wither and die unless they are accompanied, not by actions that make it easier to move autos (such as new freeways and parking lots) but by actions that make it *more difficult* to move autos. Building mazes of streets where autos ought not to pass, narrowing streets, shortening signal times, giving over freeway lanes to busses, taking actions that *cause* congestion rather than lessen it, even though this is uneconomic in conventional thought, are some possible actions.

It is important to be specific not only about what is good about the type of urban neighborhoods that Jane Jacobs wishes to see multiply, but also about what is wrong with their opposites—the auto-created suburbs. The 1970 census figures show that, for the first time in the nation's history, more people live in suburbs than in central cities. The suburbs, of course, are a product, at least in part, of people's desire to separate their homes from their work, to escape their work as much as possible. People talk about having lawns and space, but most suburbanites consider their lawns a chore, not a pleasure. People seek privacy and security in the suburbs and find, instead, virtual isolation from chance encounters with other different human beings. The suburban style of life extends the desire to imitate and emulate to its logical end.

In addition to these factors, also to be considered is the destruction of prime farmland, the willful elimination of badly needed open spaces near population centers, and the bland neon-and-plastic strip cities that result from unplanned sprawl. Further, there are incalculable economic costs from suburbs and the way they grow. Consider only two—the amount of time urban sprawl adds to travel between home, work, shopping, and school, and the cost of extending public services and utilities such as water, electricity, and sewers to housing tracts far beyond the city.

Even more significant is the impact of the suburban life style on the family. Many children are raised without knowing what their father does "at the office" or "at the plant." They do not have male models of competence. They are raised almost entirely by their mothers. Children growing up on city streets are often under watchful adult eyes. Not so in the suburbs. It is obvious to suburban children that their fathers wish to escape work. I am willing to state categorically that vital city neighborhoods in which commerce is present and men's work is apparent are better places to raise children, to teach them to live in harmony with other humans, to give them an understanding of vocation, of making one's life mean something beyond the confines of the material values of our acquisitive American homelife.

Talk of such suburban shortcomings raises the question of new transit technology and its ability to solve these problems. In considering transportation technology, the question of "efficiency" is highly relevant. Large automobiles and railroad trains obviously require considerable amounts of weight and energy to move a small number of people. The high ratio of bulk and energy required, compared to the number of persons moved, is truly inefficient. One must also remember to put the efficiency of different modes of transportation within existing systems. That is, how well a rapid transit train works for its users may depend on how long they have to wait for it at the station, or how far they have to walk to get to the station. Likewise, an automobile's efficiency can just as easily be determined by the time required to fill it up with gas, to get it out of the garage, or to find a parking place. There are also the larger measurements of efficiency of the whole systems. In his book, *The Highway and the City*, Lewis Mumford points out that the present goals of highway engineers are not related to "the essential purpose of transportation, which is to bring people or goods to places where they are needed, and to concentrate the greatest variety of goods and people within a limited area, in order to widen the possibility of choice without making it necessary to travel."

"A good transportation system," he says, "minimizes unnecessary transportation." Paul Goodman makes a related point in *Communitas*. He says that, "It is almost always cheaper to transport material than men." He points out, "If the plant is concentrated the bulk of workers must live away and commute. If the plant were scattered, the workers could live near their jobs, and it is the processed materials that would have to be collected for assembly from their several places of manufacture

. . . The living men must be transported twice daily; the material and mechanical parts at much longer intervals . . . The time of life of a piece of steel is not consumed while it waits for its truck: a piece of steel has no feelings. Supply trucks move at a convenient hour, but the fleet of trams and busses congest traffic at 8-9 A.M. and at 4-5 P.M. . . . (To the extent, and whatever, factories become automatic, the conclusion does not follow, for the chief expense is then in the automatic machines, which do not commute. Nor does it follow in the extractive and metallurgical industries, where the raw materials and the parts are very bulky, or the site is determined by nature.)"⁵

But the most important point to be made about the technology of transportation is that while efficiency, at all the levels we have been discussing it, is important and surprisingly little considered, the technology must always answer to a larger question than efficiency—What are the ends?

Goodman says that we have confused our means and our ends. "The means are too unwieldy for us, so our ends are confused. . . ." He proposes that we must begin again to ask ethical questions of our machines, our streets, our cars, our towns. "Is the *function* good? Bona fide? Is it worthwhile? Is it worthy of a man to do that? What are the consequences? Is it compatible with other basic, human functions? Is it a forthright or at least ingenious part of life? Does it make sense?"

We should all aspire toward this sort of questioning of our economy and system. Is it necessary that a democratic, capitalistic, free enterprise society produce confusion about means and ends? Has our capitalistic system doomed us to being forever unable to do anything with the answers we get to Goodman's questions? One might argue that this seeming inability is a logical extension of a system that makes so many of its decisions with the single yardstick of private profits. For profits seldom seem to have a direct or causal relationship with the ends that Goodman suggests. But this doesn't answer the question of necessity. Is it *necessary* that capitalism produce the foolishness, the inequities that ours does? It seems to me that it isn't. It seems to me that our technology is indeed flexible. But the question in a democracy is always whether or not enough people can be made to see the alternatives. We must be realistic, too, about the forces that are waged against change, even if they are in the minority. The forces are enormous and they are at the base of our deepening depression, our growing alienation, our feeling that the problems are insoluble. Looking at our urban transportation problems, it is clear that change must occur at national, state, and local levels, and that at each level there are different types of forces waged against change. There is a well-known highway-auto-oil lobby at the federal level. There are state highway departments, highway contractors and suppliers, truckers, auto dealers, auto clubs, auto insurers, real estate interests, and chambers of commerce. This list of people with an economic stake in maintaining the status quo regarding urban transportation goes on and on. Their tactics are often direct and open, but they can also be covert and unethical, and this needs to be documented and understood.

The times they *are* a-changing. People are beginning to be concerned with our basic directions. There is much talk about "the system." There are meaningful shifts in public attitudes toward "morals." There is increasing openness among the young. There is a re-awakened interest in communes and utopias. The last decade has seen a large portion of American youth seriously question our materialistic values and our rigid attitudes about such ideologies as communism and socialism. With our youth waking up to America's flaws, a process that has been immeasurably speeded by the draft and the Vietnam war, those of us who believe in the desirability of a democratic system with a maximum amount of freedom for individual, independent activity are obligated to prove that it can regenerate itself, that it can begin to use its power, its awesome technology, in the attainment of worthy, humane, and reasonable ends. If we cannot prove this ability to regenerate our system, and prove it in short order, the revolutionaries have us where they want us, and rightly so. This seems to me to be more than rhetoric. It is the essential question of the next decade. And it will be decided one way or the other. American youth is verbalizing the issue now, and where there is smoke there is fire.

NOTES

[1]"All Along the Watchtower," Bob Dylan, Copyright Dwarf Music, 1968.

[2]John R. Meyer, "Urban Transportation," *The Metropolitan Enigma*, Anchor Books, pp. 50-51.

[3]Elinor Langer, "The Women of the Telephone Company," *New York Review of Books* (March 12, 1970), p. 16; (March 26, 1970), p. 14.

[4]Paul and Percival Goodman, *Communitas*, Vintage Books, Random House, p. 13.

[5]*Ibid*, p. 83.

CHAPTER **2** THE
AUTOMOBILE
AND OUR
ECONOMY

The starting point for any analysis of the impact of our urban transportation system on our society ought to be its sheer *size*.

First, there is the size of the total auto-highway-petroleum complex. The industry that serves our space and defense business in the United States, typically called the military-industrial complex, is popularly considered huge. But the automotive "family of industries" and its direct relatives make about one-fourth again as large a contribution to our Gross National Product—a contribution of more than $100 billion per year, more than one-tenth of our total GNP, and about half of this business is the production of the auto itself.

The automotive industry is not only large, but widespread. Sales of autos and trucks run over $60 billion at retail every year now, and gasoline, tires, and accessories add another $30 billion at retail. The products are serviced and sold at over 500,000 locations. The manufacture of the auto is hardly as concentrated as generally assumed. Less than 35 percent of the passenger car assemblies take place in Michigan. The next five states—Missouri, California, Ohio, Wisconsin, and New Jersey, together exceed the output in Michigan. An additional twelve states have at least one percent of the production.

Concentration exists, instead, in terms of the number of major auto producers—four. General Motors, all by itself, has had corporate revenues or sales of over $20 billion per year

($22.8 billion in 1968, for example, when a record 9.6 million passenger cars were sold by the industry.) GM's revenues equal receipts of our three million smallest farms, or 90 percent of all our farms. General Motors, Ford, and Chrysler employ 1.4 million people, and in recent years have ranked as high as first, third, and fifth in the *Fortune* listing of the largest corporations (American Motors has lately been in the top 150.)

Size is the leading characteristic, in fact, of all modern corporate enterprise. The 50 largest corporations have one-third of all manufacturing assets and the 500 largest have more than two-thirds. By the end of 1968, *Fortune's* "500" employed 687 out of every 1,000 Americans working for industrial corporations. As *Fortune* said then, "The 500's share of U.S. business got bigger than ever last year. Their sales reached almost 64 percent of total U.S. industrial sales ... And their proportion of the profit hit 74.4 percent."[1] Furthermore, the top 50 now have nearly half of the sales and profits of the 500.

The ramifications of the size of the organizations within our industrial system are enormous. I have already quoted Paul Goodman to the effect that size does not necessarily lead to efficiency. But *at the present technological level of our industrial system*, large size *is* nearly unavoidable.

All important corporate decisions must now draw on information possessed by a number of specialists. As Galbraith puts it, "a man of moderate genius could, quite conceivably, provide himself with the knowledge of the various branches of metallurgy and chemistry and of engineering, procurement, production, management, quality control, labor relations, styling, and merchandising which are involved in the development of a modern motor car. But even moderate genius is in unpredictable supply."[2] And with the huge amounts of capital and labor associated with modern corporate effort, risk must be minimized, so planning must be extensive, and this requires again that there be variously informed specialists who can obtain and work with the requisite information concerning supply of labor and materials, market persuasion, and planning and the flow of information, for example.

In short, one of the requirements of this size, which comes from the complexity of our technology and the large requirements of time and capital involved in such technology, is group planning. Because of the depth of specialization of the members of the corporation who are involved in this group planning, a decision made by a group usually cannot safely be over-ruled by an individual, because he cannot possess all the information on which the decision was made.

Largely because of this group planning, but also because of an abundance of capital in our society—that is, an abundance of money the holders of which wish to invest in industry—the group of people who bring specialized knowledge, talent, or experience to group decision-making now possess most of the power in industry. Galbraith calls this group the technostructure. He debunks the popular opinion that the owners of companies, even the large stockholders, really control corporations anymore. He says they can now always be replaced by others who wish to invest in the organization and who will have the money to do so because of the abundance of capital. And owners can never have the depth of specialized knowledge required to make the important decisions. That knowledge is what is in short supply and it belongs to the technostructure. It provides power.

Galbraith also draws several other conclusions, all of which I found valid in covering industry for the *Wall Street Journal* for four years. Most surprisingly, he declares that the major goals of the technostructure, and thus of industry, don't include the desire to maximize profits—for the rewards of doing so fall largely into the hands of the owners of industry, not the technostructure. Instead, the technostructure first wishes to be secure and autonomous, in order to increase its power. To do this, the corporation must, to be sure, realize a minimal rate of profits or return, because if it starts to lose money, others outside the technostructure will feel free to intercede and interfere. But, more importantly, it wishes to grow by expanding its output. Expansion means money and promotions for those in the technostructure and this gives security, because it avoids contraction (or loss of jobs). This modern industrial growth usually comes through minor (not major) technological advance or innovation. The technostructure thus desires "growth" and "progress," probably our two most widely-accepted social goals in the United States.

The problem with all this is the tendency of this industrial system to become monolithic. The members of these organizations tend to substitute the organization's goals for their own, as they see power lies with the group. They also see advantage in exchanging pursuit of their own personal goals for a much smaller influence on the greater power of the organization.

While the corporation is thus bending its employees to its goals, it also is making government work for it. Government makes sure that people can afford the goods that industry produces, by regulating aggregate demand. It accomplishes this regulation through its level of expenditures, and through the corporate and personal income taxes that increase as income increases, thus curtailing demand, and fall as income falls, thus releasing spending to support demand. In addition, government purchases substantial amounts of industrial goods and implements policies that assist industry, such as import quotas and government price-fixing that exists in the oil industry (see Chapter 6). All this, of course, is contrary to the popular view of our free enterprise economy, as one without a role for government.

The problem with a monolithic industrial system that co-opts government for its own ends, distorts education for its own ends, manages the consumer's desires for its own ends, and adapts the goals of its employees to its own ends, is the vital matter of how its ends are related to the kind of society we ought to have. If its ends are simply those of the technostructure—growth and technological advance (and the public image of improvement in our "standard of living" that sustains these two goals), what is the result? Does its monolithic nature, its bureaucracy, and "groupthink," mean an inevitable stagnation? Does it mean an inability to deal with the larger problems of our society because of an inability to be creative enough to cast up the necessary *new* goods and services? What are the effects on human beings, on their frame of mind, from participating in production, marketing, and consumption of the output of an industrial system with such meaningless and empty goals as "growth" and "technological advance"?

In the case of the auto industry, it is instructive to begin by looking at the product, and then to go on to how the product is manufactured and sold. Imagine, for a moment, that you had the power to command that any kind of automobile be made. Wouldn't you require that the automobile be inexpensive to buy and operate so that it could be owned by anyone, regardless of means, and so that its ownership imposed hardship on no one? Wouldn't you also decree that it be inexpensive, easy, even simple to maintain and repair? Wouldn't you make sure that it endured over a long period of time, so that the cost of replacing it would not have to be borne often by the owner, nor the aesthetic and fiscal costs of abandoned autos and over-full junkyards be borne by society? Wouldn't you make sure that it was safe? And wouldn't you make certain that its engine didn't give off fumes that polluted the air?

I intend to deal with problems of safety and air pollution in ensuing chapters. Suffice it to say at this point that the automobile kills 60,000 people a year in the United States, and supplies the bulk of three of our five major air pollutants, roughly 92 percent of carbon monoxide, 46 percent of nitrogen oxides, and 63 percent of hydrocarbons.

But let's deal now with the other demands our imaginary philosopher king might ask of the auto, using these demands as a measure of the social purpose of the automotive industry and our industrial system. Is it inexpensive to own and operate an auto? Consider the degree to which the consumer goes in debt to buy his car. Auto installment debt in the U.S. has generally run at over $35 billion at any given time in recent years. The number of car loans defaulted, one indication of the fact the consumer over-indebts himself for an automobile, runs to more than 200,000 a year by some estimates. And defaults don't count the things that poor families give up in order to own an automobile. Nor do they speak to the fact that it is very seldom that the market value of an automobile in the second or third year of ownership is equivalent to the amount owed on the car loan. So, at any given time, a large portion of that $35 billion of auto installment debt is not secured.

And for all those people who go in over their heads to buy autos, there are millions more families who would like to own them but can't afford to. (See Chapter 7.)

Good figures on what the automobile actually costs the individual to purchase and operate just aren't available. It's my feeling that typical estimates of eleven percent of out-of-pocket family income for an average family are quite low. Many young single persons may, indeed, pay more for owning, insuring, and maintaining a new auto than they do for any other single category of expense, including housing.

The reason that good figures aren't available is not that computations of such costs don't allot reasonable amounts for purchase costs (including financing), loss from depreciation, repairs and maintenance, gasoline, insurance, license taxes, parking, and tolls. It's that any reasonable computation of costs wouldn't stop there, and most of them do. What about real property and other taxes that a person pays every year to pave streets (other than highways, paid for out of gas taxes), pay traffic policemen, pay traffic judges, pay court costs on the enormous amount of litigation resulting from auto accidents, pay public hospital and emergency service costs from auto accidents? It's true that if you don't own a car you still have to pay taxes to support such services, but is it fair to figure the cost of driving an auto without figuring the amount of taxes you pay for such services? While such taxes are seldom included in computations of individual transportation costs, even less frequently included are the costs of building garages onto homes, clearly necessitated by auto ownership. Further, many persons drive a car when it would be faster to travel by another method, simply because they prefer the comfort of the auto, don't like to associate with other human beings, or for other reasons. If one were to legitimately compute the expense of owning an auto, he would have to figure in the value of time lost because an individual chooses to drive. In short, without even pursuing social accounting at this point, it is my opinion that the automobile is a much more expensive means of transportation than is generally recognized by the public—in terms that have simple economic measurements. I think, for example, that a good economist would conclude that the average American family of four pays as much to drive as it does to eat. More importantly, because many of the costs of auto ownership and use are not included in standard calculations, whereas most of the costs of alternative types of transportation are obvious to the user, the American consumer's tendency to favor the auto over other types of transportation is increased. You have to pay a bus fare whenever you get on the bus, but you can drive your auto without a cash transaction, particularly if you have a gasoline credit card or two.

There is an economic factor that is even less-considered than those I have been discussing. That is the matter of unused capacity in the automobile system. The typical private passenger car is used less than ten percent of the time, and the space within it is generally less than 25 percent utilized when it *is* in operation. Roads and parking lots and city streets are used even less. It is all very inefficient. The American citizen living in the 1970s undoubtedly pays more for his transportation, relative to other living costs, than has any other citizen of any other country living at any other time. (All of this is said without reference to benefits, of course, but while Americans vastly underestimate the cost of the auto, they vastly overestimate its benefits.)

Too, the trend seems to be for the costs of owning and operating an auto to take an ever-greater portion of the American consumer's dollar. The cost of new and used automobiles, gasoline, and auto insurance have all been rising faster than the consumer price index over recent years. More late-model cars use expensive gasoline than in years past, and more families have two cars, and insure themselves at higher rates. Too, there is no doubt that automobiles depreciate much more rapidly now than they did, say, ten years ago. On this latter point, a very important one, examine these figures presented by an official of the National Automobile Dealers Association: in 1959, a 1956-model eight-cylinder Chevrolet with power steering and automatic transmission that sold three years earlier for

$2,556 brand-new, was selling for $1,490 book price as a used car. But in 1969, a 1966 Impala with the same equipment that sold three years earlier for $3,066 brand-new, was selling for $1,495 book price as a used car. This vast increase in depreciation (figured either in gross terms or as a percent of the original price) has not been exclusive to General Motors. In 1959, a 1956-model eight-cylinder Ford Fairlane with power steering and automatic transmission that sold three years earlier for $2,525 brand-new, was selling for $1,380 as a used car. In 1969, a 1966 model of a similar top-of-the-line Ford (a Galaxie) that had sold three years earlier for $3,069 brand-new, was selling for $1,395 as a used car. Chrysler Corporation's cars have had the same experience. In 1959, a 1956 Belvedere hardtop coupe with power steering and automatic transmission that sold three years earlier for $2,582 brand-new, was selling for $1,360 as a used car. While in 1969, a 1966-model Plymouth Fury hardtop coupe that sold three years earlier for $3,120 brand-new, was selling for $1,395 as a used car. It is unnecessary, one would think, to point out that these rates of depreciation are much higher than those for homes, furniture, or household appliances, for example.

The philosopher king designing his automobile would also want to concern himself with simplicity of maintenance and repair. If there is an accident, how much is it going to cost to repair? How difficult is it going to be for the owner of a car to diagnose and repair an operating problem? If the owner of a car can't or doesn't want to fix it himself, how difficult will it be for him to judge the work of others who repair it? This matter of repairability, or "transparency of operation" as Goodman calls it, is not simply a matter of economics. If a man is able to repair the equipment on which he depends, he has a freedom that others do not have. He can, for example, locate where there are no "experts." Similarly, our society is better off because it is considerably more flexible if its machines can be repaired by their owners. It can get away from total dependence on a monolithic and national system of production and distribution, where it desires to do so.

The automobile industry, when judged against these criteria, fails the test. The average car produced in Detroit is hardly simple—it has 15,000 parts. All Detroit cars now have heaters, 90 percent have radios and automatic transmissions, 80 percent have power steering, and 40 percent have air-conditioning and power brakes. Many also have push-button windows and seats, and movable steering columns.

In 1968, the 400,000 agencies involved in auto repairs did $24 billion worth of business, an amazing $230 for every vehicle on the road (exclusive of purchases of gas and oil). About half of the cost was for labor and about half for parts.

And these repair costs have been going up rapidly. An insurance industry spokesman told a Senate subcommittee that in a recent ten-year period, the average repair cost after an accident went up 56 percent. A fender on a standard Ford model that cost $27 to replace in 1955 went up to $49 in 1965, and $57.05 on a 1969 Ford.

How many people can repair the car they drive? Very few. Dealer surveys show that only 3 percent of all buyers look under the hood before they buy an auto, a solid indication of pure lack of knowledge. People are completely baffled by their autos and are ignorant about what makes them run. How else could the auto repair business fleece American customers for an estimated $100 million a year in fraud and extraordinarily excessive charges, as estimated by law enforcement agencies. Professor William N. Leonard, who teaches economics at Hofstra University, and is a consultant to the Federal Trade Commission, said to the Senate subcommittee investigating auto repairs, "The automobile service business has become a jungle for the consumer . . . No matter where he turns, he runs the risk of a fleecing." This could not be the case if Detroit made cars that were simple.

If cars aren't simple and inexpensive to repair, are they durable and long-lasting? Well, the "average" car on the road is only 5.5 years old (the median age of cars on the road is closer to four years than five). More than half of the cars on the road are now under four years old, while in 1958 less than half were. Figures released by the Automobile Manufacturers Association also show that at the end of 1958 over 8 percent of the cars on the road were 16 years old or more, whereas at the end of 1968 only 2 percent were that old. The number of cars on the road is growing by about 4 percent a year, but this is the result of increased sales, not more durability. The number of cars being junked is growing at a much faster rate than the number of cars on the road. Even figured as a percent of new car registrations, the number of autos scrapped in 1968—seven million (or 74.4 percent of new cars registered)—is considerably larger than the 3.5 million cars scrapped in 1958 (which amounted to 57.6 percent of new cars registered that year).

The problem is much greater than that the autos manufactured in this country aren't durable and have to be replaced often. There is the problem of what to do with them when they are junked. Because of a recent conversion in the steel industry from blast furnaces which could consume large amounts of impure scrap metal to basic oxygen furnaces which can't, the market for junked autos has been reduced. For example, between 1964 and 1968, despite increased steel production, the steel industry actually cut back the number of scrapped autos it bought from 5.3 million to 5 million at a time when, as indicated above, the number of cars being junked was going up rapidly.

A further result of the declining demand for scrapped autos has been to reduce the prices steel companies will pay for them. Instead of $40 a ton for steel scrap, the price the average processor now gets from the steel company is between $10 and $16 a ton. This means the processor is willing to pay less for junked auto bodies to the junkyard or wrecker. It also means that instead of being paid for his dilapidated car, the individual owner now has to pay the wrecker for hauling it away.

Whether the car sits abandoned on a city street (becoming a dangerous playground for children, attracting car strippers and vandals, or being used as a flophouse by tramps), or whether it gets piled into a huge junkyard to create massive blight along one of our highways, the derelict car is a nuisance and a real visual pollutant. The city of New York hauls away more than 40,000 abandoned cars a year at a cost of well over $600,000.

If some way cannot be found to inexpensively crush and

purify the scrap from junked autos, the problem is going to get much worse. The domestic solid trash discarded in this country already amounts to five pounds per day per person, and recycling is far behind Japan and Europe. In Rotterdam, for example, all trash is burned (after special treatment) and the heat from the fire is used to obtain electricity. The Japanese often use crushed trash as construction material.

Some authors have suggested that the car-stripper who sells used auto parts has to be put out of business and, instead, large stripping businesses must be combined with wrecking, crushing, and processing plants in centralized locations underground in each of our large metropolitan areas. Economies of scale might make such an operation feasible. But it is a short-term solution.

It ought to be recognized, too, that the increased use of plastics in automobiles presents a serious problem. When burned, they give off noxious fumes and toxic vapors, unless complicated scrubbing devices are used beforehand. The amount of plastics in autos has grown to over 650 million pounds per year and is expected to reach 2 billion pounds by 1975.

A close look at the automobile industry demonstrates that Detroit is not producing cars that are inexpensive to produce and operate, that are simple and cheap to repair, or that hold up well over time. Is this because Detroit is not capable of making cheap, simple, sturdy cars? The answer is a resounding "No!" The industry would only have to change some of its attitudes. It would have to stop spending so much on styling and advertising, for instance. General Motors recently spent $250 million just to change all dealers' signs to read "GM—Mark of Excellence." And the annual changeover in models now costs the industry more than $2 billion, most of which goes into styling and other similarly useless sorts of changes. If Volkswagen can make and sell cars for about $2,000, General Motors could produce autos retailing for about $1,000 that would also be very simple and durable.

But to return to the heart of the matter, those who control the auto companies do not see it in their interest to make that kind of product. If you sell 9 million passenger cars a year costing an average of $2,500 apiece, your sales are *$13.5 billion higher* than if the cost averages $1,000 per car. If your *unit cost* is higher, there can be more growth and expansion of the technostructure when unit sales go up, because more dollar revenues will pay more salaries. If the product lasts a short period of time, and if styling and other minor changes occur only to make a car appear different and obsolete, then people will change cars more frequently and the same size population will support more sales and a much larger technostructure.

Similarly, those who control our auto companies do not see it in their interest to make cars that are simple and inexpensive to repair. On the surface, it might seem that by making cars complex, difficult, and expensive to repair, and by making cars that *must* be repaired frequently, the giant auto makers only help the small businesses that repair autos, not themselves. But you have only to recall that half of the $24 billion annual repair costs are spent on parts. Who really controls the sale of those repair parts? The auto makers, that's who! If you want a Chevy part, you have to go to General Motors. They set the parts prices high not only to provide themselves with a good profit, but also because the consumer may find that he must spend a considerable amount to repair and maintain an auto that is falling apart, and consider buying a new car sooner. Furthermore, roughly one-third of all auto repairs (and most major repairs) are made by licensed new car dealers, many of which are now owned outright by the auto makers. Further, even where they have no ownership, the manufacturers publish the flat-rate manuals that set the amount of time needed for particular repairs and also authorize a "labor rate" for each of their dealers. This system, particularly the "flat rate," encourages the mechanic to beat the time set for specific repairs by using new parts instead of repairing old ones. This means sales of more repair parts.

We have been talking largely about the product of the automotive industry. What about the work required to make this product? What sort of work is it, and how does it affect the persons who do it? Obviously, the work produced by the auto industry and its effect on the worker cannot be totally divorced from the product. For if a worker reflects on the fact that he may spend his entire working life helping to produce an unsafe, polluting machine that is more expensive, more difficult to repair, and less durable than it might be, he cannot feel a basic satisfaction in his work and therefore in his life, even if his work is interesting on a day-to-day basis.

Quite frequently, the extreme specialization required by technology also robs the worker of some of the satisfaction that might naturally occur in making autos. "Men like to make things," says Paul Goodman, "to handle the materials and see them take shape and come out as desired, and they are proud of the product. And men like to work and be useful, for work has a rhythm and springs from spontaneous feelings just like play, and to be useful makes people feel right."[3] But, he says, ". . . there get to be fewer jobs that are necessary or unquestionably useful; that require energy and draw on some of one's best capacities; and that can be done keeping one's honor and dignity."[4]

Goodman is right when it comes to the auto industry. The quit rate at Ford in 1969 was 25.2 percent. Some workers just walk away in mid-shift and don't even come back to get their pay for the time they have worked. And few workers in our large industrial corporations have the sort of job they can bring into their homes in any way. Their children understand little about what they do, and their attitudes about work and its meaning, as opposed to say, consumption and its meaning, are passed along to their children.

Roger Rapoport, while a student newspaper editor at the University of Michigan, spent a week on an assembly line at the Wixom, Michigan, plant of Ford Motor Co., and wrote about it in the *Wall Street Journal*. "Working on the line is grueling and frustrating," he says, "and while it may be repetitive, it's not simple."

"I learned first-hand why 250,000 auto workers are unhappy about working conditions," he says, describing the short time for lunch, the insufficient breaks, the breakneck speed of the line, the mind-deadening routine. "Nobody seemed to take any particular pride in his work. Some workers considered some of the parts shoddy. The kick-pads that I installed under instrument panels, for example, were made of relatively brittle plastic and sometimes broke off during installation. One workman told me, 'Over 400 of them broke off one month last winter.'

"One day when I was helping the men bolt steering columns in place, the columns on a dozen cars were mounted improperly by someone up the line, so we couldn't bolt them down and men further down the line couldn't attach the steering wheels. . . .

"I saw a loose steering column fall off a Thunderbird when an inspector checked it. Later he told me that before lunch he had only missed marking up three loose steering columns, which is pretty good since 80 percent of them were going through loose yesterday. . . ."

In his 1967 article, Rapoport explains, "Because Wixom builds luxury cars priced to sell from $4,600 to over $7,300, the assembly line moves at what, for the auto industry, is considered a slow production pace of about 40 cars an hour. Some other luxury cars are built at a faster rate. General Motors Corp.'s Cadillac assembly line rolls out 50 cars an hour and Chrysler Corp. builds about 55 Chryslers and Imperials an hour. Lower-priced cars such as Fords, Chevrolets, and Plymouths usually come off the line at a rate of up to 65 cars an hour. . . ."

But while Wixom may be slower than average, Rapoport says, "An inspector who had five things to check on each car told me, 'There isn't nearly enough time to do all the inspections. I'm supposed to check shock absorbers, but I haven't had a chance to look at one in a month. . . .' "[5]

Some companies are trying "job enrichment" programs in which the worker has more say about what he or she is doing, including more responsibility for deciding how to proceed, more responsibility for setting goals, and more responsibility for the excellence of the product. This might help to make the production process more efficient and help to keep workers happier, for the man on the machine does see management mistakes and can talk about them intelligently. But this "job enrichment" has, in most companies, been no more than a sop, no more than tokenism, for the members of the technostructure are not about to give up power to make important decisions, particularly to persons who they think don't have the faculty to test the information they have (when they have sufficient information). In short, "job enrichment" is, at most, a matter of spreading the group-planning process to the workers on the line, and is highly unlikely to alter any of the basic decisions made by the technostructure. So it is not likely to alter the product of the automotive industry, for example, and therefore is not going to be able to alter the basic problem with work in the corporate system—that of lack of meaningful purpose.

A question worth asking is, How is the auto industry able to carry all of this off? That is, if the product is demonstrably inferior and over-priced, and if the work required to produce it is demonstrably dull and unrewarding, how, indeed, has the auto industry risen to the prominence it has in all of our lives? For surely, if ours is a society in which people tend to measure their lives, and the lives of those around them, in terms of goods accumulated, the automobile is the very epitome of this tendency. Tom Wolfe puts it very well: "I don't have to dwell on the point that cars mean more to these kids than architecture did in Europe's great formal century, say, 1750 to 1850. They are freedom, style, sex power, motion, color—everything is right there."[6] While he was talking about teen-agers and customized cars, he need not have limited himself.

It seems important, when you inquire into the nature of the American love affair with the automobile, that you make clear there are two very different questions involved. The first: how did the love affair come about and what were the causes? There can be some disagreement here, but it is easy for historians to offer their theories, and while I'm not a historian, I'll offer mine. The second question is much more difficult, really. How has the love affair with the auto been sustained and nurtured so well, given the considerable costs to our society from the continuation of the ardor?

The automobile and the industry that grew up around it was a phenomenon. From the auto's invention at the turn of the century, its production became the nation's largest industry by the mid-1920s. By 1929, nine million more Americans had automobiles than telephones. And during the Depression, people would go without shoes before they'd sell the family car. So it would be foolish to deny that the motorcar fulfilled some very basic and deep needs, material and socio-psychological, at the time of its introduction. It was a very useful machine—more rapid and powerful and durable than the horse, and quite quickly, more reliable. It was marketed at a price that was then quite reasonable. As John Keats put it in *The Insolent Chariot*, "In sum, the Model T was a simple, practical, tough, economical means of transportation well suited to the American mind of the time, and well suited to the income and to the roads of the period. There was never such a car before or since."[7]

But the automobile was also much more than a useful machine. There was speed and all the excitement that brings. There was the feeling of raw power at one's command. There was a machine that those with mechanical inclinations could understand, tinker with, and repair themselves. And in the first quarter of the century, rugged American individualism, and all that implies, was still dying its death, but was not yet dead. The automobile gave freedom of movement at a considerable speed to the loner, drifter, or simple individualist. The traveler was enabled, as never before, to see the world. And perhaps most importantly, the auto was, much like an article of clothing, an extension of oneself. If your car was racy, so were you. If it was solid, dependable, and dull, so were you.

But that is history. And while many of the things that were then true of the automobile are still true, the world has changed around it. There is still speed and power at your command. There is still instant mobility and freedom of a sort, and the auto is still an extension of its owner. But all of these matters have changed in qualitative terms. There are faster autos, and more powerful, but they are also more dangerous. And what is mobility and freedom if all roads and all regions of the country look and seem the same? And can anyone really say today that the ownership of an automobile can heighten your individuality? Does our modern society allow the auto to define a person in quite the same way that it once must have?

And as I have already tried to point out, the auto is not, for our time, "a simple, practical, tough, economical means of transportation." And what of loss of life on our highways, pollution, the effects of our massive freeway system and negative social, political, and environmental fallout from the oil industry, the source of fuel for the auto?

So, times have changed, and the more baffling second question is upon us. How are we *now* so easily sold these machines and the system they require? There are really two parts to the answer. The first part is the marketing and distribution ability of the industry, its ability to manage specific demand. This includes both an ability to be artful in the use of the mass media and an ability to control the distribution system right down to the very specific actions of local distributors of automobiles. The second part of the answer involves the receptivity of the American public to the auto industry's message in the media and the practices of its dealers.

As I said, the sale of autos, the management of specific demand, takes place in two basic arenas—the dealer's showroom and the media. It is important to make the point that the nation's 31,000 franchised new car dealers are largely controlled by manufacturers, particularly the 23,000 who sell only cars made by Detroit. The franchise agreement is what provides the manufacturers with the control over dealers. If a dealer doesn't perform, doesn't meet his sales quota or other requirements, he loses his franchise. Dealers are required to keep books or records in a way that provides Detroit with information it needs, but is not helpful to the dealer in analyzing his costs. Dealers are told what type of cars they will be given to sell and the number, as well as what tools, parts, and office supplies they will have. Even capital investment is controlled.

Some dealers, as a result, have become openly antagonistic toward the manufacturers. Edwin Mullane, Jr., representing the new car dealers of Newark, New Jersey, and a Ford dealer himself for fourteen years, told Senator Philip A. Hart's judiciary sub-committee during hearings on auto repairs that, "Unilaterally, the factories have complete control—sales, service, facility, location, manpower, emphasis on primary source of income, reputation, and final limitation on your life's equity position when you sell. The ultimatum becomes a powerful influence to do their bidding."

Mr. Mullane made some telling points about this control: "Both Ford and Chrysler have each invested tens of millions of dollars in land and buildings for their own retail marketing facilities to be operated as direct factory outlets or as wholly factory-controlled outlets . . . These are strategically located in the major markets of the country." Mr. Mullane complained of the disadvantage of "having to supply the factory (your retail competitor) with your monthly financial statement." He complained that such operations eliminate real competition, adding, "It is not essential for the manufacturer to make a profit from the sale of vehicles at retail. Manufacturing profits are sufficiently large to absorb retail losses without adversely affecting corporate earnings." Mr. Mullane also complained of what he called "floating performance standards," in the franchise agreements. "They move the goal posts at will. The result is: there is probably an overall majority of all auto dealers in the country which at any time is theoretically subject to cancellation for violating one or more of these very illusive performance standards . . . These precepts might be tolerable if manufacturers used their tremendous financial leverage to guide and direct the franchise system, but gentlemen, it becomes intolerable when these same manufacturers demand unquestionable loyalty from us, for their benefit, and at the same time have the audacity to compete with us."

Another of the problems Mr. Mullane and his fellow dealers have been upset about is the fact that the cars now come from Detroit in worse condition "than ever before." Mr. Mullane presented Senator Hart with a list of repairs needed on new cars recently delivered to his dealership, with serial numbers of the cars. His service manager explained to Senator Hart that the dealership would be compensated for only about two-thirds of the items it had to repair on the autos before selling them, and that much of the compensation for this "makeready" from Detroit would not cover the real costs of the repairs to the dealer. For these reasons, many repairs are never made.

Dealers also complain about the fact that their prices on new cars don't allow them enough profit, that reimbursements they receive from manufacturers on warranties don't cover the costs of doing the repairs, and that they are pushed hard by Detroit to meet difficult sales quotas.

What are the results of the control Detroit exercises through its franchise agreements? The manufacturers would undoubtedly argue that they have kept new car prices down by keeping down dealer profits, and it *is* worth noting here that the number of dealerships *have* dropped by about one-third in the last fifteen years. So this may, indeed, be partially true. But the dealers have increased used-car prices (and offered less on trade-ins) to compensate. They have also raised other standard repair costs to their customers to make up for the fact that they must absorb some of the manufacturer's costs for repairs covered by warranties.

But, most important for the purposes of the management of specific demand, the control that the manufacturers hold over their dealers forces the dealers to play their games. And not only to play their games, but also to engage in some rather unethical practices. Admittedly, not all auto dealers are dishonest. Not all of them practice the "bait and switch," in which the advertised car has somehow been "sold" when you show up to buy it. Not all practice the "bush," in which they hike the price while they are making out the papers for the sale and they have your commitment to buy in hand. Not all practice the "highball," in which they offer you more for your used car than they are willing to pay, simply to get your interest up. Not all engage in "unhorsing," in which they borrow your car, telling you they will sell it, meanwhile loaning you a car, selling your car for less than they said they would, with you being stuck with the one they've loaned you. But these practices, while not universal, are not exactly uncommon, either.

And even if the dealer doesn't resort to such dishonesty, nearly every dealer does lower himself in two significant ways: he will sell a car to anyone who can get financing, even if an objective look at the buyer's financial situation clearly demonstrates that he cannot pay for an auto without imposing severe hardship on his family or defaulting on the loan. And he will quote different buyers anywhere from two to two hundred prices on an automobile, even if a trade-in is not involved. Under this practice, the stupid and the honest-by-nature pay more.

In short, with Detroit in control, the prospective buyer of an auto who walks into the dealer's showroom finds himself with a dealer who will quote him a "variable" price, sell him the auto even if it is irresponsible to do so, underpay him for his trade-in and over-charge him for repairs in the future.

But, most importantly, the dealer finds himself obligated to play the manufacturer's games. The way he sells the car, his promotion, his own local advertising, must correspond to the national advertising and promotional campaign. The myths of masculinity and power and status must be upheld as by the maker. The dealer's very existence as a dealer is at stake.

As Galbraith says, the need to control consumer behavior is a requirement of planning. Now, let's admit from the first that any theory of consumer behavior and how it is managed consists of two parts—the management and the behavior. Without physical compulsion, which we do not have in America, the management can never be perfect. The consumer, in America, is always free to buy nothing, to opt out completely and live off the land. In between these two poles, physical compulsion and complete freedom, is a wide range of behavior. Exactly where the management of demand now is on that spectrum is a matter of considerable controversy. But just because the management of the consumer is not perfect or complete, that does not mean it does not exist. The major auto-makers do not spend hundreds of millions of dollars on advertising every year without it being somewhat useful. And, if some of the consumer's wants are given to him by his environment, instead of springing from instincts, such as hunger and the avoidance of pain, then the control of that environment and the actions within it (most easily accomplished on a mass basis through access to the mind via communications media) is significant.

The major impact of the art of mass persuasion, as practiced on television, on radio, and in the written press, is not always to make some person want a specific product. Sometimes this simply cannot be accomplished (witness the Edsel). Instead, the primary impact is to create a general desire for goods. Once this desire is set in motion, minor redesign of the product can be combined with price strategies and persuasion strategies in the dealer's showroom, for example, to accomplish the required specific ends. The consequence is that while goods become abundant they don't seem to the consumer to be any less important than when they were not abundant. It seems as important to have two cars as one.

This uncommonly strong desire for goods is a feature of our society that hasn't received much scholarly attention. Elinor Langer, who spent several weeks working for New York Bell, describes how the women who work for New York Bell discuss "objects" endlessly, and fill their leisure time not only with shopping for goods, but with talk of shopping. One interesting observation—this mania for material goods reaches its zenith at Christmastime, objectively verifiable by the fact that thievery in the lockers at the phone company goes up substantially during the Christmas season. Some of her comments follow: "The women have a fixation on brand names, and describe every object that way: it is always a London Fog, a Buxton, a White Stag . . . Packaging is also important: the women will describe not only the thing but also the box or wrapper it comes in. They are especially fascinated by wigs. Most women have several wigs and are in some cases unrecognizable from day to day, creating the effect of a continually changing work force. The essence of wiggery is escapism . . . Many of the women work overtime more than five hours a week . . . and it seems from their visible spending that it is simply to pay for their clothes, which are expensive, their wigs, their color TVs, their dishes, silver and so forth . . . The women define themselves by their consumerism far more than by their work."[8]

It is not simply the amount of advertising that people take in while they watch television, nor is it the amount of time they watch. It is also the "tone" the ad-makers give to the advertising. The tone is highly serious and emotional toward the goods being sold. It contrasts quite distinctly with the offhand, casual attitudes of our news commentators, for example.

Of course, the consumer is still free to withdraw. He doesn't have to watch television, or pay attention to the products being advertised. The problem is, of course, that the persuaders have their hands on a social weakness, and they know it. If the work you do is not useful or important, there must be some way to make your life meaningful, and that just might be through the acquisition of goods, people think. Is it a strength, among Americans, that they desire excessively powerful cars? Is it a strength to need status symbols or sex symbols instead of transportation? No, this is a society that has its ends badly perverted and confused. And while it is wrong to take advantage of such basic weaknesses, the blame must be considered somewhat less for taking advantage of them than for creating them in the first place. And it is the industrial system that has power in this society, and the people who run this system, who have the power, must be considered responsible for the way the society is. If it is the industrial system that maintains the sort of society in which people have their ends confused, and it is also the industrial system that then takes advantage of those weaknesses through advertising, it is difficult to divorce the blame of one from the other.

All of this may be slightly overstated, for the younger generation is openly rebelling against the materialistic society and its consumerism, and even among non-hippies and those who have not yet dropped out to head for a commune, there seems to be some re-ordering of priorities. The increased sales of the Volkswagen beetle are one indication that the young no longer expect the same things from an automobile that their parents did. The sales growth of other small imports, such as those from Japan, and the commitment of General Motors and Ford and the other American manufacturers to build smaller autos such as the Vega and the Pinto are other indications that there is some awareness of change.

It is wise to remember, when these rebuttals are offered, when people argue that the individual is not subject to management, and the corporations respond to his desires, that a great deal hinges on these rebuttals that uphold the theory that the consumer is king. For, if the consumer is subject to management, then the case for restrictions by government to protect the consumer is stronger. The argument that the corporate system exists to enlarge the range of choice of individual consumers and this "greater good" justifies pollution and the rigid disciplines of the large organization also falls under its own weight if the consumer is managed instead of free.

NOTES

[1] Fortune Directory, *Fortune* magazine (May 15, 1969), p. 2.

[2] John Kenneth Galbraith, *The New Industrial State*, Houghton-Mifflin, p. 61.

[3] Paul and Percival Goodman, *Communitas*, Vintage Books, Random House, p. 153.

[4] Paul Goodman, *Growing Up Absurd*, Vintage Books, Random House, p. 17.

[5] Roger Rapoport, "A Week Spent Building Cars Gives an Insight Into Industry's Problems," *Wall Street Journal* (July 24, 1967).

[6] Tom Wolfe, *The Kandy-Kolored Tangerine-Flake Streamline Baby*, Pocket Books, Farrar, Straus, & Giroux, p. 64.

[7] John Keats, *The Insolent Chariots*, J. B. Lippincott Co., p. 26.

[8] Elinor Langer, "The Women of the Telephone Company," *New York Review of Books* (March 12, 1970), p. 16; (March 26, 1970), p. 14.

[9] Donald Appleyard, Kevin Lynch and John R. Meyer, *The View From the Road*, M.I.T. Press, Copyright 1964.

CHAPTER 3 VIOLENCE AND THE AUTO

When writing about violence and the automobile, you have to start with Ralph Nader, and you might as well end with him, too. His book, *Unsafe at Any Speed*, while now a little bit outdated (and isn't it sad that it isn't more outdated) covers all the ground and not only covers it, but strikes the right attitude, the right tone. You can't help but admire how coherently Nader outlines goals and places responsibility, as in this passage: "In accidents involving all modes of transportation—motor vehicles, trains, ships and planes—the motor vehicle accounts for over ninety-two percent of the deaths, and ninety-eight percent of the injuries. This mass trauma represents a breakdown in the relation between the highway transport system and the people who use and control it. From an engineering standpoint, when an accidental injury occurs, it is a result of the failure of the technological components of the vehicle and the highway to adapt adequately to the driver's capacities and limitations. This failure is, above all, a challenge to professional engineering, which in its finest work has not hesitated to aim for total safety.

"Automatic elevators are the safest transportation system known to man; anyone can use them with the assurance that accidents will be at an absolute minimum ... In the aviation and space fields, the meticulous anticipation of possible breakdowns in man-machine interactions and the development of fail-safe mechanisms are the fundamental orientations. In the space field, waiting to learn from accident reports is an unthinkable procedure; in aviation it is a last resort. . . .

"The stated goal of General Motors of 'no injury-producing accidents' is attained in a number of their plants each year. This plant safety has produced dividends in the form of greater quantity and consistency in production, less worker training, fewer breakdowns in the production process, and lower insurance costs.

"But the dead and injured consumers of automobiles do not interfere with production and sales."[1]

If this seems a little strident and harsh when taken out of context, it certainly does not seem so in the context of Mr. Nader's richly detailed book. He not only documents the possibility of adapting the vehicle and highway "to the driver's capacities and limitations," but he makes it clear that it is to feather Detroit's nest and only to feather Detroit's nest that this adaptation has not occurred. His documentation is not shallow journalism. It does not consist of stating a conclusion then throwing out a few non-supportive facts that make it seem you know what you are talking about when you don't.

Take this paragraph, part of what he says about the all-important point of how much money, time, and effort the auto companies put into styling their cars, to the neglect of safety:

> Other manufacturers agreed to an innocuous bumper height standard, but Haynes (Alex Haynes, Ford's executive engineer in charge of safety) fought until the end against even the principle of including the bumper under any safety standard. Haynes's engineering background must have taught him the great potential in safer bumpers for the significant energy-absorption of impact forces. Prior to 1958, his engineering associates at Ford had worked on such safety bumpers. But this background obviously receded before Ford management's desire to defend the unfettered flexibility of company stylists. For their part, the stylists seem dedicated to the proposition that the function of the bumper is to look nice—and to protect the bumper. (Ford's engineering skills labored under no such inhibitions in its

work on energy-absorptive mechanism for the aerospace field. Its aeronutronic division developed in 1962 and 1963 an "impact limiter" for the Ranger project, designed to modify the tremendous landing forces to levels that protect the most delicate instruments in the lunar-landing spacecraft.)[2]

Not only is his book well-documented in this fashion, but Nader does not leave any of the arguments of the auto companies alone. Take the following statement concerning the key argument of the auto industry that the consumer doesn't demand safety features and auto makers are out to give the consumer only what he wants. To rebut this he speaks of "the industry's long practice of not introducing safety features as standard equipment unless there is compulsion or threat of legislation or regulation. Haeusler (Roy Haeusler, Chrysler's leading automotive safety engineer) wants the compulsion of the marketplace instead of the compulsion of the law. The consumer, who is expected to buy more and more products each day, is also expected to exercise a purchasing sophistication that is wholly unrealistic. In 1850, the consumer's day was twenty-four hours long and a purchase was a major event. Today the day is still twenty-four hours long, but purchases come in rapid succession—purchase of much more complex products . . . Haeusler wants the consumer to demand not just 'safety,' but those limited safety features which the companies decide to reveal to the market."[3]

But Nader is not satisfied with destroying every inch of ground the auto industry has to stand on. He is not satisfied with taking someone like Roy Haeusler, just about the only direct and forthright auto safety engineer in the business by Nader's description, and pointing out that his limited honesty is not worth much in terms of making progress because it rests within the confines of limiting philosophy. No, Nader also takes on the "independent" auto safety researchers (universities and foundations) for not publicizing their ideas and findings in order to compel action. He takes on the "safety establishment," the auto clubs and the insurance companies for leaving the auto companies alone. He takes on doctors and lawyers for being more concerned with the revenue that results from accidents than in preventing the accidents. He places blame squarely and directly. He does not shirk from moral and ethical judgments.

What, exactly, can we say about the impact of Ralph Nader's fine book on the way the auto industry operates, on the way government treats the auto industry, or on the way society views the automobile? We can start by saying that in 1965, the year *Unsafe at Any Speed* was published, there were about 50,000 deaths from automobiles on American highways and there are now around 60,000. This seems enough evidence that the progress has not been sufficient, in fact that it has been mostly superficial.

This is not to say that there has been no progress. The rate of deaths per 100 million miles of travel declined to 5.2 deaths in 1969 from 5.5 in 1965. Among the improvements that Nader's book helped to produce are padded dashboards, headrests, seat belts, shatter-proof windshields, and collapsible steering columns. On their own initiative the auto companies have made some other improvements—some Chrysler autos now have a rail inside the door to protect passengers from side collisions. Ford has developed an anti-skid braking system and Chrysler an automatic rear window defroster. One of the next developments, and a very important one, is likely to be the installation of "air bags" that automatically fill with air in a collision, quickly inflating to a size large enough to protect passengers from bumping into the steering wheel or dashboard. They are due to be installed on all cars built after July 1973.

But while these changes are important, because every life is worth saving, they are not indicative of fundamental changes in the viewpoint of industry, government, or the public. Albert R. Karr had this to say about the improvements since Nader's book in a December 17, 1969, story in the *Wall Street Journal*. "From the start, Congress was reluctant to furnish money and people for the National Highway Safety Bureau. This year President Nixon's budget hold-down hit the young agency especially hard.

"The 20 original passenger-car safety standards, considered modest by many, were written early in 1967, and were expected to be only the forerunners of a massive improvement program. But they constitute the bulk of the Bureau's standards-drafting accomplishment."

Mr. Karr goes on to say that, "The critics say scarcity of funds loom large in the record so far. The Safety Bureau's annual budget is about $25 million; the Defense Department spends that much on public relations. The bureau's financing does seem small against the scope of its assignment . . .

"For its efforts to cut the highway toll, the Safety Bureau has a staff of 518; by contrast, the Federal Aviation Administration, for which safety is a major concern, has a staff of 48,000. (Total aircraft deaths last year were 1,750.) . . .

"The bureau's staff has a four-year backlog of work in writing new and revised safety standards. It is still checking initial test failures of 1968-model cars and equipment, while only lately starting 1969- and 1970-model testing. Only 25 persons handle the entire compliance-testing program. Says Mr. Armstrong, the program's head: 'We're monitoring the largest individual segment of American industry with a handful of people.'"

It probably ought to be noted that even when standards go into effect, they take five to seven years to cover half of all the cars on the road (the average car is six years old).

The list of what still needs to be done by government to force industry to take specific action is very long. Other than the "air bags," which are needed now, not in 1973, the Safety Bureau might concentrate on speed governors, body structures that won't crush so easily in a collision, energy-absorbing bumpers, more extensive interior padding, elimination of dangerous protrusions on auto exteriors (some 8,000 of the annual U.S. deaths from automobile accidents are pedestrians), replacement of all "stick" gear shifts, wrap-around seats, reduced glare from windshield wipers and body paint on the hood, higher positioning of brake lights, and headlights that turn with the steering wheel. One of the more interesting proposals is for a tri-light system on brake lights instead of just the usual red lights that flash when the brakes are applied. Green lights would go on when the driver's foot is on the accelerator, amber lights when the foot is removed from the gas, and red lights when the brake is touched. This would give more warning to drivers behind the vehicle.

With such an agenda of items, all of them within easy technological reach, with used-car standards not out at the time of writing and without a comprehensive government crash-testing program to compare how each make of car will come out of an accident, it seems clear that the basic attitudes of industry and government are still the same. There are three other solid indicators that this is so—continued rash of defects in new autos, the continued production and advertising of "hot" or "muscle" cars, and the continued lack of adequate safeguards by auto-makers, such as enough road testing, guidelines for transport to the dealer and dealer inspection rules.

"Hot" or "muscle" cars mean speed. Speed is not as great a problem in accidents as past safety advertising has indoctrinated all of us to believe. Studies indicate that some 87 percent of accidents take place at speeds under 40 miles an hour. The problem, of course, is that high-speed accidents are more damaging both to passengers and to the automobile itself. Insurance companies now commonly have posted surcharges of 20 percent to 50 percent on high-horsepower cars and a young man may now have to pay $1,000 a year for insurance on his Corvette, GTO, or Mustang. Extensive study has demonstrated that costs of claims on such high-powered cars average 56 percent more than on typical American cars.

It is not as if Detroit isn't aware that this is the case. But it keeps using the argument that high-powered cars allow you to flee from danger more quickly. And every other year or so it comes back to emphasizing "hot cars" in its advertising after swearing off because of criticism from safety advocates and insurance companies. The reason Detroit likes to sell high-horsepower cars is that they bring in more money and offer opportunities to sell such highly-profitable options as heavy-duty springs and shock absorbers and special rear axles. In addition, some market researchers now believe "performance" has become nearly as important as styling in selling autos in the medium-price range between a Chevy and a Cadillac. Speed and racing have become symbols of masculinity in our society and "hot" cars now make excellent showroom come-ons, just as convertibles do for somewhat similar reasons.

The model year 1969 brought out the most recent big splurge of advertising for "hot" cars. In a six-page advertising spread appearing in several auto magazines, Chevrolet introduced its new models by announcing that Chevy is "No More 'Mr. Nice Guy!' " It called one car "the class bully" and said that racing stripes painted on another model symbolized "a mean streak." Ford advertised that its new Cobra model, with the same name as the well-known racing car, was "the hot one" and "belts out enough torque to leave two black lines right out of the horizon." American Motors showed drivers in its AMX model ("ready to do 125 m.p.h.") wearing racing helmets. Chrysler was more careful. In ads for its "Wailer," described as "no kiddy car," it inserted the plug, "Safety is no accident. Drive with care." Such gratuitous last-minute thoughts about safety remind one of all the soft-drink company advertising asking people to throw their bottles and cans that can't be reused in trash cans. Somehow, the role of producer of unsafe cars or nonreturnable bottles can be justified, but the role of people who use them in ways that can be clearly determined beforehand by the producer is not justifiable.

It may at first seem important to distinguish between safety problems that result from the design of automobiles and those "defects" which result from failure to execute the design properly. But, in reality, it is nearly impossible to separate the two. When you have hundreds of makes and models with hundreds of options on each and when cars become more complicated with more parts on them every year (15,000 parts per car now), you are thereby decreeing more defects, because it will be more difficult to standardize production and to eliminate problems with design.

The putting-together of a car, both design of the production process and the process itself, is an enormously complex job, under the conditions that the auto industry has decided are most profitable. Ford Motor Co. figures there are 18 billion possibilities for error every day its production schedule calls for 10,000 cars, because each of the 15,000 parts and assemblies has an average of 100 critical characteristics. It figures there are "only" three billion chances for "human" error every day during assembly. Chevrolet technicians sat down one day and computed the number of possible combinations in which a car's parts could be assembled. The figure came out with 125 zeros. And, of course, the faster the car is put together, the more profit for the auto companies.

Then there is the matter of craftsmanship, and here too it is impossible to really separate worker performance from the way in which Detroit has decided to run its business and design its cars. When workers play no decision-making role, when they know that the auto they are building differs from others only to allow its user to imitate and emulate other car-owners, they can have little commitment to perform their jobs effectively. Similarly, when designers understand that the company views their role as designing cars that people will buy because of styling and because they are "hot," designers will worry little about making quality products that are safe, economical, and trouble-free. This becomes even more true when they come to understand how much money the auto companies make from replacing parts and how much the industry relies on the fact that its automobiles become obsolete rapidly.

Thus, a high number of defective automobiles, defective in their design and defective in their production, come out of Detroit because of the fundamental way Detroit runs its business. Detroit decides that it would rather have less safety and less reliability than less profits. Safety-related trouble forced the recall of 14 million vehicles in 545 different campaigns in the first three years the government's Highway Safety Bureau began monitoring the process. During 1969, when Detroit built 8.8 million passenger cars, it recalled 7 million. American Motors recalled 27,242 AMX and Javelins because chafing of the clutch system against the brake line caused the brakes to fail. Chrysler recalled 4,981 of its models after finding that some of its cars' wheels might fall off because of an improperly heat-treated part. Ford recalled 354,000 Cougars which the firm decided had hoods that would fly open while driving. General Motors found 2.6 million Chevrolets built over five years time might allow exhaust fumes to enter the body and three million cars and trucks had been equipped with carburetors which could cause the throttle to jam in an open position.

All of these figures say nothing about the "lemons," the cars which may not have had inherent design problems, but which just weren't properly put together. Sometimes these problems occur in very expensive cars. Ralph Nader received a letter from an owner of a 1969 Cadillac Sedan de Ville (price $7,000) who, when at his "club," was "very embarrassed when the leather door handle came off in my hand when I closed the door." And a Miami stockbroker wrote him to say that he spotted the leaky roof on his $6,000 Corvette when rain water dripped "on my Brooks Brothers suit."[4]

While Detroit claims it has added more inspectors on its production lines, is emphasizing quality more and spent less on styling changes on its 1970 models, people who have road-tested the new models find as much to complain about as ever. One *Wall Street Journal* reporter who spent weeks testing new 1970 models reported a long list of defects, including the following:

"The combination air conditioner and windshield defogger on a $5,600 Ford Thunderbird quit minutes after being turned on during a rainstorm. Since designers have eliminated the little vent windows that used to provide air for defogging, the only way to keep the windshield clear was to open the main side windows. That let rain pour in on the driver and a passenger.

"In a big four-door Chrysler New Yorker, the front seat belts were improperly installed in their containers on the floorboard and couldn't be pulled out for use . . .

"An American Motors Corp. Hornet compact shed a piece of a plastic air-conditioner outlet when the car hit a bump. On another bump, the glove-compartment door popped open. On a third, a plastic container of windshield washer fluid dropped from under the hood and hit the road with a splat. When the driver pulled up the door lock button to leave the car and retrieve the container, a small plastic molding around the button came loose . . .

"On three of four Mercury Montego models inspected, the stick-on simulated wood dashboard trim was peeling back at the edges, and on one Buick Skylark smears of gooey black windshield sealer were spread along the dashboard near the edge of the glass."[5]

Other industry critics don't think much progress is being made. Bob Knoll, head of the automotive testing division of Consumers Union, the organization that evaluates consumer products, recently told a reporter that, "We certainly have found no improvement in the quality of Detroit cars in the last few years."

It's really not too surprising to find that Detroit isn't worried enough about the quality of cars to do anything about it. For one thing, dealers are profiting from the recalls. Tim Metz reported in the *Wall Street Journal* that, "the auto makers and their dealers are finding that callbacks have a silver lining. They are helping the industry sell more service—and even new cars in some instances."

"We find that four out of every ten callback customers order extra work to be done," says Michel Tarbuck, a Buick-Chevrolet dealer in Calumet, Minn. Harold De Brandt, general manager of a St. Louis Pontiac dealership, says callback letters sent out by Detroit's manufacturers have had the same effect as a good direct-mail advertising campaign, boosting his service business 'by three to five percent over the past few months.' "[6]

In addition to the continued emphasis on "hot" cars and to the continued rash of auto defects, there is a third indicator that Detroit has not changed its basic attitude about its business—how it treats the car after production. It continues to road test a very small fraction of the cars it produces—about one percent. Then it ships them to the dealer in a very casual manner. Frank R. L. Daley, Jr. head of service research development at General Motors' Warren, Michigan, technical center, figures that 60 percent of the shortcomings found in cars reaching dealers stem from transportation damage. General Motors found that a large number of its wheel bearings were damaged in transport by the jostling they received in one year.

Once the cars get to the dealer, there is supposed to be more testing to see that the car is in shape, and there are prescribed tests for each car. John C. Bates, director of General Motors' technical center marketing staff, says an annual survey shows only about 75 percent of the dealers perform these inspections properly. Mr. Bates says that only about two-thirds of the dealers have adequate service facilities in the first place. And most of the problems are in the critical urban areas where dealers have large volumes.

Detroit's attitude about auto safety is often mirrored in Washington. Consider the wheel failures on certain 1960-65 General Motors trucks that Albert Karr pointed out in his December 17, 1969, *Wall Street Journal* article. The failures represent a clear case of the lack of political support for action the National Highway Safety Bureau wanted to take. Safety bureau engineers insisted that the wheels were inherently defective, that many failures occurred without overloading and that GM should notify all 217,000 owners of recall. But Transportation Secretary John Volpe held up the move and agreed to a compromise with GM in which it would pay only for replacement of the wheels on some 50,000 trucks whose owners had campers or other special bodies on them, on the reasoning that such customer "overloading" was responsible for wheel failures. Mr. Volpe argued that there was some doubt on the matter and noted that GM could file a law suit and tie the matter up in court.

Detroit has traditionally "gotten off easy" when blame is placed for the lack of auto safety. This obviously isn't changing, in substance. But that is not to say that there aren't some other safety problems in which Detroit plays only a peripheral role. These include tire deficiencies, unsafe highways, confusing road signs, lack of a rational way to treat the drunk driver, lack of adequate auto inspection and lack of decent systems to quickly transport injured persons to a place where they can receive good medical care.

Testing of automobile passenger tires by the National Highway Safety Bureau is a farce. The inspection, which is based on tests developed by the tire industry itself, tests for puncture resistance by slowly driving a ¾-inch steel shaft into the tire; checks to see if the tire comes off the wheel rim when subjected to sidewall pressure such as occurs when a curb is struck; and tests for endurance and speed by running two tires overloaded against a steel wheel with the room temperature at 100 degrees. The tests don't even look at a tire's traction or skid resistance, so, as Ralph Winter pointed out in the June 4, 1970, *Wall Street Journal*, a bald tire could pass the test but clearly be unsafe for driving on the road.

Even more importantly, the federal testing program gives the buyer no useful guide for selecting among the 1,300 types, brands, shapes, and sizes of tires. With 180 million passenger tires produced annually, it is a ridiculous situation when William W. Jordan, the head of the tire branch in the Safety Bureau answers the question, "What rule of thumb might the consumer use?" in this fashion: "There is literature put out by tire companies which indicates that this or that tire was designed to perform for a man doing this or that type of driving. And I think the buyer should dig into this literature. He should have the salesman produce the literature and look it over himself rather than be sold perhaps on the basis of price. He should take the time to analyze available data against his own particular situation." Elsewhere in the same interview, Mr. Jordan says there is no tire grading, that the average tire buyer cannot assume that the more expensive tire is the better tire, and that the "average tire merchant" isn't capable of helping. "I might even point out," he says, "that a second-or-third-line tire of one company might be equal to or better than the premium tire that's being sold under that nomenclature."

In other words, Mr. Jordan admits the tire buyer is at a complete loss. There is no guide or rule of thumb, no grading. Tire companies are dishonest enough to sell poorer tires for higher prices and the merchant often doesn't even know what is going on. How the tire companies are allowed to maintain such a situation when people's lives are at stake is a mystifying question. As many as 1,000 lives a year are lost from tire failure that causes accidents in this country, but don't count on the government to give the consumer a chance to assure himself he won't be among the victims of the tire industry.

Unsafe highways present some of the most difficult-to-solve safety problems. There are expressways all over the country that lack median barriers. There are numerous cases of inadequate mixing of pavement materials. There are many highways where turnouts are not wide enough. There are inadequate freeway access and egress lanes. There are bridge piers in the medians of highways and also many closely adjoining the roadside. All of these matters are easily identifiable and it is not difficult to avoid them when building highways. But it is expensive and difficult to correct them once they are in place. There should be tougher national standards on building highways and rigid enforcement procedures.

Confusing road signs or the lack of sufficient road signs are even easier problems to identify and correct. The Dallas, Texas, sign that read "advance green when flashing" instead of "turn left on flashing green" is a classic example. Signs that identify highways only by a number or don't really give sufficient information about where the road goes are equally dangerous. So, too, are the short ¼-mile leeways given on many new freeways between the turnoff and the turnoff sign. However, signs can also get expensive and they are often numerous. In an urban area freeway interchange, the signs can cost $150,000. In cases like this, it is well to remember that many fatalities occur from people striking sign posts. It is perhaps too simple just to say that more thought has to be given to road signs by road builders and designers, but that is the case.

Authorities blame drunk drivers for about one-half of all U.S. traffic fatalities, but this problem will yield to solution at a much slower rate than any other safety problem. To take away a man's right to drive because he has what most medical experts now acknowledge to be an "illness" is not the answer to the problem. To rehabilitate the drinker is the answer, but we are a long way away from being able to accomplish that on a scale large enough to deal with the safety problem. There are, however, some in-between solutions that may help automobile safety. The National Highway Safety Bureau is currently involved in nine demonstration projects, including expanded apprehension of drunk drivers with breath-analyzers, and the confirmation of a past history of drunk-driving convictions with computerized data. But the projects that seem to hold out the most hope for dealing with the problem logically are those testing devices that would become equipment on the cars of past offenders. One example is an "alcohol sniffer" that won't allow the ignition to be turned on if there is an alcohol smell present. In another project, the offender has to push a series of numbered push buttons, in order, before the car will start, a very difficult task when drunk.

But, in a very real way, these devices are acceptance of defeat. They indicate that our society is not yet ready to deal with the alcoholism problem in any meaningful fashion. We still treat the alcoholic as a criminal, not as a sick man. Of all U.S. arrests by police, 28 percent are for drunkenness. The use of police and court time to deal with the skid-rower is phenomenal, and if there could somehow be a shift in the way the alcoholic is viewed by society, the resources that now go into processing him through the courts and keeping him in jail, could go to rehabilitating him and, peripherally, making substantial progress on the drunk-driving problem. One answer is increased funding for detoxification centers—places that concentrate on "drying out" the drunk, giving him good food, a clean bed, medical attention, and counseling. St. Louis was the first city in the country with a detoxification center, opening it in November 1966 with the aid of a U.S. Department of Justice grant (the $275,000 annual budget is now borne by the city and state). Some fifteen other cities have since opened similar centers and many others are currently considering them. The centers, hopefully, are indicative of a trend to treat the alcoholic as a medical and social problem. Maryland and North Carolina laws have recently been changed to treat alcoholism as a disease rather than a crime, for example.

Many drunk drivers aren't skid-rowers, however, and may need more than drying-out centers. There is a real need for programs to help the alcoholic after he gets out of a detoxification center or a hospital. These include halfway houses to live in, vocational training, and continued intensive counseling and guidance. Programs that help him deal with welfare and social security and other government and private service agencies would also be helpful. This is how the alcoholism-auto safety problem can really be solved. And it is gratifying to see that Senator Harold Hughes' (D.-Iowa) legislation, aimed at such solutions, has been enacted into law.

If the drunk-driver problem is very difficult to solve without massive expense, so too is the problem of inadequate automobile inspection. All states are now required to carry out regular safety inspections of automobiles or forfeit federal highway aid, although some states have been slow to set up the inspection process, knowing full well that the federal government won't use its muscle on the safety issue.

There are now two prevalent types of safety inspections. One consists of random checks of autos by state police or other state officials. How effective such checks are depend entirely on how many cars are checked, how thorough the inspections are, and how much teeth is put into a law requiring the owner to bring his car up to standards. When I was recently stopped for an inspection in Oregon, the officer discovered that my left signal light wasn't working, but he didn't cite me or take any action to see that I got it fixed. The inspection was perfunctory at best.

The other alternative currently in practice is to require mandatory annual inspections and stickers demonstrating such inspections have been made. These inspections are usually carried out by garages which are licensed by the state. Ralph Nader says such inspections are "tailor-made for graft and sloppy work," largely because the garage will try to require unnecessary repairs because of the business this will bring in. A *Washington Post* reporter visited sixteen auto-inspection garages in two counties in Maryland and found "vast variations in inspection fees, procedures and results." Repair estimates on the reporter's car ranged from zero, at five garages where the auto was approved without repairs, to $77.50. The car failed a special inspection by Maryland state police after it had been approved by ten

Maryland garages, some of which collected fees for minor repairs.

Some states already have mandatory annual inspection that is carried out by the state, not private garages, and this seems the best system, if it is run properly. It might also be a good idea to have state-run garages to repair the problems found by the safety inspection.

Improvements are also possible in the whole area of emergency medical services to accident victims, but, again, state and local governments must act. Standards must be established for the training of ambulance attendants and for the equipment of all licensed ambulances. Emergency care in hospitals continues to be shameful in many cases. Public health officials must be made to see their responsibility in this field and take it. An electronic communications system permitting early detection of emergencies, rapid dispatching of helicopter service (with doctor aboard) and continuous contact with ambulances and hospitals is required. This is the sort of service we give our servicemen in Vietnam. It must be extended to victims of the automobile here at home. The reasons it is not being extended are not all that complex. Listen to E. M. Johnson, then president of the American Association of State Highway Officials, speaking at the National Conference on Highway Communications for Service and Safety in August, 1967, "Our highway program is to the point of refinement and sophistication where we are now considering emergency communications and services, safety and beauty.

"All of this is coming at a time when documented highway needs are at least two and one-half times as great as the financing in sight. There is a certain amount of money available for highway purposes. It is for this reason that we want to take a long hard look at the expense involved in a communications system, and whether or not one can rationalize spending substantial sums of money out of the available highway funds for such a system and defer the other needed highway improvements."

In short, new highways and the profits that come with them are the first priority. The value from decent systems to inspect autos, to save lives, to help persons injured in accidents and to help rehabilitate drunk drivers isn't so easily measured in economic terms. And those are the only terms our government, as embodied by our state highway officials, understands.

It is possible, of course, to measure the economic costs of highway accidents (Ralph Nader says that in 1964 there was $8.3 billion worth of losses from property damage, medical expense, lost wages, and insurance overhead expense and that indirect costs probably doubled this figure, bringing it up to about two percent of our gross national product). But it is also possible to measure the large gains to the gigantic service industry that handles the direct and indirect consequences of accident injuries—medical, police, administrative, legal, insurance, automotive repair, and funeral services. It's worth noting, for example, that our courts spend more time on litigation resulting from auto accidents than on any other single classification of work.

Auto insurance rates have nearly doubled in the past twenty years. Insurance companies blame construction of autos for much of the problem and cite the 50 percent inflation in auto repair costs in the last ten years, as well as increased medical and hospital costs. Undoubtedly, the auto companies must share some of the blame, but the insurance industry certainly ought not to come off like the knight in shining armor. The industry still cancels policies and refuses to renew after accidents. Its major companies reject no-fault insurance out of hand. It continues *sub rosa* racist policies by discriminating against occupational and residential factors that reflect racial distribution. And it uses all its power to see that its investment earnings aren't included in state rate-setting calculations. Virtually all major auto insurance companies are in excellent financial shape if one considers what they do with the money they take in from premiums. But often they have "underwriting losses," and, unfortunately, it is underwriting income that states use to determine rates. All insurance companies have reserves on which they earn much money—unearned premium reserves, loss reserves, and claims expense reserves. These are not profits from past activities that the companies then invest. They are policyholder premiums which they hold in trust. Senator Philip A. Hart stated in a speech to an insurance group in Chicago in 1968 that the net investment income of auto insurance companies from 1958 to 1967 was more than $7 billion. He said, "When someone turns one pocket inside out to show you how empty it is, but has $7 billion in the other pocket, it is difficult to take their claim of poverty too seriously."[7] Ignoring net investment income from reserve funds when giving the public financial statements is only one way the insurance companies have of poor-mouthing their situation and keeping the rates high.

So, it is easy to see that, taking just one portion of the fantastic service industry that profits from auto accidents, there is "good reason" for our society to continue to fail in efforts to prevent auto accidents.

But it was only fitting that the funeral industry provide what may be the final irony—for it was Hirschel Thornton, an enterprising Atlanta, Georgia, undertaker, who recently announced that his concern had adopted the drive-in window approach to corpse viewing.

NOTES

[1] Ralph Nader, *Unsafe at Any Speed*, Pocket Books, Simon & Schuster, Inc., p. 129.

[2] *Ibid.* p. 138.

[3] *Ibid.*, p. 141.

[4] Ronald G. Shafer, "Luxury Car Owners Say Lemons Can Come in All Price Ranges," *Wall Street Journal*, p. 1.

[5] Charles B. Camp, "Reporter Finds Flaws Are Many in 1970 Cars During Months of Tests," *Wall Street Journal*, p. 1.

[6] Tim Metz, "Detroit Finds Recalls of Cars With Defects Can Bring Dividends," *Wall Street Journal*, p. 1.

[7] Gilbert B. Friedman, "Why Automobile Insurance Rates Keep Going Up," *Atlantic Monthly* (September 1969), p. 60.

CHAPTER 4 AIR POLLUTION AND THE AUTO

Discussions about air pollution can get to be a bore in a hurry. Everyone seems to be against it—as long as they aren't affected by action to stop it. People who understand the real effects of air pollution, not just in terms of individual health or personal irritation, but in its gross shaping of the entire atmosphere, usually are without much real power. They tend to be the kind of people who ride bicycles instead of drive cars, not because they want to make a symbolic point, but because they really believe it will help. Such people may have an appropriate feeling of *mea culpa*. But our air pollution problem is more complicated than that, for it is not going to be solved by a series of individual acts of conscience. Instead, these people must somehow obtain enough power to coerce large numbers of other people to stop taking actions that pollute but are personally convenient, and to coerce industry to look at something beyond its profit and loss statement for once.

Just how serious is our air pollution problem becoming? Well, we Americans are now hurling more than 150 million tons of contaminants into the atmosphere every year, by federal estimates, up from 140 million tons or so last year and 130 million tons two years ago.

But what does this mean to us, other than a little more stink and a little more eye irritation? First of all, it means many more premature deaths, particularly in places like New York City and

Los Angeles. Robert N. Rickles, Commissioner of Air Resources in Mayor Lindsay's administration in New York, estimates that 2,000 people a year die prematurely in New York because of air pollution. Like other places, New York's worst air pollution crises occur during periods of temperature inversion which trap polluted air close to the ground. Late 1953, early 1963, and over Thanksgiving weekend in 1966 were three of the worst periods. Dr. Leonard Greenberg, former Air Pollution Control Commissioner for the city and now a professor at Albert Einstein College of Medicine, has studied all three incidents for the number of deaths compared with normal periods. According to press reports, he has concluded that air pollution caused the deaths of 220 persons during the first inversion, 300 to 350 during the second, and 168 during the third. All figures are well below the estimated 4,000 deaths that occurred as a result of the three-day inversion in London in 1952.

Los Angeles, the epitome of our automotive culture, is, of course, the smog capital of the world, and things there are getting worse instead of better, despite heroic efforts by an Air Pollution Control District to clean up industrial air pollution. Roger Rapoport explains in *Esquire*[1] magazine that, according to the Los Angeles County Medical Association, doctors are advising at least 10,000 people a year to leave the area for their own health, and one-third of the physicians are seriously thinking about going with them. The death rate from emphysema is doubling every four years and chest physicians are seriously overworked.

Of course Mr. Rapoport points out that amazing action that made front-page headlines across the country when it occurred: on July 1, 1969, the Los Angeles County Board of Supervisors decreed that the 1,675,000 local students at 2,250 schools must be "excused from strenuous indoor and outdoor activities when the concentration of ozone in the atmosphere reaches .35 parts per million." Between July 1, when the order was issued, and the opening of school the next fall, there were 27 days when the level was high enough to curtail activities.

Mr. Rapoport quotes Wilburt Hallett, former chief of the chest clinic at Los Angeles County General Hospital thusly:

"You have to understand that when we set an adverse ozone level of .1 ppm (parts per million) we are saying that animals constantly exposed to ozone concentrations higher than .1 ppm don't grow well. In industry, the maximum allowable eight-hour concentration of ozone is .2 ppm. But on many days a guy walks out of the factory and breathes fresh air that is worse than that." Indeed, during 1968, Los Angeles air exceeded the adverse ozone level on 188 days, the adverse particulate level on 166 days and the adverse nitrogen oxide level on 132.

But the most amazing part of Mr. Rapoport's article is not his citing of Los Angeles' problems, but how those problems are spreading. He picked up this letter to the Los Angeles *Times*, for example, by Santa Monica meteorologist Jay Rosenthal, reporting on a June 27, 1969, flight he took from Denver to Los Angeles: "After leaving the transparent skies of the Rocky Mountain area, I was surprised to notice a widespread haze covering the terrain of extreme southwestern Colorado. As we flew across southern Utah, the low haze thickened and began to obscure and color land features . . . This haze became denser all the way to the mountains surrounding the L.A. Basin. Here, large quantities of smog could be seen flowing through passes in the mountains."

Los Angeles smog has already spread so far that it has infected about 1.3 million stately Ponderosa pines in the San Bernardino National Forest near Lake Arrowhead, 83 miles east of Los Angeles. The U.S. Forest Service has already allowed the logging of over 1,000 acres of these trees.

Estimates of crop damage from California's smog vary from $30 million to $100 million a year. Lettuce and other leafy vegetables can no longer be grown successfully in Los Angeles County. Vineyards and orange groves around Los Angeles have had their production cut in half by smog.

When Los Angeles smog floats past the Continental Divide, it can merge with that in Denver, that city once billed as the mile-high city where you could see forever. In point of fact, Denver's weather conditions are more conducive to smog than those of any other U.S. city except Los Angeles. Like most Western cities, it also has a high ratio of cars to people.

A recent *Wall Street Journal* article[2] citing air pollution problems throughout the West, in Arizona, Oregon, California, etc., adds this about Denver, "And Denver has one other problem: the city's altitude causes the internal combustion engine to work less efficiently, thus pumping more pollutants into the air. A gallon of gasoline burned in Denver produces up to 60 percent more carbon monoxide than the same engine in Los Angeles, for example. It also produces 30 percent more hydrocarbons in Denver . . . The result is that Denver's smog problem has been growing worse every year. In January when Governor John Love was about to give his state of the state message to the legislature, Denver became enveloped in a brown haze. Visibility fell to a block. 'It was awful,' says a state air pollution official. 'You couldn't even see the buildings.' The governor devoted much of his message to the state's increasing air pollution problem."

Because of the omnipresence of the automobile, the West, once famed for its clean air, will continue to have serious air pollution problems. Ratios of cars to population are much higher in the West. Even a smaller city like Portland, Oregon, which is not among the nation's thirty largest metropolises, has levels of carbon monoxide in its downtown area that are dangerous.

The spread of air pollution is much more extensive than the growth of urban centers would indicate. Over the Pacific Ocean the dustiness of the air increased 30 percent in ten years, and the dust fall in Central Asia, as measured by Russian scientists, is nineteen times as great as it was in 1930.

The major danger from increasing air pollution, in fact, may not be the specific and, at least in part, isolated dangers to health and well being, but instead the gross effect on climate and worldwide energy systems. Recent government-sponsored tests near St. Louis and Chicago indicate that air pollution has large and measurable effects on weather conditions. The most significant effect of air pollution thus far documented is increased precipitation and thunderstorms. What happens is that tiny dust particles strongly attract water vapor which condenses and freezes on them, forming ice crystals. These, in turn, form clouds which can eventually cause rain. Belleville, Illinois, ten miles downwind of St. Louis, where winds are usually from the northwest, receives about 7 percent more rain annually than areas upwind of St. Louis where the air is cleaner. And La Porte, Indiana, is similarly southeastward and downwind of Chicago and Gary. Between 1946 and 1967 it averaged 47.1 inches of rain a year, 47 percent more rain than fell at stations upwind of Chicago and Gary. In both Belleville and La Porte, rain patterns generally match days of haze and smoke, occurring on weekdays when auto and industrial activity is highest. On the 83 days in the past eighteen years that Belleville had rainfall of at least a quarter-inch but St. Louis did not, 82 were weekdays.[3]

Some violent weather is also thought to be caused by air pollution. Downtown St. Louis has five more days of thunderstorms a year than a rural area thirteen miles upwind with less pollution, for example. And La Porte has had 130 days of hail in fourteen years, four times as many as surrounding weather stations.[4]

Scientists also see, but cannot yet prove, much more gross effects from the pollutants in the air. They think that the increased cloudiness brought on by the dust particles is contributing to the worldwide cooling trend. Since 1940 the average annual temperature of the world as a whole has dropped by one-third to one-half a degree. The latest ice age was brought about by similar temperature drop of only four or five degrees. Reid A. Bryson, University of Wisconsin meteorology professor, recently pointed out the dangers of continued air pollution—"Looking at the climate of the past, it is clear that small changes in the past 10,000 years had very large ecological effects and they can happen bloody fast. The end of the ice age took less than a century—kapow! It's fast, and that worries me because we don't know but what in a few years we could have a significant change that would disrupt our entire climate."[5]

How much of the air pollution is due to the automobile? No one has done enough testing nationwide to give us accurate figures. But the best guess is as follows—researchers list five basic types of air pollutants and the internal combustion engine produces four of these. Autos are probably responsible for about eight percent of all particulates (bits of solid matter including lead); 46 percent of the nitrogen oxides; 63 percent of the hydrocarbons and 92 percent of the carbon monoxide. The fifth air pollutant is sulphur dioxide, a deadly gas that comes mostly from the burning of coal and fuel oils.

The main pollutant from the auto is carbon monoxide, which is dangerous because it slows down the delivery of oxygen to body tissues. In high dosages, it kills quickly. At lower concentrations it brings on headaches. Nicholas Gage, writing in the *Wall Street Journal*[6] about air pollution in New York, had the following to say about carbon monoxide: "New York state guidelines warn that levels should not exceed 1.5 ppm more than fifteen percent of the time during an eight-hour period. But after four months of measurements in midtown Manhattan it was determined that carbon monoxide levels remained above that level all day, every day.

"During daytime hours when traffic is heaviest, the carbon monoxide level in Manhattan often soars to between 25 and 30 ppm, having an impact on the lungs equivalent to that of two packs of cigarets a day. In some areas of the city, such as the Lincoln Tunnel and the approaches to the George Washington Bridge, the carbon monoxide level reaches an astronomical 100 ppm—nearly seven times the "safe" level.

"According to medical studies, exposure to this much carbon monoxide, even for short periods, can cause headaches, nausea and dizziness. After 90 minutes of exposure to only 50 ppm, the ability to make certain visual discriminations and time judgments is impaired—indicating that high carbon monoxide levels on streets and highways may be a factor in traffic accidents. Even exposure to levels as low as 15 ppm may have an effect on mental and sensory responses, researchers say.

"The celebrated surliness of some New York City taxi drivers and policemen may actually be a symptom of carbon monoxide exposure, according to some authorities. Cab drivers and traffic policemen must be in the streets constantly, often in areas where concentrations of the gas are highest. 'Every time I work days I wind up with a headache,' says one cab driver, Robert

Uzak. 'So I've asked to be put on nights permanently. I've been held up twice while on night shifts, but I would rather risk getting shot or stabbed than dying slowly from all the poison in the air.' "

Nitrogen oxides, researchers are discovering, may be nearly as bad as carbon monoxide. Researchers at the University of California at Los Angeles have learned that nitrogen oxides reduce the oxygen-carrying capacity of laboratory animals' blood by up to 38 percent, and can also induce inflammation of the respiratory tract in laboratory animals. Higher doses can restrict breathing. In addition, nitrogen oxides act as fertilizers and induce a harmful overgrowth of algae in lakes and streams after they settle out of the atmosphere.

Nitrogen oxides combine with hydrocarbons in the air to form ozone or photochemical smog, the stuff that is so damaging to plants.

Isn't it surprising, considering these facts, that Detroit still produces automobiles with internal combustion engines in them? And it is even more amazing that all of us let them do it. But Detroit is wily. Auto manufacturers know their power. And they know the affinity of the American public with their creation. They started out by halfway denying that their dirty little engine was really dirty. In 1953, a Ford Motor Company executive told Los Angeles pollution control officials, "these vapors are dissipated in the atmosphere quickly and do not produce an air pollution problem." Since that time there has been a pattern to Detroit's action that might be characterized as follows, "Pretend to give more than you are giving in the way of meaningful remedies, but give as little as possible. Pretend to be working on the problem, but stall as long as possible and fight real change with political muscle, because the profit and loss statement is at stake." The auto industry has yet to do anything voluntarily that would favorably affect the health of the American public.

A story by John Wicklein in *Washington Monthly*[7] quotes S. Smith Griswold, who served many years as director of air pollution control in Los Angeles, "We decided we had to make the manufacturers control emissions. The companies said it couldn't be done. So we got independent companies to design emission control devices and ordered the auto makers to put them on their cars. Then we discovered the auto makers *had* the devices, and finally, when they were forced to, they put them on."

A study by the California Air Resources Board shows those hydrocarbon emission control devices installed on 1966 to 1968 models failed. Hydrocarbon emissions are reduced to the required level for only the first 4,000 miles on 1966 and 1967 cars and the first 8,000 miles on 1968 cars. (The devices affect output of oxides of nitrogen not by reducing them, but by increasing them, and the Los Angeles County Air Pollution Control District reports that the increase is creating a type of air pollution that differs only in kind, not necessarily in severity.) In addition, the exhaust devices installed are designed largely for freeway driving like that found in Los Angeles. Studies show that in New York City the devices cause cars to burn ten percent more gasoline because of stop-and-go driving, at least partially offsetting any supposed gains.

And in another much more serious way Detroit is still misleading us with its efforts to clean up its dirty little engine. As the newer air pollution control devices become more effective (assuming they do, which from past experience is not a safe assumption) the amount of emissions *per car* will fall by as much as 60 percent in the next decade. But this is *not* the important figure in terms of people's health and well-being. The important figure is the gross or total amount of pollution in the air. And after Detroit has cleaned up its internal combustion engine as much as appears technically feasible to experts outside the industry, all gains (in gross or total terms as opposed to gains per car) will be offset by the fact that the number of cars on our highways are expected to double in the next decade. Then, following the end of the decade, the gross amount of air pollution will begin to rise again *sharply*.

Finally, in recent months, after two decades of stalling and duplicity on the matter of cleaning up its dirty engine, Detroit is beginning to realize that more and more people understand what it has been up to. So what has been its latest evasion? To turn around and point a finger at the oil industry, and the gasoline it produces.

It's not that what Detroit says about gasoline isn't accurate. Oil companies could make unleaded gasolines that leave less deposits inside auto engines. Those deposits now cause greater emissions of unburned fuel, and depending on who you listen to, cause the internal combustion engine to burn from seven percent to 35 percent dirtier (the seven percent estimate is by a maker of lead compounds for gasoline). In fact, American Oil Co., a subsidiary of Standard Oil Co. of Indiana, has been making unleaded gas for some time. This gasoline is only slightly more expensive (one to two cents a gallon), but the oil industry estimates that it would cost $4.25 billion to convert all refineries to the production of unleaded gasoline. Some oil companies are already making the conversion. They see what's coming. The California Air Resources Board, for example, has recommended legislation prohibiting leaded gasolines, and the Nixon Administration has supported such action at the federal level.

Lead is not the only problem with gasoline, either. The butane content of gasolines is also worth considering seriously. Butane helps gasoline to evaporate as it passes through the carburetor, something that is necessary because the internal combustion engines actually burn gasoline in vapor form, not liquid. But high butane content, according to General Motors engineers, makes gas so volatile that large quantities evaporate into the air without ever being burned. Now, just as lead makes engines "knock" less, butane in gas increases the volatility of gasoline, making the engine "perform" better. And just as taking lead out of gasoline, taking butane out will raise the cost a cent or two a gallon. But General Motors engineers say a study of 1,800 drivers showed that most couldn't tell the difference between the way their cars operated with more or less butane in them. And they add that the fumes in the Los Angeles atmosphere, for example, could be cut by twelve percent immediately by lowering volatility. Oil companies do vary their gasoline volatility now with seasons of the year and areas of the country, but butane is in oversupply and putting less of it in gasoline would increase the cost of gas, and, heaven forbid, that might cause the public to buy less gas or something, and oil companies have a profit and loss statement too, don't forget. Nevertheless, Jersey Standard has developed an evaporation control device costing from $5 to $7 for cars and the California Air Resources Board required it on new cars in 1970 and similar federal standards went into effect in 1971. For the next ten years, of course, all of the cars made before 1971 will spew out quantities of gasoline fumes, unless Detroit succeeds in getting the states and the federal government to regulate butane content, too.

Detroit's "holier-than-thou" attitude toward the oil companies is motivated by more than simple evasion of the onus of pollution-producer. As Mr. Wicklein puts it, "The auto industry executives took a look at the 1975 standards of the Air Resources Board in California (where better than ten percent of the nation's autos are sold), consulted with their technical research people, and decided they could not meet them without removing the lead that clogs control devices. So, to save their technology, they jettisoned the oil industry."

What Mr. Wicklein means by "to save their technology" is very simple. He means that Detroit intends to delay and stall the day when it will have to give up on the internal combustion engine. If there is any sanity at all left in the political processes of this country, that day is coming. For, as Detroit admits, it is only possible to make the internal combustion engine so clean (even with unleaded, low-volatility gasolines). And that is not clean enough to offset the pollution that will be produced by the vastly increased number of cars expected on our highways. The reason Detroit wants to delay the end of the internal combustion engine is that it is going to cost a lot to change production to another form of propulsion. The cost may not be simply financial. The $5 billion Chrysler estimates it would cost the auto industry to retool for, say, gas turbine engines may sound big at first, but Detroit normally spends about $2 billion each time it accomplishes a complete model changeover. And as Ralph Nader recently pointed out to a Congressional committee, General Motors spent $250 million to change its advertising signs at dealer locations and elsewhere to read, "GM—Mark of Excellence." (All of these figures may pale beside the simple cost of clean-up and material repairs from air pollution, not considering health and the loss of life. That figure is estimated at $20 billion a year by some sources.)

The cost for Detroit will not simply be a financial one. There is also the tremendous psychological effect of having to give up its pride and joy of 60 years—the internal combustion engine. Somehow, when Detroit is forced to take this step, and it is obviously going to have to be forced, it is no longer going to be able to retain its aura of invincibility and infallibility. Perhaps progress will then become possible on other fronts, as well.

There is a very important theoretical debate concerning moving to another energy source for the automobile. It does not, interestingly enough, center around what the alternative will be, but rather focuses on exactly how government ought to be involved.

First, let's look at what the alternatives are. There are three basic alternatives now being discussed—the steam engine, the gas turbine, and the all-electric car. There is the additional alternative of moving to natural gas within the internal combustion engine. (This has already been accomplished on tour vehicles at Disneyland, on some autos of the U.S. General Services Administration and on the entire fleet of cars and trucks of the Pacific Lighting Corp., a large Los Angeles utility holding company. Most of these vehicles are being equipped to use compressed gas, not the less bulky, longer-lasting liquefied gas.)

All of these alternatives have technological problems. Natural gas, while it is a cleaner-burning fuel and costs less than gasoline, nevertheless, evaporates rapidly (two to five percent a day) and if liquefied, requires heavy, bulky tanks for insulation purposes.

Steam engines, while they provide less air pollution, get better mileage using less expensive fuel, and have superior acceleration and braking characteristics, are, nevertheless, as bulky as the internal combustion engine, have major lubrication problems, and require auxiliary power to operate heaters and air conditioners when the car isn't moving. There are also problems in keeping the fluid used in them from freezing and in finding a compact condenser to convert the steam back to fluid again.

All-electric cars have a short range and their conventional lead-acid batteries wear out quickly.

The gas turbine engine, which Chrysler Corp. researched for a dozen years, is probably currently the leading choice as an alternative. It would be much cleaner because fuel is burned much more thoroughly in it than in the internal combustion engine and there is thus less residue to dump into the air. It has fewer moving parts than the internal combustion engine, and would use less expensive fuel (probably kerosene) but Chrysler says that it would consume more fuel, accelerate poorly, and might be more expensive, even though simpler, because the metals needed for some parts are currently in short supply.

But, while there are serious technological drawbacks to all of these alternatives, there is no doubt that they are possible, even feasible, alternatives.

The technological problems could be overcome, experts agree. Ford and General Motors are already producing gas turbine trucks, and Chrysler produced and tested passenger autos with turbine engines.

The questions then become: when? And, who pays? There are those who feel that the auto industry has made its money on polluting machines and it should be forced immediately to use this money to produce a non-polluting machine. The logic of this argument is hard to fault, but it is necessary to point out that action on such a major scale is without precedent, and given the power of the auto lobby, highly unlikely.

There is also another side to this question. If Detroit is simply told to develop a non-polluting engine and put it in its autos, it is likely to make air pollution the single and only item for consideration (outside, of course, of the effect on its own pocketbook). But the choice among alternatives will have serious ramifications aside from air pollution. The effect of the decision on producers and distributors of gasoline, the safety of autos using the new energy source, the obsolescence factor, the side effects of the energy source selected, are all-important considerations which Detroit is perfectly capable of ignoring, perhaps even likely to ignore. Consider, for example, the effect that moving to electrically-propelled autos would have on the electric power shortages we are currently experiencing across the country, or on the demand for new nuclear power plants with all of their possible radiation dangers. Given the current bent of our system, the government can only control these factors by becoming involved in the research and study of alternatives and their ramifications. It cannot force Detroit to consider these things with the general welfare of the public in mind. But if it once considers these things itself, government can force Detroit to act according to its guidelines, and to pay the cost for such action.

Thus, critics of President Nixon's plan to provide $9 million for research of alternatives to the internal combustion engine (the Department of Health, Education, and Welfare has so far been spending its money basically on ways to clean up the internal combustion engine, not on alternatives) should forget about criticizing the use of taxpayer money. They should focus instead on what sort of research will be undertaken. Such research should obviously concern itself with much more than the technological problems involved for the auto industry, but at this point it is unlikely to do so.

The efforts of the Nixon Administration to use the courts to fight air pollution are, unfortunately, nonexistent, although such tactics might help. The Justice Department in the Johnson Administration instituted a suit in U.S. District Court in January, 1969, charging the Automobile Manufacturers Association and the four largest auto-makers with conspiring for fifteen years to limit the development and installation of emission-control devices. But the Nixon Justice Department signed a consent decree in September, 1969, in which the manufacturers neither admitted nor denied the allegations, but agreed not to engage in such practices in the future. In August, 1970, however, twelve states picked up the ball, filing a suit in which they ask the U.S. Supreme Court to require auto manufacturers to develop effective pollution-control devices or clean engines as soon as possible. The suit charges a similar conspiracy in restraint of trade, with the attempted elimination of competition not only among auto-makers themselves in the research and installation of control devices, but also limiting competition by other makers of such devices, by the purchase of patent rights. The suit doesn't seek damages but asks instead for an injunction requiring auto-makers to speed up development of effective controls or a pollution-free engine "at the earliest feasible date as shown by the evidence." The Supreme Court is also asked to require the defendants to install, at their own expense, effective control devices on all cars of their manufacture sold in the U.S. during the period of the alleged fifteen-year conspiracy.

If the Supreme Court does not take action, perhaps stronger legislative action will be forthcoming. Former Representative Leonard Farbstein from New York and Senator Gaylord Nelson from Wisconsin have both introduced legislation designed to outlaw the internal combustion engine, Nelson by 1975, Farbstein with a phase-out from 1975 to 1978. To pay for the changes, Nelson also introduced a sense of Congress resolution suggesting that the auto industry make no more yearly style changes until it develops a low-pollution alternative. Nelson said, when introducing his bill, that the air pollution problem is growing toward "a disaster of colossal proportions," while the auto industry has "skillfully filibustered and sweet-talked the nation out of forcing them to do anything meaningful." He added that, "Expert after expert outside the automobile industry has confirmed that we can produce alternatives to the present automotive engine that are efficient, economical, quieter, and virtually pollution free."

However, anyone who holds out much hope for the passage of the Nelson or Farbstein bills would do well to take a close look at what happened in the California legislature when State Senator Nicholas Petris introduced a bill to ban the sale of motor vehicles with internal combustion engines in California after January 1, 1975. The bill passed the Senate by 26-5. But then the auto industry sent in its well-financed lobbyists and the bill was killed (by one vote) in the Assembly Transportation Committee. Detroit spokesmen complained that they had no alternative. "The know-how isn't there to do the job," said one industry official.

Of course, it is not only in the highly-visible executive and legislative branches of our national government and larger state governments that efforts to fight air pollution are lagging. Gladwin Hill, a reporter for *The New York Times*, recently took a close look at what is going on across the nation. Some of his conclusions follow:

"—States and localities generally still have penalties for air pollution that are little more than a wrist slap."

"—Administration in many places is still muddled. Both the city of Chicago and Cook County have agencies concerned with what is essentially one air basin."

"—Although federal law for two years has required auto makers to provide vehicles with fume control equipment, few states have done anything to assure their effectiveness, after a car has left the factory, by providing for regular inspection of the equipment."

"—Public officials in many places still seem to consider flurries of complaints from citizens preferable to the complaints they might get from instituting effective air quality programs . . ."

Has our laissez-faire system of unregulated private enterprise locked us into a worsening spiral of environmental destruction with local and regional efforts remaining piecemeal and ineffective? This is the case so long as people think like Robert Rickles, New York's Commissioner of Air Resources. He said in a newspaper interview[8] that, "There's no question in my mind that possibly 2,000 people die prematurely in New York City each year. We have a lot of groups that come in and say, for example, 'Ban the automobile in Manhattan,' and I'd like to—public transportation in Manhattan is quite capable and there's no real need for an automobile, except possibly taxis, and those we could convert to a low-pollution mode—but I haven't seen the public pressure. When the mayor tried to get a $10 use tax on cars in the city he couldn't do it because of public pressure in favor of the automobile.

"I understand when a few people say, 'My God, if people are really dying prematurely, why don't you shut the city down?' And I'm not averse to this. But I don't think anyone can sensibly expect the mayor to do this, or for me to recommend it to him, unless we saw the great public outcry."

Mr. Rickles misplaces the blame and misunderstands how our system works. If auto manufacturers were about to lose their business, would they wait for any great public outcry to the contrary? They would be out there creating it. Similarly, men like Mr. Lindsay and Mr. Rickles have the obligation to do more than propose and then speak for such measures. There must be no waiting for a "public outcry," because it is *not* coming. The "public" will adapt, even to massive loss of life—history tells us that. So let us not talk falsely now. The hour is getting late.

NOTES

[1]"Los Angeles Has a Cough," *Esquire* (July 1970).

[2]Earl C. Gottschalk, Jr., "Many Areas in West Once Famed for the Air, Befouled by Polution," *Wall Street Journal* (April 21, 1970), p. 1.

[3]Richard D. James, "Scientists Charge That Increased Air Pollution Is Altering the Weather," *Wall Street Journal* (December 31, 1969), p. 1.

[4]*Ibid.*

[5]*Ibid.*

[6]Nicholas Gage, "New York Atmosphere Points Up the Hazards of Big City Pollution," *Wall Street Journal* (May 26, 1970), p. 1.

[7]John Wicklein, "Whitewashing Detroit's Dirty Engine," *Washington Monthly* (June 1970), p. 10.

[8]Stephen MacDonald, "Concerning a Sore Throat and the Air," *Wall Street Journal* (July 23, 1970), editorial page.

CHAPTER 5 FREEWAYS FOR OUR AUTOS

Some people have truly earned the right to be called prophets. One such is Lewis Mumford. In 1958 in an article in *Architectural Record*, he said, "When the American people, through their Congress, voted last year for a 26 billion dollar highway program, the most charitable thing to assume about this action is that they hadn't the faintest notion of what they were doing. Within the next fifteen years they will doubtless find out; but by that time it will be too late to correct all the damage to our cities and our countryside, to say nothing of the efficient organization of industry and transportation, that this ill-conceived and absurdly unbalanced program will have wrought."

There is no doubt that it is too late to correct the damage. There is no doubt that thousands and thousands of Americans have come to deeply regret major aspects of the interstate freeway system. It is very easy to find freeway haters these days. Perhaps because of the emotions involved, the verbiage that spews forth from the press and others about battles over freeways sheds more heat than it does light.

To avoid this, it is good to be precise about what we are discussing, namely, roadways with controlled access. As Mumford points out, Benton MacKaye, the regional planner (not a highway engineer) was the first person to put together all the essential features of the freeway, calling it a "townless high-

75

way." However, he added greenbelts to his freeway, in both the median and bordering it, to be used for footpaths and bicycle paths. (See *The New Republic*, March 30, 1930. A controlled access highway was built in Brooklyn as early as 1906, however.)

Freeways, in one sense, are a very small part of our roadway system. We have, in the United States alone, some 3.7 million miles of streets and roads. That's enough pavement to cover 15 million acres of land, or the entire State of West Virginia. We have one mile of highway pavement (to say nothing about parking lots) for every square mile of land in the country. In these terms, the whole interstate freeway system is very small, for it is designed to contain only 42,500 miles of roadway and at the time of writing only 30,000 of those miles are completed. Some of the rest is not yet even in the acquisition of right-of-way stage.

But, the interstate freeway system's percentage of our total road mileage (1.1%) is more than a little misleading, for freeways will carry about 25 percent of all traffic by 1975 and the 42,500-mile interstate system, when and if it is ever completed (some are now saying 1978), will cost about $75 billion, a great deal more than the $26 billion figure Mr. Mumford used. The clearly stated aim of the interstate system is to connect some 90 percent of all cities of 50,000 and more, by high speed, high volume, limited access roads. It is, in short, the largest single construction project ever undertaken by man.

Freeways just can't be compared with other types of roads. First, they are bigger. They always have at least two lanes going in each direction. A simple four-lane freeway with a moderate-sized median strip takes 17.4 acres of land every mile. Now this matter of size is more important than it first sounds. Somehow, an eight- or ten-lane freeway is not just four or five times larger than a two-lane road. And it is not simply the median strip down the middle, or the right-of-way boundaries (which always extend well beyond the pavement). There is a geometric progression in the impact of a freeway when it reaches beyond four lanes. All that concrete and all that land for the extra lanes somehow compound each other, somehow make the thing "out of scale" with the human beings or natural elements on or along the roadway. Part of this is simple psychology, I am sure. But part of it is the fact that freeways are always built for truck travel. What this means is flattened grades, flattened curves, ponderous bridges and supports, thicker grading beneath the highway, larger intersections, and roughly triple the expenditures by the estimates of some highway engineers. It should be noted here that, contrary to conventional wisdom, the more lanes a freeway has, the less efficient it becomes in terms the highway engineers understand—moving traffic. Lane-switching and the slowing down this causes make each lane added to a freeway able to handle fewer cars than the lane previously added. A four-lane freeway (two lanes each direction) is really more efficient per lane than a six-lane freeway (three lanes each direction.)

So freeways, by their very nature (their size, their adaptability to truck traffic, their high-speed, high-volume design), are, in a very important way, inherently destructive of the landscape through which they pass, be it urban or rural. And most unfortunately, this inherently deficient tool, the freeway, has been the sole property of American highway engineers. As Ian McHarg says, ". . . surely it is the highway commissioner and engineer who most passionately embrace insensitivity and philistinism as way of life and profession."

Here we have the world's largest construction effort, the biggest single physical task ever undertaken by man. You'd think maybe this would be some inspiration. But William Bronson can hit the nail on the head by flatly stating, "Perhaps the most telling indictment against the highway program is the fact that there is not one mile in a hundred that can be considered anything more than a means to an end. You will find no romance, no beauty, no majesty. There will be no sentimental ballad written for Interstate 5. Where in the freeway system can one find that element of nobility characteristic of man's great works of the past?"[1]

But it should not satisfy us to simply condemn the freeway system and the American highway engineer, for that is too easy to do. And we can be much more precise about what freeways are doing to us, their destruction of what lies in their path, their psychological effects on users, their aesthetic roles in our urban and rural landscapes, their effects on how cities work and function. We must also go beyond what they do to take a look at why they do it. To take a look at exactly who participates in the planning process for freeways, at what that process is and what factors it considers in freeway design and location. And we must extract from the experts a set of design rules to make freeways aesthetically sound and a pleasure to drive on and look at. Finally we must consider the economics of freeways, what their real costs are and what their real benefits are; who pays for them and who gets the benefits. (Elsewhere we will consider in detail what happens to people who are removed to make way for freeways and what sort of political process works to keep production of them sustained at current qualitative and quantitative levels.)

It requires no unusual artistic perception to see that our freeways are ugly things. Probably the easiest way to do this is to compare them to fine highways built in the past. Everyone must have a favorite drive, one that he truly enjoys taking as a drive, not just as a way to get somewhere he wants to go. For me, there are two such drives. One is the old highway up the Columbia Gorge near my home city of Portland, Oregon. The road clings to the hills and presents breathtaking vistas high above the Columbia River. It darts in and out of wooded areas and the trees overhang the narrow two-lane roadway. Where it runs along a sharp drop, there are natural rocks placed along the edge to keep autos from going over. The bridges are thin and graceful, in keeping with the lovely falls they sometimes reveal behind them. The men who built it were sensitive and they loved the land, for there are no sharp cuts through hillsides, no unnecessary bridges. They knew the country was dramatic and they let it tell its story, from the road.

Another road that has always been even more special for me is the Wilson River Highway that connects my present home, Portland, with the small town where I was born and raised, Tillamook. In all the times I have traveled over it, there has always been something pleasant and appealing about the going itself. While the road is winding and often filled with sharp curves that must cling to the mountains, it is not a particularly well-engineered highway at any point. There are some cuts and fills that may have been unnecessary and irrelevant. But in analyzing my attachment to the drive from Tillamook to Portland, I find that it stems from the fact that the road always helps to give a sense of place, to define where you are. Going West, toward Tillamook from Portland, there are flat lands, once only lush farmland, today randomly spotted with suburbs, and there the road is flat and straight, with the smell of alfalfa often in the air. Then, just before entering the Coast Range, there are orchards on rolling hills and there the road rolls and sweeps with the hills, presenting a variety of angles to view the orderly fruit fields. Then, on leaving the rugged Coast Range and the famous Tillamook Burn, ghastly scene of one of the world's largest forest fires, one literally bursts out into the Tillamook Valley and its green pastures. Coming the other direction, into Portland, just before one gets to the city, a traveler used to pass through what seemed to be a dense forest but actually harbored dozens of well-hidden homes on its hillsides. Then, the road was closely bordered by trees, and one was barely aware that he was entering a metropolis of half a million people. But today, the highway engineers have widened the highway and pushed the trees far back on the right-of-way, so one loses completely the amazing feeling of this deserted green forest lying directly up against a large city. And instead of first viewing the city, with Mt. Hood in the background, beneath a beautifully arched bridge, the visitor now leaves the forested hills through a tunnel to find before him a few concrete freeway ramps, and too many oh-so-informative road signs.

If one compares the experience of driving the Columbia River Gorge Highway or the Wilson River Highway with time spent on any of the country's freeways that have so far been my privilege to drive (and that is a good portion of them) there can be no comparison. The freeways are clearly a means to an end. They have no feel for the land, nor any regard for it. They seldom provide a sense of place, or concern themselves with how best to present this vista or that one. I look back on the nine months that I spent commuting 26 miles to work on Los Angeles freeways, using the Long Beach freeway, the Santa Ana freeway, and the Hollywood freeway for 45 minutes each day as one of the most aggravating, irritating experiences of my life—dull, dangerous, stupefying and demoralizing, all at the same time.

It's important to distinguish, of course, between the rural freeway and the urban freeway. In our sprawling metropolitan areas there is no countryside to place the highway in scale, no dramatic hillside or vast plains. On the other hand, the effect of our cities, these days, is to make most places look the same. My reaction to spending time behind the wheel on our urban freeways is, I am certain, shared by many others. A recent study in the San Francisco Bay area, in which a group of men were wired for 24 hours a day with instruments that tested and recorded the amount of nervous stress and tension they were undergoing, demonstrated that those who had a freeway commute, without exception, underwent the greatest degree of stress during their daily time spent driving on the freeway.

It may actually be pleasant to take a long-distance drive on our freeway system. But I am not alone in feeling that bus or rail transit is preferable in the urban area. It offers an opportunity to read or work or observe the passing scene, while driving on an urban freeway requires attention to the rather unpleasant experience of doing that driving. This does not mean that our rural freeways are well-designed. But a poorly designed rural freeway presents a much different sort of problem than an urban freeway. Freeways in urban areas are almost inherently destructive, and good design can simply ameliorate the ill effects. Poor design of rural freeways can do great damage. But good design of rural freeways can produce a "good freeway," something that would be nearly a contradiction in terms in a city.

Without first taking a look at the freeway engineer's position, we can use two case studies to demonstrate further what freeways do. The first, an urban case, comes from an article by Richard J. Whalen in the *Saturday Evening Post* of December 14, 1968. Mr. Whalen writes about a planned three-mile section of Interstate Highway 40 in Nashville, Tennessee. He notes that it would disrupt 234 Negro-owned businesses with a gross annual volume of $11.7 million, representing more than 80 percent of all the Negro-owned businesses in Nashville's home county. Along Nashville's Jefferson street, it would level 650 houses, 27 apartment buildings and several churches, walling off an area of almost 100 square blocks. Customers have already fled from those businesses not marked for destruction. The removal of these businesses is compounded by the shortage of commercially-zoned property in other Negro neighborhoods and racial discrimination in the white neighborhoods. The route was briefly discussed at only one poorly advertised public hearing and the state then committed $10 million to engineering studies and land acquisition, telling Negroes that the route was preliminary and subject to change. Mr. Whalen adds that, in Nashville, "It is also true that interstate and arterial routes were carefully fitted around such white institutions as Vanderbilt University and Peabody and Scaritt Colleges, while Interstate 40 will divide and tend to isolate the campuses of three Negro institutions." It will cause several dead-end streets, the destruction of part of the only park in black North Nashville and put the only branch library there across a walkway. Mr. Whalen concluded that, "The road will be most useful to white commuters from the suburbs of East and South Nashville on their daily trips to work in West Nashville's growing industrial complex. The unemployed and underemployed Negroes of North Nashville, who number one in four of the working-age population, will be able to sit on their crumbling porches and watch the white men's cars whiz by." The Supreme Court of the United States issued an order that temporarily froze construction. Highway officials conceded that no economic study was made in the Negro area, although detailed economic studies were made elsewhere in Nashville.

It is not always in an urban area that such destruction occurs. Consider the case of Highway I-Lak-89-D in Lake County, California. In a story in *Cry California*,[2] the journal of California Tomorrow, a statewide conservation organization, Joseph Engbeck wrote about the roadway's effects on local agriculture.

The California Division of Highways laid out four alternative routes that cut through Big Valley between Kelseyville and Lakeport. Local residents, aware of the Class One soil in Big Valley, the only Class One or "prime" farmland in the area, fought for a route that ran above the floor of the valley and its fine Bartlett Pear orchards. Despite heavy local opposition, the Highway Commission decided on and built a route cutting right through the heart of the valley.

The following arguments carried the day for the highway engineers and enabled them to convince county supervisors to sign contracts condemning land. (Mr. Engbeck implies there was also subtle pressure involved, to the effect that the road wouldn't be built if it didn't go where the Highway Commission wanted.)

1. The route down the center of the valley is 1/10 mile shorter than the route above the valley floor.

2. It would be the cheapest right-of-way. (However, estimates of right-of-way costs by the engineers turned out to be wrong. They were less than half the actual cost.)

3. It would be the cheapest to construct. (Possibly true, but the construction of the route the people favored would also have improved over a mile of state highway.)

4. It would have the highest user benefit.

Mr. Engbeck says this item "carried great weight in the minds of the engineers because it is the only item that clearly favors" the route selected. Yet, he adds, "the user benefit argument is the most questionable of all." User benefit was said by the highway engineers to be $3.1 million over the next 20 years. "User benefit" is an interesting term that describes the economic benefit in terms of savings by users from increased speed and decreased operating costs. The engineers do a traffic study and develop "flow line charts" showing where people now go and where they want to go. In Big Valley, these "studies" showed that three-fourths of the traffic was local and that it would use the route down the heart of the valley but not the other public-supported route. However, the so-called "benefits" being given by the highway are not identified as "benefits" by the people they are designed to be benefits for. For it is the people of Lake County, and not the highway engineers with all their studies, who understood exactly what the effect of the highway was to be. The users didn't want "user benefits."

The Division of Highways used a figure for the loss of pear orchards, situated where the road was to go, of $45,602 a year. However, Mr. Engbeck points out that this figure of $45,602 was for pear trees already producing and did not include those planted but not yet in production, a calculation which should have brought the figure up to $63,338. As he points out, this calculation also does *not* account for the growth factor. Several of the acres taken by the highway did not have any pear trees on them, but assuming increased demand and the historic growth of the crop in Big Valley, much of the acreage would have been in production during the next 20 years. In addition, and even more importantly, the Highway Division's figures completely disregarded the multiplier effect in the economy. The University of California Extension Service figures that for every $1.00 the farmer receives for his pear crop, another $2.80 worth of economic activity is generated for allied industries and businesses, including shipping, processing, packing, merchandising, etc.

The route through the center of the valley touches 50 ownerships and ten of these are bisected, leaving small odd-shaped pieces on opposite sides of a fenced-off, high-speed expressway. As a result, many of these small pieces are no longer agriculturally workable and some 150 acres of them were taken out of production.

There are other hidden costs to farmers, too. Consider the safety factor, for example. Harvesting the Big Valley pear crop alone requires 12,000 round trips from the orchards, one-third of which lie south of the new route, to the packing sheds, all of which lie north of the new route. Special low-bed trailers are used during the harvest season to transport pears from the orchards to the packing sheds. Mr. Engbeck says that, "Product damage occurs if the tractor-drawn trailers exceed 10 m.p.h. Studies indicate that after stopping at the grade crossings, 26 seconds will be required for these vehicles to get across the expressway. During the same amount of time an automobile traveling 65 m.p.h. would cover nearly half a mile. To make matters worse, harvest season coincides with the peak of the tourist season."

The costs involved with the new highway, as pointed out by Mr. Engbeck, are clearly measurable, and it is only the narrowness of the Highway Divison's standards that precludes their measurement.

There are also many less tangible factors which the Highway Division did not measure. For example, how much will the new highway speed the urbanization of the Big Valley area? Mr. Engbeck quotes a Dave Dresbach of the Soil Conservation Commission as telling the Highway Commission this: "Customary formulas for monetary value should not even be attempted here ... because a body of alluvium such as Big Valley is the creation of many geologic generations. It is actually priceless." Fine fruit that cannot be duplicated elsewhere in the world may be priceless to Mr. Dresbach and to some others. But nothing is without its price to our highway builders and the price is always right for the taking.

If one momentarily disregards how freeways can destroy the economic structures of neighborhood and countryside, he can isolate the visual qualities of freeways. In their definitive work on the subject of freeways, (only a portion of their book) "Man-Made America, Chaos or Control," Christopher Tunnard and Boris Pushkarev note that highways can be analyzed in structure, function or form. Structure involves soil mechanics and the resistance of pavements, function includes such economic matters as discussed above. Form, and they really mean visual form, has been recognized in this country only in lip service, they say. With some objects, like jet aircraft, the form is not a concern as it derives necessarily from a rigorous expression of function. The highway, on the other hand, leaves the designer, "considerable freedom to give the object intuitively a more refined and unique expression, beyond the bare minima of utilitarian standards."

When condemning how highway engineers design the form of our freeways, you must be careful not to identify the highway engineer as too much the evil villain. He may often be a pedestrian bureaucrat who does his job and no more, but we must not fault him too much for his failure to have a larger vision. For he is not encouraged or trained to have a larger vision. And the rewards of taking pains with highways, of doing more than is asked for, are totally negative. He becomes the engineer who always wants to spend a little more money, or take a little more time, than is "necessary" to build a highway. And no one in the road bureaucracy wants roads to be more expensive. For then, heaven forbid, there might be fewer roads, and what would happen to the road-builders or the asphalt salesmen. That there is a basic fallacy in the penny-pinching approach of the road bureaucracy—namely that as Tunnard and Pushkarev say, "the public in general believes its experts," and will pay almost whatever they say is necessary—is not the fault of the highway engineer. Our politicians cannot escape blame, but highway engineers can be relegated to a somewhat shallower level of our hell, for they did not decree the evil. They are only carrying it out.

In talking about the roadway and its visual impact, there are some facts that are often ignored, yet are basic to the perceptions of the driver and the onlooker. In their fine book, *The View from the Road,* Donald Appleyard, Kevin Lynch, and John R. Meyer note that, "The modern car interposes a filter between the driver and the world he is moving through. Sounds, smells, sensations of touch and weather are diluted in comparison with what the pedestrian experiences. Vision is framed and limited; the driver is relatively inactive. He has less opportunity to stop, explore, or choose his path than does the man on foot." Further, the driver can make body motions within the vehicle which are irrelevant to his motion through the landscape, unlike when he is on skis or a motorcycle. Because the car interposes this filter, if surrounding objects are too far off or featureless, a superhighway can induce sleep, frustration, or excessive speed.

If the car as filter is one basic concept, a second one is the highway as guide. The highway must be seen before it can be traveled on. Being seen is an integral part of its purpose.

There are also psychological considerations in the visual design of highways. For example, as the authors of *The View from the Road* say, "One of the strongest visual sensations is a relation of scale between an observer and a large environment, a feeling of adequacy when confronted by a vast space; that even in the midst of such a world, one is big enough, powerful enough, identifiable enough. In this regard, the automobile with its sense of speed and personal control may be a way of establishing such a sense at a new level." But, they suggest, even more than a feeling of significance is possible. They ask, "Would it be possible to use the highway as a means of education, a way of making the driver aware of the function, history and human values of the world?" It could expose working parts, pick out symbols or landmarks. Signs could give real information, and the most powerful experiences could come when things are working in unison, "when a tower rooted in community history is the visible goal of a trip and the visible pivot about which the road turns."

The driver does seek meaning. When he is in the country he wants to see country people and country life, but our freeways are progressively denying this meaning to him.

The View from the Road sees three important but neglected objectives of highways: 1. to present the viewer with a rich, coherent sequential form—"intricate dances" are seen in which, "landmarks may move against a background or a foreground, be caught in a moving frame, be masked and revealed, or rotate first one way and then another"; 2. to clarify and strengthen the driver's image of the environment; 3. to deepen his grasp of the meaning of his environment.

To reach such positive goals, so unlike what we usually hear from the freeway haters (blend roads into landscapes, control billboards, cover up the scars of construction) it is simple enough for the literate highway engineer to seek out Fritz Hell in *Die Strasse* to discover that highways have both an external and an internal harmony. Tunnard and Pushkarev believe that each form of harmony presents two opportunities for the highway designer, two sources of beauty. The internal harmony, the visual quality of the alignment of the roadway itself, regardless of its setting, can first have a harmonious rhythm to its curves, their form, scale, and three-dimensional co-ordination. Secondly, it can have pleasant shapes formed by the median strip, the horizon, and the pavement. In short, "internal harmony," is an important factor, whether the highway is in the city or the countryside, whether it is in the mountains or on the plain. And this "internal harmony" is always in the control of the designer. He can always influence the curves and rises, how sharp they are, how wide the median is, and so forth. But there is also the "external harmony" of how a road relates to the objects in the environment that are not in the control of the designer. Should it cling to a hillside or run down in the valley? Should it present this view of an important landmark or pleasing vista, or should the highway present a different view? Tunnard and Pushkarev say that, in the designer's mind, the internal harmony should take precedence over this external harmony because "An ugly house in a pretty garden is still ugly."

They credit J. R. Hamilton and Louis L. Thurstone with deriving from the general principles of vision five propositions that are necessary to understand how to design harmonious highways.

1. As speed increases, concentration increases. Therefore, by pointing the road in different directions, a highway designer can offer variety, but he cannot really distract you away from the roadway. The road must aim the eye if the designer wants you to see something.

2. As speed increases the point of concentration recedes. The driver concentrates generally on objects 600 feet away while driving 25 m.p.h., but 2,000 feet away at 65 m.p.h. So it is easier to direct a driver's attention to faraway objects at high speeds, and difficult to distract or get his attention for objects nearby.

3. As speed increases, peripheral vision diminishes. At 25 m.p.h., the driver's eye encompasses about 100 degrees

horizontally. But at 60 m.p.h., it encompasses only 40 degrees. Therefore, if highways are designed in a straight line, they can become hypnotic. There should be some lateral movement of the highway or objects around it.

4. As speed increases, foreground detail begins to fade. At 40 m.p.h., the driver can discern detail 80 feet away. But at 60 m.p.h., he can discern only detail that is beyond 110 feet. (If one combines points three and four, it becomes obvious that at 60 m.p.h., the driver sees detail only within an angle of 40 degrees and only at a distance of 110 to 1,400 feet, an interval that is traversed in less than 15 seconds. As a result, elaborate detail is meaningless for the freeway driver, for it is gone before he can spend the time needed to perceive it fully.)

5. As speed increases, space perception becomes impaired. So the fewer clues the highway offers for judging speed, the more likely the driver is to lose judgment of space and motion—for example, he may come up too fast on cars slowing down in front of him.

In addition to these basic visual rules, designers should keep in mind that on a six-lane freeway at high speeds the sky occupies one-half the visual field, the roadbed almost one-third and the roadside the remaining one-sixth. If the roadside is flat and does not rise above the horizon, it shrinks to a tiny five percent of the visual field. Because of these facts, divided highways offer much more opportunity for visual variety, making a visual interplay of the two ribbons become an important factor, reducing the dominance of the sky and roadbed.

Because of the principles cited above (but actually ignored by American engineers) Tunnard and Pushkarev favor what they call "curvilinear" alignment, meaning that they would like to see curves that are at least 1,000 feet long, curves that end in spiral transitions into other curves, rather than the typical American short curve-long tangent alignment. They want "a continuous curvilinear alignment" in which topography is used to control the circular arcs. They are not dogmatic about this in cities, and it is obvious that many of the rules they apply to freeways are most applicable in the countryside. For, in the city, considerations of a social and economic nature will usually be more important than that a freeway have some "internal harmony" to its design. Nevertheless, they note that the circular arc brings more roadside into view, shows the driver a changing panorama and arouses a sense of anticipation for what is beyond. As it is now, individual pieces of what should be a flowing ribbon are evident separately. The ideal, they say, might be to have a freeway with no straight sections. The driver would have to adjust his steering, of course, but he must make minor adjustments on straight highways anyway.

And then, buried in the middle of this section of theirs on American highways, Tunnard and Pushkarev make a short revealing statement that they, with typical understatement, say is "often overlooked."

Besides all the visual and aesthetic reasons to build continuous curvilinear highways with no straight sections, there is a sound economic reason to do so. The economic reason they cite, when one thinks about it, is so common-sensical and basic that it definitively demonstrates the utter incompetence of American highway engineers to really do well even what they say they do well—build cheap highways. If the beginning point and the end point of a highway are given and one builds a highway with sharp curves and straight tangents, the result of the sharp curves will be to make the actual length of the pavement longer than if a curvilinear alignment is used in which there are no straight sections and therefore the curves are not sharp but flowing. They might be said to have given us a new axiom—straight lines are *not* the shortest distance between two points *(see diagram)*.

Tunnard and Pushkarev also make a very convincing argument for wide medians, despite the fact that such width means that the freeway will take a bigger swath of land. They note that wide medians reduce the headlight glare, reduce cross-median accidents and break up the visual impact of our ever-widening roadbeds. Wide medians also permit a much better fit with the landscape. The narrowing and widening of median width at propitious locations can also be exciting.

When it comes to the external harmony of a freeway, how it fits the landscape, Tunnard and Pushkarev have some equally

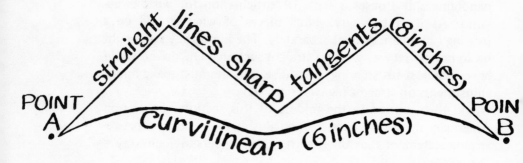

perceptive observations about plantings, textures along the roadway, and noise.

Planting, they say, is important, but must be determined by climate and can be a safety hazard. (Albert Camus died when his auto struck a roadside tree.)

For aesthetic reasons as well, man-placed planting should be used with restraint. "The Freeway in the City: Principles of Planning and Design," a report by a group of distinguished architects, planners, and engineers to the U.S. Department of Transportation, has this to say about plantings, "Urban freeway planting should normally be limited to ground cover for erosion control and to drifts of native shade and flowering trees." The study notes that individual trees and plants are meaningless and calls for "variation in tree-enframed spaces rather than evenly spaced trees with their soporific rhythm." Tunnard and Pushkarev suggest that designers look for upward slopes to put trees on, reducing their danger and accentuating the steepness.

About texture along the roadway, they say that the most common, yet the worst imaginable, way to articulate the shoulder and access lanes is to pave them and then paint lines on them. Textured materials such as brick, block, and concrete contrast handsomely with asphalt, and could be used instead of painted lines to show where shoulders are.

Tunnard and Pushkarev also believe that a lake, a river, a factory, or a skyscraper must all be set back from the freeway a sufficient distance for respect. The need for this is functional as well as aesthetic because the freeway generates noise, fumes, and headlight glare at night. To save on right-of-way acquisition, highway departments occasionally let houses stand in an impermissible proximity to the freeway. One study about noise showed that at a distance of 300 feet from the pavement, passenger cars at 55 m.p.h. are about as loud as acceptable for a residential area. Accelerating trucks are about four times too loud. Another study of residents toward highways in Westchester County, cited by Tunnard and Pushkarev, indicates that within 100 feet of a well-landscaped parkway, 54 percent felt it a nuisance, 35 percent between 100 and 200 feet, 18 percent between 200 and 300 feet and 4 percent over 300 feet. Assessment of the parkway as a convenience went from 27 percent to 50 percent to 63 percent to 75 percent at the same distances, with the people living farthest away considering it more convenient.

"The Freeway in the City" has many sound suggestions regarding the external harmony of a freeway, its bridges, overpasses, fences, tunnels, and other physical aspects. The study seeks to find means by which the sheer area and mass of the freeway may be reduced to a more human scale.

About fencing, the study notes that "insistent and obtrusive fence line in the landscape can be softened or completely screened with plantings. This is particularly important on side-hill shoulders or terrain crests where the fence would otherwise 'read' against the sky."

About bridges and overpasses: Quoting Elizabeth B. Mock in the *Architecture of Bridges*, "Since the function of a bridge is simply the continuation of a roadway over a void, its structure is both means and end, and its reality lies not in space enclosed, but in structure itself." Therefore, "it is capable of extraordinary purity."

When the scale or proportion of a bridge seems wrong, the fault is usually one of brutality. "Even in a powerful landscape, where heavy structures might seem to be in keeping, the contrast of slender bridge members and profile is usually more pleasing," the study says. Bridges which can be viewed as a thin ribbon or which show a light silhouette over the roadway or stream below generally create a pleasant impression. Further, bridge designers should minimize the amount of superstructure above roadways. For this reason "deck" bridges are preferred. "As a safety measure and to improve the visual characteristics of the highway wherever feasible, bridges should span the entire width of the roadway, including shoulders," the study declares. When intermediate piers are eliminated at medians, the cost of overpasses only goes up about 5 percent.

Bridges in a freeway system have both an individual and a collective impact and an orderly pattern of overpass design is commendable. Consideration must be given to the underside of a bridge, where details should be kept as simple as possible. Girders that are curved to fit a curving overpass are handsome.

The study adds that bridge railings should be designed in height, material, and section to provide maximum visibility for travelers on the bridge. "The views of many of our nation's most spectacular land and water crossings are denied the traveler simply because these views were never considered in the design of bridge railings," it says.

My home city, Portland (Oregon), provides ample proof of the wisdom of these recommendations on bridges. For in the last five years what must be the world's worst bridge has been built right here. The Marquam Bridge was designed to carry interstate freeway traffic across the Willamette River. It does so in full view of six other bridges crossing the Willamette, but it is at least twice as high as they are and completely out of scale, not only with the other bridges, but with the complete urban environment. It is a two-deck bridge, four lanes wide at its widest point on both decks, with the two decks connected by ugly diagonal trusses. Its supporting piers are massive and it reads cumbersomely heavy against the sky. But worst of all is its unnecessarily large scale. How did it get so big? A witness at the hearing on its height, who is a member of the city planning commission, recalls that a junkyard just upriver from the bridge asked that the bridge be built that high so ships could get in and out. Someone at the hearing asked a question that went something like, "But couldn't the ships cut down on their mast height as they came upstream?" The junkyard spokesmen replied, "That would be a terrible nuisance," and the highway engineers promptly decided to build this huge, ugly bridge more than 50 feet higher than it needs to be.

It is necessary to talk about the visual qualities of freeways at this length not just because the subject is one that draws a lot of heated discussion. Architects and planners talk about "ugly" freeways, and I have tried to cite the best explanations I could find of exactly what that means. I think that the above set of principles regarding the design of freeways and their appurtenances do more than bring this discussion down to a concrete and specific level. These basic rules, about such things as curvilinear design, slender bridges, and wide medians, do more than make it obvious that the common-sense principles that ought to be observed regarding freeway design are found more often in their absence than their observance in America. For freeway design, as closely as one can tell, is in the control of people with uniformly narrow vision and aesthetic sensitivity, from the top man in the Bureau of Public Roads to the lowest of the lowly highway bureaucrats. This should tell us something fundamental about the kind of society we have. We have spent more on highways than on going to the moon in the last decade. Our freeway system is the world's most gigantic construction project, yet we have executed it totally without regard to the simplest of design principles—principles that can be understood and observed by any layman, principles that the American public would pay for if their highway experts and politicians would only ask, principles that, if followed, could have lightened the burden of living in this difficult time.

Having noted the massive damage that can be done by freeways in urban areas (like Nashville) and rural areas (like Lake County, California) and having noted how unnecessarily ugly freeways are, it is worth asking exactly how they get this way.

You have to start with the fact that the federal government, in giving out its money (90 percent federal for ten percent state on interstate freeways), sets up certain rules for the use of its money and has certain design specifications. However, the Bureau of Public Roads does not and cannot dictate where a freeway is to go, for local or state money and a contract from local officials must be present for a freeway to be built. So it must then be pointed out that state highway commissions are particularly isolated and independent bodies. This fact historically stems in part from a desire to avoid graft and also in part from a desire by state legislatures to insulate highway commissions from all of the local governments and politicians competing for road monies. Further, local politicians are under heavy political pressure not to fight highways, for highways are thought to help the local economy.

What this means (and we will take a closer look at it later) is that the highway engineers are free to operate within their very narrow set of guidelines for determining route location and designing the highways. The method traditionally used for route location by the Bureau of Public Roads and promulgated by it among the State Highway Departments is the old user-benefit or cost-benefit ratio method, cited above in the Lake County case. Cost benefit analysis would not be necessarily evil in itself if the categories of "cost" and "benefit" were not narrowly defined. But they are. Benefits considered include only savings in time by drivers, savings in operating costs by drivers and reductions in accidents. Costs are simply those of acquisition of right-of-way, construction, and maintenance. Any factors beyond this analysis are considered *after* the cost-benefit ratio has been determined and are then put only in descriptive terms, not included in the magical figures.

If the engineers calculate the benefits at $120 million and the cost at $100 million, using the factors cited, the ratio is 1.2:1.0. What is an acceptable cost-benefit ratio may be in question. Some sources say any ratio over 1.0 to 1.0 is acceptable, while others say that 1.2 to 1.0 is required. But it matters not, for the calculations are too narrow and are only guesses anyway. The costs may have a high degree of accuracy (though anyone connected with the engineering business can tell you about plenty of bad estimates) but the benefits are surely only guesses. The benefits must be calculated over a period of time (often twenty years) and the growth of traffic must be calculated to determine the benefits. The freeway will always create some new traffic, so the benefit estimate won't be as far wrong as an estimate of how the lack of a freeway would fail to produce benefits. But even with this in mind, the highway engineer who can accurately predict land use development, that his highway does not directly cause, has yet to be found. And land use development determines highway use.

Even given these inherent difficulties with the cost-benefit or user-benefit ratio used by highway departments, its principal problem remains its monumental narrowness. Ian McHarg, the Scottish head of the Department of Landscape Architecture and Regional Planning at the University of Pennsylvania, has laid out a pretty good list of suggested criteria for Interstate Highway Route selection in his book, *Design With Nature*. Here is the table he presents:

BENEFITS AND SAVINGS	COSTS
Price Benefits	*Price Costs*
Reduced time distance	Survey & engineering
Reduced gasoline, oil & tire costs	Land & building acquisition
Reduced vehicle depreciation	Construction & financing
Increased traffic volume	Administrative, operation & maintenance
Increase in land & building value industrial, commercial, residential, recreational, institutional, agricultural	Reduction in value (land & buildings) industrial, commercial, residential, recreational, institutional, agricultural
Price Savings	*Price Costs*
Non-limiting topography	Difficult topography
Adequate foundation conditions	Poor foundations
Adequate drainage conditions	Poor drainage
Available sand, gravels, etc.	Absence of construction materials
Minimum structures required (bridges)	Abundant structures required
Non-price Benefits	*Non-price Costs*
Increased convenience	Reduced convenience to adjacent properties
Increased safety	Reduced safety to adjacent populations
Increased pleasure	Reduced pleasure to adjacent populations
	Health hazard and nuisance from noise, glare, dust, toxic fumes

Non-price Savings	*Non-price Costs*
Community values maintained	Community values lost
Institutional values maintained	Institutional values lost
Residential quality maintained	Residential values lost
Scenic quality maintained	Scenic values lost
Historic values maintained	Historic values lost
Recreational values maintained	Recreational values lost
Surface water system unimpaired	Surface water resources impaired
Groundwater resources unimpaired	Groundwater resources impaired
Forest resources maintained	Forest resources impaired
Wildlife resources maintained	Wildlife resources impaired

The value of Mr. McHarg's criteria and much of his other study about planning is that it takes into account specific factors about the ecology of an area in a most detailed and thorough fashion.

Mr. McHarg uses a set of transparent maps, one for each factor listed above, darkening the areas where the freeway would, if it were located there, produce price or non-price costs or reduce price or non-price benefits. Then, when he lays the transparent maps on top of each other, the area that has the least color, that is the lightest area, is the alignment of minimum social cost. The problem with this method is obvious to even the least educated layman. Each value in the list is given the same weight. So that a map for bedrock foundation will have an equal part in determining the route with a map for say, "community values." There is also some difficulty in determining the proper way to calculate such things as social values. For example, do you make cost of the house a positive or negative factor in determining where a road goes, or do you consider it at all? (McHarg makes it a positive factor, that is, freeway routes should avoid more expensive housing.) Nor do I really even wish to suggest that McHarg's list of criteria is complete.

In fact, this whole area of setting criteria for freeway routes is much more complex than even Mr. McHarg suggests. It gets all tied up with what the goals of our society are or ought to be. Without determining our values and goals, we cannot even begin to suggest what the criteria ought to be, let alone how each of the criteria ought to be weighted. It's easy enough to list possible goals, all right. Catherine Bauer Wurster, for example, suggests housing choice, job accessibility, better mixes of class and race, productive efficiency, individual opportunity, family welfare, privacy, security, cosmopolitan stimulation, quality of communications, adaptability to further change, social relationships, responsible citizenry and range of environmental choice. All of these undoubtedly ought to be considered as possible goals by the planner and politician. But then comes the question of how you move toward those goals you decide upon, and which goals are the most important. And who is to decide which are most important and who is to decide how you move toward them? How do you involve experts like architects and planners and sociologists and economists, yet recognize the necessity of consulting the so-called general public? These are interesting questions for theoreticians, and I do not have the final answers, but you can set up a few general guidelines about how the process ought to work and you can describe how the process works now and the success of efforts to change the process.

So far, I have tried to make two basic points. First, for a variety of reasons, the rules that would enable outstanding visual and aesthetic design of our freeways are not being followed and it is likely that the people now designing our freeways have never understood those rules. Second, the processes that are now used to determine freeway route location and design do not allow for consideration of a broad range of social and economic factors, and the people making these decisions are satisfied with the narrowness of their tools.

Before going on to a discussion of efforts to change the way our freeways are designed and located, I wish to make four more broad arguments, all of which bear on the need for change and how that change should take place.

First, planning goals ought not to be uniform throughout the nation. Some people value cosmopolitan stimulation more than others. Some people feel they have a history worth preserving while others do not. Some areas will contain prime farmland and others will not. The criteria used in planning freeways ought to shift enough to respond to these local values. This would mean that the federal government must insist that the local governments not only have the means, but are *required* to articulate local desires and attitudes. It is true that the federal government has frequently had to become involved in changing local values, whether those local values involve disregarding racial freedom or disregarding the importance of a unique ecological setting. But, unfortunately, the balance in our interstate freeway system has almost entirely disfavored local interests. When the state and federal government can control whether or not money is spent for highways in an area, they can control, if they want, *how* it is spent, because the local governments, desiring the money to come in, won't argue too strongly about *how* it comes in. This power has been badly misused. This is not to say that the local people will always make a wiser decision, only that they should be allowed to have more input.

Second, it is not practically possible to completely divorce decisions about major public expenditures, such as freeways, from the political process. Every freeway is a political statement and that is going to continue to be true. The political statement that our freeways now make is that the almighty dollar rules, that our values have largely to do with preserving the "rights" of certain social classes to use highways to further economic ends by saving time or reducing transportation costs. Or preserving the "right" of certain private business interests to increase their profits through the construction of a highway or its location at a given place. It may be true that our state and national legislative bodies, our city councils and even our governors are regularly and consistently denied access to decision-making powers on highway location and design and even on the amount of pavement to be laid down. But this is so because the private interests, who desire highway commissioners and engineers to make route and design decisions with the same speed and authority they have in the past, have been successful in establishing and defending their authority to do so. It is not an accident that practically the only body to be allowed any input in early decisions about freeway location in most states is the Chamber of Commerce and its various road committees. Nor is it an accident that state after state governor has tried to obtain more power over road decisions and has lost. In the State of

Washington, popular Republican governor Dan Evans has four times introduced and fought for legislation to put the highway department into an overall transportation department where it would have to respond to broader political input. Governor Evans has failed. Most states have gasoline taxes that, like the federal gas tax, are "dedicated" only to highway uses. Proponents of change in the way freeways are located and designed tend to forget that every highway is now a political statement and that there is massive political power supporting the continuation of the current location and design process, the way it goes about making decisions, and the speed with which it produces more pavement.

Third, another important principle is that freeway planning must start from its gross effects on land use and traffic patterns. This may seem obvious, too obvious to be stated. But the most fundamental rules about how highways work are largely forgotten by the people who are generally acknowledged to know how they work—the people who now design freeways. If it is so obvious, for example, that freeways affect land use radically when they are built, why don't highway-builders acquire rights-of-way far ahead of the development so that the location of the development can be influenced in a rational fashion. If you tell me that they can't afford to, I'll laugh.

And if it is so obvious that freeways affect land values, why do we continue to allow the increased land value, produced by government expense, to accrue totally to private interests when such land value increase could become a logical way to raise the money to reduce the damage done to communities by freeways?

And if it is so obvious that freeways act as guiders and classifiers of traffic, why do we continue to permit, even encourage, major interchanges within urban cores, so that people must often drive downtown into all the traffic in the core in order to get to a place that is nowhere near the core city? Why don't we locate our belt or circumferential freeways to serve as "interceptors" to distribute through traffic or divert it away from the core? And when a freeway absolutely *must* pass through the core or central business district, why do we insist on having entrances and exits right downtown within that central district? None of these actions makes sense, even within the framework of the designers' ostensible goals—inexpensive, time-saving freeways.

Fourth, a flexible and just method of financing freeways must be found. The federal government now pays 90 percent of the cost of interstate freeways through the highway trust fund. All federal gas taxes are put into this trust fund to be spent only for highways. Proponents of the trust fund argue that it is "fair" because each user of highways pays in proportion to his use of it. However, the basic assumption that gasoline consumption measures "use" of highways seems questionable at best. If I am the owner of a business and I profit from the traffic the freeway brings right to my door, am I not a "user" in a much more significant way than the amount of gas I buy might indicate? And when the 75-year-old pensioner who never buys a gallon of gas goes to the grocery store and pays a price for his goods that is lower because of the freeway system, is he too not a highway user? The idea of a "trust fund" is poor in the first place. Under the theory that gasoline taxes should be spent only to provide additional benefits for the buyers of gasoline, one might argue that all liquor taxes should be spent only to build bars. Finally, no gasoline tax yet devised discriminates between those who use highways when they are crowded and those who use highways when they are empty. All vehicle use of the highways is now charged the same amount per gallon of gas used, although it is clear that some uses of the highway are more "important" or are "worth more" economically than others. If use of major expressways were measured by devices (already developed) that kept a record of where each driver got on and off the road, and at what time of day, and the driver was then billed more for his use during times when highway demand was high, he would begin to pay the real "cost" of his highway use. For all rational cost analysis recognizes that time is money. In fact, as pointed out earlier, time savings is an important part of the Bureau of Public Roads' method of measuring the benefit of a freeway. Understandably, highway proponents aren't interested in intro-ducing this very real factor of time loss from congestion into any equation, for the true cost that would result might discourage use of highways.

These four principles constitute an attempt to point some new directions and indicate major deficiencies. There are, of course, signs of hope that new directions will be more than charted. The so-called "freeway revolt" has been widely discussed and written about. Freeways have been stopped in New Orleans, San Francisco, Cambridge, and elsewhere. And there have been sincere efforts to do a better job with freeways, particularly in Baltimore and Chicago. But it is also easy to get these hopeful signs out of perspective. We are still building over 1,000 miles of interstate freeway a year and almost all of it is uniformly bad. The people with immediate power—those at the head of the Bureau of Public Roads and State Highway Commissions—remain in basic disagreement with the reformers. Secretary of Transportation Volpe has tried to speed up, not slow down, construction of the interstate system. The easiest lesson to take from the so-called freeway revolt is that our democratic system of government is no longer responsive to demand for change.

Nevertheless, discussion of the urban design team concept, as begun in Baltimore and Chicago, is important in understanding how we can *eventually* progress in the business of locating and designing freeways. The truly innovative elements of the Chicago and Baltimore experiences are the efforts to establish a process to broaden the scope of factors considered in the location and design of freeways. Obviously, this means in part that persons *capable* of designing and locating freeways, with larger economic, social, and aesthetic considerations in mind, had to be brought into the process. In each city, design teams were formed to include four separate architectural and engineering firms. And each team employs members of all four design professions—engineers, architects, landscape architects, and planners—as well as social scientists (sociologists and economists) and experts in graphic design, noise, lighting, and traffic.

A second important step forward, taken in both cases, was to give each team a mandate to consider land along the right-of-way within the scope of design. This is a simple response to past freeway design, which has been similar in logic to designing a hospital corridor before designing the rooms, or to determining the size and carriage design for an elevator before the rest of the building is designed. So each team was instructed to draw up a "joint development" program that would actually improve the neighborhoods through which the freeway would pass, that would attempt to evaluate and analyze the impact and relationship of the freeway in terms of the intimate human activities that occur in those neighborhoods.

Now experience should tell us that these two innovations—design teams and joint development—do not insure success in freeway design or location. They are necessary to success, but that is different from insuring success. Neither design teams nor joint development will insure that the location and design of a freeway and its impact on the surrounding city will conform to community values and socio-political goals. And, perhaps even more importantly, even if goals are conformed to, use of a design team or joint development do not insure that the goals are reasonable or moral or humane. Given such goals (and they don't exist anywhere now), it would be necessary to establish design teams and to provide for joint development. But design teams and joint development are no substitutes for the goals.

This is not to denigrate some of the advancements that appear to have resulted from events in Chicago and Baltimore. In Baltimore, despite the fact that a route for the city's east-west freeway had already been established and condemnation of land had occurred through Rosemont, a middle-class Negro neighborhood in West Baltimore, the design team asked for and received the right to consider alternatives to the condemned route. They recommended that the freeway bypass Rosemont. The 530 owner-occupants whose homes had already been condemned were given the option of staying put or selling to the city for impartially-appraised value plus a subsidy of up to $5,000. As reported by James Bailey in the March, 1969, issue of *Architectural Forum*, the new route recommended by the design team would displace a total of 800 residential structures instead of 2,000, some 1,200 families instead of 3,800, some 200 commercial and industrial buildings providing 3,000 jobs and entailing taxable property assessed at $14 million instead of 350 such commercial and industrial buildings providing 4,500 jobs and taxable property assessed at $28 million. (Another Negro area, the Franklin-Mulberry ghetto, was also disliked by the design team, but a twenty-block corridor had been vacated ten full years in advance of planned construction.) The historic Federal Hill area of Baltimore has evidently been saved, but some question remains about equally important Fell's Point across the Harbor. It should probably be pointed out that a citizen's group called Movement Against Destruction (MAD) *opposed* the new route of the design team.

In Chicago, there are no historic areas within the Crosstown Corridor, no communities of eighteenth and nineteenth century houses such as Fell's Point and no harbor to be crossed or not crossed. But there is a middle-class Negro neighborhood in a section of the Chicago corridor and the entire area is heavily populated. The Crosstown Design Team was brought into existence in the wake of a public outcry over a proposal that called for an elevated, eight-lane freeway structure—a giant 120 ft. wide monster that was to rise as high as 83 feet in some sections. It was quickly labeled the "Stiltway" and the American Institute of Architects' Chicago chapter issued a statement saying it would be "a costly, ugly and inefficient blot on the cityscape—a monument to poor planning and gross insensitivity to urban values." Daley's government came back with a proposal that was equally disliked and then the Design Team was formed.

The design team, in the first 3½ mile segment it put forth of an eventual 22 miles, has not only chosen a route that would minimize relocation and put forth some interesting proposals for joint development, but has come up with an entirely new concept, which it calls the reverse-flow split alignment. (See diagram.) The design team called for splitting the eight-lane freeway into two four-lane legs, one replacing Cicero Avenue, a sleazy commercial and industrial strip, and the other using a largely vacant space running alongside the elevated Belt Line

Normal Freeway

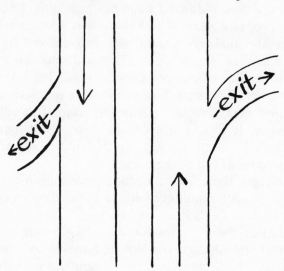

Reverse-Flow Split Alignment

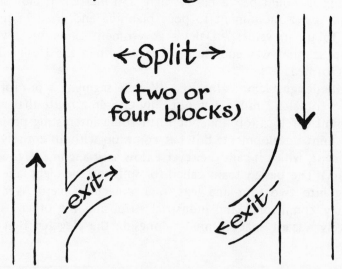

←Split→

(two or four blocks)

Railroad. The two four-lane legs are four blocks apart. But then the design team did something even trickier—it transposed the alignment, so that the four lanes on the right run to the left and the four lanes on the left run to the right. In an interview, Milton Pikarsky, Chicago's Commissioner of Public Works, explains the reverse-flow alignment: "One of the problems with any freeway is that it becomes a boundary. So, if you're going to have a boundary, if you use a reverse-flow split alignment, you can put a buffer strip of trees and parkland on the outside edges of both sections and the frontage and access roads won't cross it. Instead the exits and frontage roads can all run off to the inside, or the four block area between the two legs." Mr. Pikarsky adds that, "the first reaction to the reverse-flow alignment from the members of the large and traditional engineering firm participating in the design was that such an alignment would cause confusion and would therefore be unsafe and that was why it had never been done. But we found a somewhat similar situation in Montreal and the reverse-flow there had been well-accepted by the citizenry and there had not been an unusual number of accidents. This is logical, of course, because from the driver's-eye view, these portions of freeway are simply one-way portions because the driver can't see the other portion."

Pikarsky also points out that the split alignment makes air rights development over an expressway feasible. To put an air rights structure over a conventional expressway 300 feet wide is quite a project, but air rights construction over the 100-foot and 150-foot one-way channels of the 3½ mile segment of the Crosstown are practical, and, indeed, probable according to Pikarsky. In addition, the narrower channels will allow all bridges to span the whole width of the expressway to maintain an "open" feeling. For safety, there need be no piers in medians, because there are no medians as such.

By picking relatively vacant spaces for the channels, the design team minimized relocation of residences—only 69 in 3½ miles. With the concentration of eight lanes, the median strip, the mass transit facility alongside and the frontage roads for access, the total space taken would have been more than a block wide, and if run along either Cicero or the Belt Line, would have required the taking of hundreds more residences.

At the time this is written, Pikarsky is still determined to get a new type of joint development, one that will allow the freeway-builder to buy land away from the freeway, but within the same neighborhood, on which can be built homes of value equivalent to those removed by the freeway. Similar action would be taken for industrial plants and commercial sites. For such relocatees, Pikarsky would subsidize interest rates that were similar to what the home-owner was paying, even if at four to five percent. Pikarsky further notes that renters who are relocated could, in some cases, be "moved-up" to become homeowners. Because the housing supply is being decreased, and to cover the inconvenience, up to $1,500 could be available to a renter for a down payment on a home. Pikarsky may not get his way on all of these matters, but legislation that would allow use of highway monies for such acts is now being proposed in the Senate by Jennings Randolph, who has generally had the support of the highway-auto lobby for what he has done.

Chicago's design team has taken the "joint development" projects—for street improvement (particularly cross-streets that would have to bear the burden of on-and-off-the-freeway traffic); for new shopping centers, for parks (48 acres of land for parks would be acquired along the 3½ mile stretch); for mass transit facilities (not a new concept in Chicago where rail rapid transit already runs down the median strip of several freeways); for a small industrial park and more parking near Midway airport; and for a proposed high school or college campus which the city's Board of Education is studying. One of the parks, right at the intersection of the Crosstown freeway and the Adlai Stevenson freeway, would be a large "hill-park." It would be made of earth removed in building the highway, and the savings in earth-hauling (not having to go further away with the dirt from the depressed freeway) would probably pay for it. In winter, it would provide a sled and toboggan slide half again as high as the highest one now available in the Chicago area.

Even this cursory look at what has come out of the design team concept in Chicago and Baltimore is favorable enough to call for legislation providing for such teams and their financing throughout the nation.

But, again, we ought to be very careful about how enamored we become with the idea, because design teams can easily produce bad recommendations or be totally impotent to implement good ones. The value of design teams depends upon what goals are established for them and what guidelines are set up for their operation.

In Chicago, for instance, Mr. Pikarsky says a decision was made to "concentrate Chicago's growth along corridors of high accessibility."

In a speech he declared, "In too many cases in Chicago, commerce, industry, and residence are all mixed up together. This results in confusion, traffic, noise, and even danger . . . the corridor concept suggests that we equip a few main transportation routes with a full range of transportation options, then concentrate our high-traffic activities along them: shopping centers, industrial parks, high-rise apartment projects, community centers. This is not only more convenient for these activities, it also means less traffic, less noise, less danger in the blocks of single-family homes and low-rise apartments away from the corridor."

This approach may coincide nicely with the whole idea of "joint development." But, as an approach, it is not sound and condemns Chicago's design team effort to producing poor results. For, as Jane Jacobs has so thoroughly documented, neighborhoods *thrive* where there is a mixture of primary uses—residential, commercial, industrial. Such mixes make the street safer because it is heavily used at all hours. Such mixes produce variety, diverse and vital streets. To take all the high-traffic uses out of neighborhoods and place them in a freeway corridor would be to rob residential neighborhoods of elements they need.

This approach Mr. Pikarsky puts forth also neglects a very important effect of freeways. People always talk about how freeways split neighborhoods, and this can be true. But, more importantly, freeways create what Jane Jacobs calls "border vacuums." These vacuums deaden the areas adjacent to them, making them less lively places and therefore less desirable to live in and around. So to put high-traffic uses next to freeways is to waste at least one side of the high-traffic use. A community center with shops and other high-traffic uses in the middle of a residential neighborhood can create *foot* traffic in *four* directions from itself, enlivening all of those streets. But a community center bordered on one side by a freeway can probably create significant foot traffic in only one direction from itself. And, because it is near a freeway, the community center will probably draw people in cars who otherwise might come on foot, again reducing foot traffic and making things unpleasant for people who do walk.

In short, Mr. Pikarsky's corridor concept demonstrates how wrong-headed goals can negate the positive effects that a design team might produce.

On the other hand, Chicago's efforts to set up *operating* guidelines for the design team have been far more successful than efforts in Baltimore and elsewhere. Part of the reason for this is spelled D-A-L-E-Y. Since the federal government and state government don't do much meddling in Mayor Richard Daley's territory, coordination goes quite smoothly. But there are other reasons too. There is a regular review of design team work by a planning committee made up of officials of six city agencies and five county, state, and metropolitan bodies. There is much early intermingling of ideas, and members of the design team can get rapid political decisions about what their goals ought to be.

Chicago also seems to have taken some wise steps to eliminate problems that might crop up in the formation of a design team. It chose, for director of the project, an individual who had not been connected with any of the firms involved on the design team. He has both architectural and engineering degrees. Chicago also amalgamated the working quarters of all members of all four firms participating in the project. "With architects working alongside engineers, and with none vying and no firm as leader, we feel we have gotten the best out of all participants," says Mr. Pikarsky.

Baltimore, in contrast with Chicago, had serious problems in structuring a proper working context for its design team. The design team reports to the Maryland State Roads Commission, although the funding is federal and most of the political pressure has come from local groups. The lack of communications was most obvious when at one point, the Baltimore design team was recommending one freeway route alignment to the mayor while the local planning and housing agencies were notifying the mayor they favored a different route.

Andrew F. Euston, Jr., director of urban programs for the American Institute of Architects, has suggested that what is needed is not one team to be called a "design team," but three teams—the design team, a "citizen's or community team" (consisting of neighborhood and local citizen representatives) and a "decision team" (consisting of city, state, and federal agency representatives).

The need for a "citizen's team" is obvious. Citizens directly affected by freeways have been screaming for a long time. Now, joint development and liberalized relocation assistance provides the means to respond to them, at least in part. Federal laws require "hearings," but there is no way citizen participation is institutionalized and guaranteed. A citizen's team would do this. Even in the case of Chicago where a design team was involved, the need for citizen participation was obvious. While the 2,000-plus residents who showed up at hearings on the 3½ mile segment of the Crosstown Freeway uniformly liked what they saw of the plans, a couple of groups found items that the planners, in all their wisdom, had overlooked. Mothers, for example, wanted some additional pedestrian overpasses so their children could cross the freeway to schools or playgrounds. Not only will local citizens know their own problems best, but only if the public is truly consulted in a systematic way (and hearings don't necessarily do that) will the planning take into account social and cultural differences from community to community.

The need for a "decision team" ought to be equally obvious. It could have dealt properly with the communications problems in Baltimore, for instance. Local government officials have long complained that, in the area of freeway location and design, they have been shut out of the decision-making and forced to negotiate with the state and federal government highway agencies. These bodies hold all the cards, in the sense that they can, at any time, decide not to spend funds in a given locale. Decision teams would be a way to involve local government in a meaningful, institutionalized, systematic fashion.

Decision teams can make it easier to implement recommendations of design teams. Financing will always be the key to joint development of the freeway corridor. The decision team can be a mechanism for working out the pooling of funds on projects. A highway dollar and a housing dollar spent separately may only buy half as much as the two dollars spent together.

Decision teams can make design teams function better by providing them with the goals in the first place and then reviewing their work regularly in terms of those goals.

Decision teams, citizen teams, and design teams all have their role in the "systems" approach to designing freeways. The systems approach uses systems analysis to tie together all of the interdependent factors and functions involved. It is characterized by adherence to the scientific method and by doing the work according to a prescribed formula or a prescribed sequence of jobs. A systems approach to designing a freeway might follow these steps:

1. Definition of task or problem and the goals involved, by the decision team.
2. Assembly of design team and statement that the decision team will make the final decisions about whether or not the work of the design team conforms to goals.
3. Development of procedures to attack and study the problem, by the design team.
4. Investigation and analysis with visual aids, computers, models, etc., by design team. Input from citizen's team comes here.
5. Decision making by decision team from alternatives and recommendations of design team.
6. Implementation by the decision team.

Such a process insures that the decisions will be properly political—political in the sense that community input through the political process is possible. The systems approach outlined here also provides for citizen's participation. And it provides for the use of a broad range of disciplines in finding the solution and developing alternatives. It almost goes without saying that the wider the definition of the task, the better the chance of success. A systems approach to total urban transportation would be far more productive than a systems approach to designing a freeway.

And this really brings us to the major question of this chapter. For the problem is obviously greater than "How do we design and finance and locate a freeway best?" The question must also be whether we aren't putting far too much of our resources into freeways, autos, oil, etc. Shouldn't we slow down the construction of freeways until we are guaranteed that they will be done much better than they are now.

Once again, it becomes important to distinguish between urban and rural freeways. A system of freeways connecting our major urban centers has provided undeniable economic benefits, and their social costs, while great, have not been enormous. It is still pleasant to take a trip in an automobile, and it is nice to be able to drive from St. Louis to Los Angeles in three days or whatever. The going can still be enjoyable and relatively inexpensive.

But the social costs of urban freeways, as they are now being financed, located, and designed, far outweigh the gains from them. The basic debate might go something like this—Side A (my side) says that highways clearly take land out of a higher economic use and take land off the tax rolls. Side B says, yes, that may be true, but all of those costs from taking land out of a higher use and taking it off the tax rolls are more than offset by the increase in land value that results near interchanges of new freeways, for example. Side A replies that there are huge intangible costs from freeways, such as those entailed in the relocation of people, the destruction of community life and spirit, the destruction of often irreplaceable natural environment, the destruction of open space and historical landmarks, etc. Side B answers that those values are, indeed, intangible and unmeasurable, and the mobility and flexibility and time saved that result from our highway system are social goods that may offset those social costs.

It must be obvious that deciding with any degree of finality whether or not more freeways are needed is not possible, in the abstract. The answer about whether freeway A or freeway B is needed or not is a different matter. It probably can be decided with some finality. My *opinion* is that if we start making that decision in a large enough context, and we consider alternative ways the funds might be spent to fill transportation needs, we would build far fewer urban freeways in the next decade than we are likely to under present circumstances. For this reason, a politician who called for a total moratorium on freeway building would probably be more right than wrong. For once the freeway is built it is not likely to be torn down, and once it is built it is likely to stimulate demand for more of the same. I say let's have a moratorium on urban freeways.

NOTES

[1]William Bronson, *How to Kill a Golden State*, Doubleday & Co., Inc., p. 104.

[2]Joseph H. Engbeck, Jr., "I-Lak-89-D Across the Fruited Plain," *Cry California* (Summer 1966), pp. 25-29.

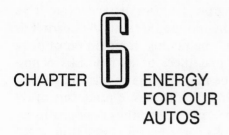

CHAPTER **6** ENERGY
FOR OUR
AUTOS

In analyzing the impact of the automobile on our society, it is difficult to know where to stop. One could write in detail about the highway-construction business, the rubber tire business, or the trucking industry, for example. In this chapter, I'd like to take a single auto-related industry, one that depends on the auto for well over 50 percent of its business, and demonstrate what one finds by taking just one of the many tangents available to a chronicler of the problems presented by over-reliance on the automobile.

The oil industry has long been synonymous with big money and high-powered politics. With the possible exception of the defense and aircraft industry, it has carried the level of sophistication of power politics to its highest order. Whether it is involved in trying to save its own special tax treatment, to defend itself from conservationists and others who believe that our environment must come before oil industry profits, to defend its protective import quota and government-run price-setting system, or to maintain the privileged position of the automobile and highway construction industries so it can continue to sell more gasoline, the oil industry knows how to play the political game better than anyone. It is also probably the prime historical example of how vested interests can use their power to mollify and dissipate reform interests.

In some ways, it is not an aberration. The large oil companies are not unlike the 500 to 1,000 major corporations that comprise our industrial system. They rely on planning, specialization, and organization. But the large requirements of capital and time to get oil out of the ground, refine it, and bring it to market require that there be no doubt that the market is controlled, that "competition" be neither competition of price nor competition of quality, that there be as few risks as possible. So, the highways must be there for the people to drive on, or people will not buy gasoline. The domestic producers of oil must protect their market, their prices, and thus their profits by keeping out cheaper foreign oil. The inherent risk of drilling for oil must be reduced or eliminated by special tax privileges and rationing of production that keeps marginal operators in business. And, as John Kenneth Galbraith has so aptly pointed out in *The New Industrial State*, it is increasingly the State that must absorb the risks and pay the costs. The State must establish a trust fund to build highways, must set up import quotas to protect oil markets, must provide tax privileges to make drilling for oil essentially risk-free. For technology, in all its manifestations, and largely because of the time and capital required, leads to the necessity of planning, and as Galbraith says, technology "may put the problems of planning beyond the reach of the industrial firm" and into the hands of the state. He says that technological compulsions, not ideology or political wile, require industry to seek this help and protection from the state. But the costs we pay for this are not only the obvious ones—irrational maintenance of a seemingly sacred gasoline tax trust fund for highways only, higher consumer costs for gasoline because of import quotas that keep low-cost oil out, the loss of tax revenue because of special oil-tax privileges, or ocean waters polluted by oil. No, the costs are much greater than is readily apparent. The oil industry's special tax privileges contribute to a huge over-investment and misallocation of the nation's resources toward the finding and production of oil. The industry's requirement that it have a growing market for its product has contributed substantially to the over-emphasis upon the automobile as means of transportation (45 percent of the oil industry's product goes to gasoline and about ten percent or so to auto lubricants and truck diesel fuel). And the manipulation and control of government to serve the oil industry has given us, or helped to give us, a politics that talks one way and acts another, a politics that has made millions of Americans distrustful of its ability to respond, to lead, to act ethically and honestly for worthwhile ends.

The history of the oil industry in the United States has been one of vast over-drilling. The United States now has about 550,000 oil wells, compared with about 1,500 in the entire oil-rich Arab world. Because of the nature of oil, the more wells you drill into a pool of oil, the less pressure there will be to push the oil up the pipe to the surface. If an operator understands the location of the oil reservoir and the subsequent pressures within it, he can extract most of the oil in it with one or two strategically-placed wells. So by overdrilling, money is wasted partly because of the number of wells drilled, but also because nature's forces, that would normally send the oil to the surface, must be augmented by pumping.

Overdrilling was much more severe in the United States prior to 1933. The legal nature of oil, as defined in the United States, combined with the then unrestrained nature of our free enterprise system, caused waste and uneconomic development. The legal nature of oil in the United States is that it is "fugacious," meaning that it flees, and is subject to "capture." The law allows any property owner to take out any oil he can get from wells on his property, even if he is sucking it from the earth below his neighbor's property. So, historically there was no reason to wait or dally, or the oil that you could get through your well might be lost to a neighbor.

In the East Texas field, the richest in the Continental United States, this over-drilling reached its absurd limits. The small town of Kilgore, Texas (population 12,000) has 1,000 oil wells, with one downtown business block containing 32 wells. Oil economist Paul Homan estimated recently in the *National Observer*[1] that there are ten to fifteen times as many wells drilled in the East Texas field as are needed to drain the reservoir. These wells, most drilled in the early 1930s, led to a glut of oil just as the depression was settling on the nation. Prices fell catastrophically and out of this era grew production controls and "prorationing." In "prorationing" each of the 31,000 wells in Texas, for example, now gets statewide production quotas or "rations" of how much oil it can produce each month. The production controls were initially enforced by the state militia, but this is no longer necessary. Texas now has what is called the Texas Railroad Commission, a three-man statewide elective body that sets the quotas each month.

It obviously made good sense for the states to begin to regulate production, in the name of "prevention of waste." But the states of Texas, Louisiana, Oklahoma, Kansas, and New Mexico, which produce most of America's oil (Texas produces more than 1/3; Louisiana almost 1/4), have clauses in their statutes that define this "waste" as "the production of crude petroleum in excess of . . . reasonable market demand." By thus tying these production quotas to market demand the oil-producing states, in effect, make certain that supply never exceeds demand, so that no more oil is produced than can be sold at current prices. The states tie the production levels to market demand by having each owner of wells ask for the amount of oil that he knows he can sell that month. Price-fixing is never mentioned. It doesn't need to be. If supply never exceeds demand, prices are fixed.

This intrastate regulation wouldn't be effective in controlling supply by itself, of course, but the federal government helps out by banning "hot oil" in interstate commerce and by limitations on imports of foreign oil.

But before discussing the subject of import quotas, it is important to note one effect of the state prorationing system. The way the prorationing system works contributes importantly to the over-investment, the over-drilling that continues in the oil industry, but could have gone out in the 1930s. The effect of the complicated system is to use the most expensive oil first, and the least expensive oil last. If production is cut back for a state, all wells in that state are not cut back equally. All reduction is concentrated in the highest-producing wells. The marginal or stripper wells, those that can't produce more than ten barrels of oil a day, are never cut back. About half of the wells in Texas are of this low-producing variety, although they produce only about fifteen percent of the oil drilled. Obviously, the oil these wells produce is more expensive because it takes more wells, more capital investment, per barrel. Even among the wells that produce more than ten barrels per day, the prorationing system discriminates against the more economically efficient, higher-producing wells. It does this by giving each well a "top allowable" amount of oil it can produce on any given day. Furthermore, this "top allowable" limit (which really, because of its limitations, starts out by saying that *no* high-producing well can achieve its top rate of efficiency) is determined by using yardsticks that are nearly totally irrelevant. The law says that a well of certain depth, say 2,500 feet, would get a "top allowable" of 22 barrels a day if it were set on a ten-acre tract of land, and a "top allowable" of 74 barrels a day if drilled on a 40-acre tract. If it were deeper it would be allowed more barrels for each of the same-sized tracts. The problem is that the depth of the well has nothing to do with how much oil a well can produce. And the acreage is only roughly related, because the pool of oil underground may or may not be contained by the acreage above ground. The ability of a well to produce oil really depends only on the quantity and richness of the oil sands it has tapped. As a result, many wells can never reach their "top allowable" production for their acreage and depth, while those wells that can exceed their "top allowable" aren't allowed to because it is illegal.

This uneconomic encouragement of poor-producing wells may *seem* illogical. But it is not illogical to the thousands of Texans and residents of other oil-producing states who own the land that these poor-producing wells sit on and who know that if the prorationing system didn't protect them the way it does, the low-producing wells on their land would be plugged up in a minute and the royalties they receive from the production of these wells would stop coming in. It is these royalty receivers who continue to re-elect men to bodies like the Texas Railroad Commission to see that such uneconomic policies are maintained.

While such a system can be praised for protecting the little man, the small independent producer with marginal wells, at the expense of the major producers who can diversify their exploration, it also should be roundly condemned for another important side effect—the encouragement of continued over-investment in oil. The oil industry has historically had a very high profit return—on its sales. An April, 1969, study by First National City Bank of New York[2] showed that when 2,250 manufacturing companies were divided into 41 categories, the 99 oil companies were second in profit return *on sales* with 9.0 percent, compared to 2.8 percent for 55 aircraft and space companies and 5.8 percent for auto and truck companies, for example. But the oil industry always points out that such percentages of sales figures don't show the cost of producing those sales, and industry spokesmen add that the oil industry has to maintain a very high investment to produce its sales. Indeed, the same bank study showed that the average rate of return (or profits) as a percentage of investment or net worth was 12.9 percent for oil companies, slightly below the average of 13.1 percent for all 2,250 companies studied.

One reason that the oil industry must spend so much money, must invest so much money, to produce its sales and eventually its profits, is that its prorationing system continues to encourage marginal, inefficient wells, as described above.

But there is a second and even more important reason for over-investment—the industry's special tax treatment. Walter J. Mead, professor of economics at the University of California at Santa Barbara, explained this effect before a Senate subcommittee, "... favored tax treatment ... substantially raise(s) the expected after-tax profit rates on oil industry exploration and development investments, in what would otherwise be submarginal uses of scarce capital. ...

"Oil industry spokesmen have defended their various subsidies with the question, 'If we receive all the subsidies which our critics allege, why is our rate of return on invested capital not substantially higher than other non-subsidized industries?' The answer to this question is that a subsidy will raise the profit rate at the point in time at which it is conferred.

"Its effects, however, are eroded away with time as producers react to their more profitable situation by expanding into otherwise submarginal areas. This expansion leads to a decline in the rate of return toward a normal yield and to resource misallocation as well."[3]

Petroleum tax rates have generally been about half of the tax rates paid on profits by other industries. Atlantic Refining Co., and then the merged Atlantic Richfield paid the United States no income tax at all from 1962 through 1967, although its net profits in that period aggregated almost half a billion dollars. As Ronnie Dugger pointed out in his fine article on oil and politics in the September, 1969, *Atlantic* magazine, "It is a fair question to ask how much U.S. income tax, on both foreign and domestic profits, is paid by the five international majors that dominate the U.S. industry, Jersey, Texaco, Gulf, Mobil, and California Standard. The answer is that during the five years from 1963 to 1967 these companies paid on total net profits before income tax of about $21 billion (U.S.) federal income tax of about $1 billion. Their five-year U.S. income tax rate was 4.9 percent. They paid foreign governments more than five times as much . . ."

Even after the much-publicized tax reform law that passed in December of 1969, the oil industry retains three very special tax benefits. The infamous depletion allowance remains the biggest one. The economic theory on which depletion allowances rest is as elusive and fleeting as is the oil in the ground. As Mr. Dugger says, it "depends on the assertion that an oil venture's capital is not the same thing as its capital investment. Oil, it is explained, is an irreplaceable 'wasting asset,' a limited quantity of an elusive substance that is being depleted. Therefore, we are told, when oil is discovered in the ground, it becomes capital that should be valued on the basis of its selling price." Because, as Jersey Standard President J. M. Rathbone has said, ". . . when a prospector found an oilfield and produced that oilfield, he was in effect going out of business."

The investment that a company makes in its business, in actually acquiring the equipment necessary to do business, it has historically been thought, should not be taxed in the same way as the inventory or goods that are sold by the business after having been produced or purchased. Thus, the grocer's truck that he buys is not taxed in the same way as the inventory on his shelves or the profit that he makes from the sale of that inventory, even though the truck is as much a part of his assets or net worth as is the inventory, or the revenue from the sale of the inventory. So what the oil industry is claiming is that the oil it discovers is more like the grocer's truck than it is like his inventory, and should be given special tax advantages. It is more like the grocer's truck, because it can become totally depleted or used up, like the grocer's truck, the oil industry's theory holds.

However, it is clear that there are also some strong dissimilarities between the grocer's truck and oil in the ground. The most important one is that the grocer must buy his truck—it is related to his out-of-pocket costs. In the case of oil in the ground, unlike the well which is used to drill for the oil, there is no relation to out-of-pocket cost of the prospector. Thus oil companies, when they deduct from their taxes a portion of the selling price of the crude oil which comes out of the ground, can, and often do, end up deducting from their taxes many times more money from a well than they actually spend to drill the well. In fact, prior to the 1969 tax reform law, the U.S. Treasury estimated that for each producing well in the ground, oil companies were recovering from these depletion allowances nineteen times the cost of the well on the average. A grocer can deduct his truck until it is fully depreciated and he has thus recovered its cost, but only once.

The second way that oil isn't similar to a groceryman's truck is that its sale is the principal object of the oil business, just as the sale of groceries (not the truck) is the object of the groceryman's business. Income derived from the sale of oil is clearly "business income." For all purposes other than the depletion allowance, it is treated as business income, just like the sale of groceries. As Ronnie Dugger put it, ". . . when the time comes to tell the stockholders how much money has been made, oil companies figure it out in the ordinary way. By investment they mean their actual costs. Profit is income in excess of those costs. The effect of percentage depletion in the financial accounts is a reduction in taxes and a higher net profit."

The final question about the depletion allowance is, that even if you said the oil companies' theory is correct, how do you set a rational percentage amount that can be deducted each year. Until the tax reform law, oil companies were able to deduct from their taxes each year up to 27½ percent of the money they received from the first sale of crude oil from their wells. However, this deduction could not exceed 50 percent of the company's profits. Thus, if gross revenues or sales on a well totalled $100,000, the producer could take a "deduction" of $27,500, that is, take it away from profits before he figured out what taxes he had to pay. However, he could take that deduction only so long as the net income or profit from the well after expenses was $55,000 or more. If, however, profits were only, say, $50,000, the deduction could only by $25,000 (only half of the profits).

As a result of this depletion allowance, in the decade 1960-69, oil companies received tax deductions that put some $20 billion of profit out of the tax collector's reach, meaning that at a 48 percent tax rate on these profits, other taxpayers forked over an extra $10 billion or so in the decade. And what Congress did to the depletion allowance in December of 1969 was essentially to make only a symbolic cut in the privilege. It cut the depletion allowance from the magic 27.5 percent figure to 22 percent. This may sound like a substantive cut. But during the debate on cutting the allowance a "Heard in the Street" column by Dan Dorfman in the "Wall Street Journal" shed some light on why the cut turns out to be more symbolic than substantive. Dorfman pointed out that oil industry analysts, such as Bache & Co., expected a cut to 22 percent to affect industry earnings by "less than 2 percent." The reason that the impact would be so small, Bache said in a wire to its offices telling them *not* to worry that stock prices of oil companies would be affected too much, is that most oil companies don't utilize the full 27.5 percent benefit because of the aforementioned restriction that it can only go up to 50 percent of profits. Bache said that, "a widely accepted figure for the actual or effective depletion allowance currently utilized by the industry is about 23 percent."[4]

Congress did put a little bit more bite in the reform by also placing a ten percent tax on the amount by which the depletion allowance exceeds the federal income tax of an individual or corporation (after subtracting actual depletion of investment costs, such as the materials needed to drill an oil well). Thus, if a company has depletion allowances of $1 million (after sub-tracting its investment costs) and these depletion allowances reduced its taxes from $1 million to $500,000 it would have to pay an additional ten percent tax on the $500,000 difference between the depletion allowances of $1 million and its taxes of $500,000—or a tax of $50,000. But even this bite combined with the cut to 22 percent will not cut the effect of the depletion allowance by more than about one-fifth, according to oil industry sources themselves. The depletion allowance, for all practical purposes, remains untouched as a special privilege.

And the depletion allowance is only one privilege. Of the three other major privileges, the Tax Reform Law of 1969 touched only one. It did eliminate so-called "carved-out produc-tion payments," which allowed oil companies to sell their oil production in advance, thus allowing the companies to shift income from one year into another at will, and get better use of the depletion allowance. But the oil companies were able to use the loss of this tax dodge as a bargaining tool to maintain the deduction for intangible drilling costs and to maintain foreign tax credits.

In oil and gas, the costs of dry holes, wells that don't produce, can be deducted from taxes. And if a well does come in, up to 90 percent of the costs of drilling it and developing it can be deducted in the year *they are incurred*. These so-called "intan-gible costs" include labor, fuel, overhead, land clearing, and all costs other than equipment that has salvage value. Expenses similar to these "intangibles" in industries other than natural resources, when they can be written off at all, must be capital-ized and written off over a number of years, not in the year they occur. The recent U.S. Treasury tax reform study says the tax loss from this deduction is $300 million a year from oil alone.

Also left untouched by the reforms were foreign tax credits that U.S. companies receive. Investments of U.S. oil companies abroad are enormous. Jersey Standard, for example, takes in as much as 49 percent of its income from foreign subsidiaries in a given year. The debate in this area centers around whether U.S. companies ought to be allowed to continue to claim against U.S. taxes "credits" for "taxes" paid to foreign governments on a dollar-for-dollar basis. A tax "credit" is subtracted directly from the amount of tax to be paid. A "deduction" is subtracted from profits before taxes are figured on those profits, and, therefore, at the current corporate tax rate on profits of 48 percent, it is worth about half as much as a "credit." Opponents of this foreign tax credit system say that many of the payments that U.S. companies make to foreign governments are actually more like royalties than like taxes, and thus ought to be treated as "deductions" against U.S. taxes, not as dollar-for-dollar credits. Royalties paid to *domestic* landowners are deductions, not credits, they note. (Royalties are payments for the use of land, much like rent, and are a normal part of production costs.) These opponents point out that, on the advice of oil companies, oil nations in the Middle East and elsewhere make their royalties seem like taxes by basing their "tax" schedule on "posted prices" which the governments set arbitrarily. These "posted prices" are almost always higher than the price the companies actually get for their oil. Thus, at the very least, the portion of the so-called "tax" that is paid on the part of the "tax" schedule above real prices ought to be considered a royalty that can be deducted, not a tax that can be credited, they argue.

It is worth pointing out in passing that oil companies can also claim depletion allowances on foreign production and can write off intangible drilling costs incurred in foreign lands—against their U.S. taxes. All of this is something of a foreign aid program. The U.S. treasury, with those write-offs, in effect pays for the costs of exploring for oil in these countries, and then the foreign countries claim whatever taxes there are to be claimed on the profits of the exploration. Perhaps the practices could be better justified if the benefits from them accrued more to the foreign countries and less to the oil companies.

These tax advantages to the oil industry have considerable social, political, and economic side effects. They help to encourage the overinvestment in oil, as mentioned before, and the misallocation of resources. One solid indicator that such over-investment does exist and is not just talk, is the multiplication of drilling funds—companies that sell shares in oil drilling operations to investors in much the same way that mutual funds are sold. Hundreds of these funds have cropped up in the last five to ten years, providing individual investors in high tax brackets with the advantages of depletion allowances and deductions for intangible drilling expenses. In a recent article the *Wall Street Journal* said, "The infusion of so much money is having an enormous impact on the oil industry. According to some estimates, one-third to one-half of all the drilling in the U.S. by the nation's 10,000 to 12,000 independent oil operators is being financed by funds."[5] Indeed, these drilling funds can be considered inherently wasteful in their exploration because, in order to provide investors with much advertised tax write-offs, they must spend available money quickly on drilling—even if no promising exploration properties are immediately available.

But in talking about the advantages provided the oil industry and their effect, we have so far left almost unmentioned probably the most important and most questionable privilege—the oil import quota system. I leave it to last because the way in which it is administered leads neatly into a discussion of the impact of our oil policies on our national politics. But first a discussion of what the import system is and how it works. In June of 1969 that bastion of business world boosterism, *Fortune* magazine, featured an article by Allan Demaree that started out this way, "The quota system that chokes off the free flow of oil into the U.S. costs the nation billions and shelters gross inefficiencies in the domestic crude-oil producing industry. Imposed in the name of national security just a decade ago, it has become the object of mounting discontent. It has given government officials the power arbitrarily to parcel out enormous fortunes to individual companies. . . ."

That's *Fortune* magazine you're hearing from, and that's the oil industry's Pet Program it's talking about. One of the things *Fortune* complains about, and the oil industry admits, is the huge cost to consumers of this restrictive import policy. *Fortune* says it is "impossible to determine exactly; but reasonable estimates put the price tag at about $4 billion a year." How does *Fortune* get anywhere near that fantastic figure? Here's how. By erecting quota barriers, the U.S. limits the foreign oil brought into the country to about 21 percent of domestic consumption. This helps (with prorationing of domestic oil as explained earlier) to keep the wellhead price of U.S. crude oil at about $3 per 42-gallon barrel, more than twice the price of Middle East crude. As *Fortune* notes, "Middle Eastern and Venezuelan crude has been landed on the east coast in recent years for $1.25 to $1.40 less per barrel than crude produced in Texas and Louisiana." Obviously prices in the U.S. would go down drastically if unlimited foreign crude were allowed in.

How is the import quota system administered? The government, namely the Interior Department's Oil Import Administration, divides the foreign oil among refiners by dispensing import allocations or "tickets" as they are known. A ticket to import a barrel of foreign crude is worth about $1.25 at the time of writing, the difference between domestic and world prices. How the tickets are awarded is obviously an important question. Big companies get fewer tickets compared to their total output than do smaller refiners, but the total number of tickets big companies receive is also much higher in absolute terms. Thus Jersey Standard has received tickets valued at over $300 million since the program began, for example, and other major companies are over $250 million.

Quite a trade has developed in the tickets. All refiners receive tickets whether or not they process foreign oil. Many inland refiners can't process foreign crude because of transportation costs, so they trade their tickets to coastal refiners for domestic crude and pocket the $1.25 difference on each barrel.

How did we get import quotas? Well, the oil industry got President Eisenhower to put them in effect in 1959 when voluntary quotas "didn't work" in the late 1950s. Foreign oil was being imported in large quantities and domestic prices were dropping. Eisenhower had first put a voluntary program into effect by using the power given him under the National Security Amendment of the Trade Agreement Extension Act of 1955.

So "national security" became the key phrase for the oil

industry in the debate over import quotas. The industry's contention is that the nation's economy would be in trouble if domestic facilities were allowed to lie idle because of a flood of cheap foreign oil. It feels that the United States can't afford to depend on other countries in the Middle East and South America for a supply of oil, because such a supply would be cut off in times of crisis. And it worries about the impact of the balance of payment situation that might occur if we started buying large quantities of oil from abroad. These are the main arguments in its so-far-successful battle to save the quotas.

But critics of the quotas seem to me to have a sounder set of arguments, and they are rooted in a basic questioning of the oil industry's interpretation of what the nation's security or defense needs are. "Does the world situation really require us to be so protective of our position?" is the question at the root of the matter. But, even given that we do need to be so paranoid a nation, is it wise for the United States to use up its own reserves when it could save them and buy cheap foreign oil instead?

Dozens more questions assault the logic of the import quotas. The discoveries in Northern Alaska give us more oil than we thought we had in the 1960's. New technology could make shale oil, of which we have trillions of barrels in the U.S., feasible in the near future. What of the growth of atomic energy? And what of the experimentation with other sources of energy for the auto? These may reduce our need. And if national security must be our concern, there are alternatives that may be cheaper than the import quota system. *Fortune* suggests that the U.S. could diversify foreign sources to limit risk, stockpile oil in storage tanks underground, or pay companies to explore for oil on federal lands and hold these reserves for that "security crisis."

Besides national security, the oil companies also claim that the oil import quotas give them an incentive to explore for oil in the United States. But with the current overinvestment in the oil business, it is long past time to reduce this incentive.

One of the rules of American politics has long been that real power flows to those who can create enclaves where important decisions can be made solely on a political basis. The Interior Department's Oil Import Administration is just such a preserve of power politics, an agency with the power to grant highly profitable privileges with few checks or balances. In 1965, for example, the administration awarded Phillips Petroleum the right to establish a $45 million petrochemical plant in Puerto Rico that would be allowed to process exclusively foreign oil, and then ship 24,800 barrels a day of gasoline "byproduct" to the east coast, the latter privilege alone being worth an estimated $11 million a year. Then Secretary of the Interior, Stewart Udall, said that such a special import allocation was needed to bring job-creating investment into Puerto Rico. Udall brushed aside a request by Texaco to build a refinery there, although Texaco is Puerto Rico's largest distributor of gasoline. Later, however, Udall also awarded Sun Oil, Union Carbide and Commonwealth Oil valuable rights to process exclusively foreign oil in Puerto Rico and ship products to the mainland. Unlike the award of oil leases or contracts, these deals are negotiated privately and not subject to competitive bidding.

As Mr. Demaree put it in *Fortune*, ". . . suspicion pervaded the capital when well-connected Washington lawyers and influential politicians were associated with one request for special privilege after another. Oscar Chapman, a prominent Democrat, Secretary of Interior under Truman, and now a Washington lawyer, was instrumental in putting together the Puerto Rican deal. . . . Puerto Rico was represented by Arnold, Fortas & Porter, the firm co-founded by President Johnson's close confidant, Abe Fortas, who had been intimately connected with the island's affairs since World War II."

But the Puerto Rico situation pales beside the one regarding the Virgin Islands as an example of political favoritism. Hess Oil & Chemical won from the Oil Import Administration the right to ship to the mainland oil products refined on St. Croix. Simultaneously, Udall turned down a request from Coastal States Gas Producing. If he had tried to cite the building of the economy in the Virgin Islands, Udall would have been on weak ground, as employment in the Virgin Islands was so high that workers had to be imported to build the refinery and man it. And when Udall turned down the Coastal States application, he said he wanted to permit no other refineries there "to protect and conserve the incomparable reefs and beaches." It ought to be pointed out that David T. Wilentz, a director of Hess Oil and Chairman Leon Hess's father-in-law, was a powerful figure in Democratic politics in New Jersey.

Formal opinions aren't issued on these decisions and while the Oil Import Administration does hold hearings, it doesn't follow with a report of findings. As import controls have become more and more involved in this web of wheeler-dealing, some strange things have happened—the Oil Import Appeals Board, the three-man administrative panel that hears appeals of the Oil Import Administration's rulings, has handed out tickets to two small refiners that had been shut down for many years, as Mr. Demaree claims in *Fortune*, "Hoping the handouts would help them pay off their creditors and reopen their plants." Another company bought an abandoned refinery from Mobil in Wyoming, encountered unexpectedly high costs in rehabilitating it, and so was helped by import tickets by the Appeals Board.

In all of this, the Interior Department is often seen bargaining to get the corporations to do something in return for their special privileges. So Phillips promised to reinvest $55 million in satellite plants in Puerto Rico, which would use the petrochemicals Phillips produces as feedstocks; Hess agreed to pay $2.7 million a year to a conservation fund on the Virgin Islands, and so forth. It is quite reminiscent of the way in which the various urban renewal agencies all over the country negotiate with private firms for sale of low-priced, high-valued land and other special privileges (instead of entering into competitive bidding) and then claim that this approach is justified because it enables the local government to get special considerations from private enterprise in return for the privileges. One begins to expect that, over the long run, the companies doing business with the public agencies fare far better than the public. But this is the way our system works—corporate executives talk about free and competitive markets, the free enterprise system and the glory of private enterprise, but in reality they expect the government to restrict and manage the economy so that the risk-taking is reduced and the chance of larger and more consistent profits is much enhanced.

And as for conflict of interest, such as that which appears to be present in the oil import administration's awards to companies which are politically favored, this is nothing new to the oilmen. For a long time they have had good reason to consider Congress their own private domain. Robert Kerr was the epitome of this in recent times. The late Senator from Oklahoma, as the second ranking Democrat on the Finance Committee, for years protected the depletion allowance while profiting from it himself. Kerr and his family owned about a fourth of the huge company called Kerr-McGee Oil Industries, Inc. In the seven years just prior to Kerr's death, that company paid less than 13 percent income tax on total aggregate profits of $77 million. Senator Kerr, when charged with conflict of interest, would simply reply with the argument that the people of Oklahoma knew he was in the oil business and approved of what he was doing.

Senator Russell Long of Louisiana holds the more contemporary counterpart position to Kerr's position in the 1950s and early 1960s. Ronnie Dugger goes into Senator Long's position at considerable length in his *Atlantic* article. He notes that Senator Long is chairman of the Finance Committee that considers tax bills, and therefore Long must manage any major tax bill on the Senate floor. Through all of this, he ardently defends the oil depletion allowance. Dugger says:

> Senator Long is also an oilman. He readily acknowledges that he inherited valuable oil and gas properties and that he has participated in drilling thirty or forty wells. He says his income from the inherited properties exceeds what he makes in the Senate. . . . (He) has participated with his mother, brother and sister, in the drilling of thirty or forty wells in Louisiana's Sligo field and in De Soto Parish south of there. . . .

> Long was elected to the Senate twenty-one years ago. How much has he made from this drilling? "I guess we're probably ahead, but not by a great deal," he says. "In drilling and producing we've probably made . . . we're doing . . . at least it's made me conversant with what we're talking about. . . ."

Long sees no conflict or impropriety in the situation. "I come from an oil-producing state, and if I was not cooperating with oil against those people who are out after it, I really don't think I'd be representing my state," he says. . . .

Once he and Senator Eugene Millikin of Colorado were discussing this very subject, Long says, and Millikin told him that any time he, Millikin, has a financial interest in something "parallel to the best interests" of his own state, he never worried about it. By that doctrine, Long says Millikin told him, the Colorado senator had an interest in shale oil. . . .

He contends, "We just haven't come down to the thing yet that a legislator has to have no interests or dispose of his outside interests. Theoretically a legislator is not expected to be unprejudiced and unbiased. . . . If someone has a conflict of interest, that's something that should be considered when he's up for re-election."

Long's theory, basically that our system allows you to get away with what you can get away with, coincides very nicely with the idea that if you can create agencies that control profitable privileges, like the Oil Import Administration, then you have the right to profit from them. In short, anything goes, as long as it works.

And it isn't very far from blatant and direct conflicts of interest, like those involving Senators Kerr, Long, and others, to the financing of political careers with huge campaign contributions in return for support of special privileges. One reason that it isn't very far, of course, is that senators like Thomas Dodd insist on converting political contributions to private use. But there isn't much difference, anyway, between trading principle for personal financial gain and trading principle for personal political gain.

With election reporting laws, and the many ways that they can be circumvented, it is difficult to document the real extent of contributions of such oilmen as H. L. Hunt, for example. But even with the unbelievably inefficient reporting laws, Dugger is able to point out that the Mellons of Gulf Oil gave the Nixon campaign $215,000 and the Pews of Sun Oil contributed $84,000. He can add that, "Officials of twenty-nine of the largest (oil) companies gave (in sums of $500 or more) a recorded $344,997 to Republicans and $14,650 to the Democrats in the 1956 general election campaign. That same year, three family groups whose wealth is associated with oil—the Mellons, Pews, and Rockefellers—contributed $469,554, all of it to Republicans. In the year of the Kennedy-Nixon campaign, officers and directors of the American Petroleum Institute gave Republicans a recorded $113,700 and Democrats $6,000; in 1964, a significantly different situation, $48,310 to Republicans and $24,000 to Democrats. And these figures are just the spray from the gusher."

The fantastic amount of money the oil industry spends in electing candidates is paralleled by the amount it spends lobbying those candidates after they are elected. Even in state legislatures these expenditures are huge. Al Shults was, in 1966, one of six lobbyists in Sacramento, California, for the oil industry. He reported $53,411 in salary and expenses for just six months of California's legislative session that year. Mr. Shults was paid in a typical month $4,500, and got another $4,000 for entertainment, and that's just what he reported as directly related to lobbying efforts. His salary and expenses were almost matched by the other five oil lobbyists in California.

Oil money also shows up by the barrel in ballot measure races, particularly those asking voters to transfer state highway trust funds to uses other than highways. In the relatively small state of Oregon, for example, eight national oil companies spent $83,390 to successfully fend off adoption by voters of a measure that would have imposed a one-cent-a-gallon gasoline tax for four years. The money would have been used to purchase private beaches for the public.

When one gets to criticizing the oil industry and its effects, it is difficult to know where to stop. Consider the matter of pollution. There is air pollution from the internal combustion engine. There is air pollution from oil heaters. There is air pollution from oil refineries. There is air pollution from oil well fires offshore, which are increasingly common. Then if you want to go to water pollution, oil must be the primary single water pollutant in the entire world. There is also the pollution of plastics that doesn't break down in the environment, and many plastics come from petrochemicals, or oil. There is the visual pollution that results from ugly gasoline stations and their signs cluttering our landscape. And one could go on.

The problem with public attitudes about much of this pollution is that the public tends to look at such environmental problems in a vacuum of sorts. They don't very often relate the amount and nature of the pollution we face in the United States to the type of economy we have—consumer oriented, affluent, an economy that treats natural resources as if they were endless, an economy that values growth above nearly everything else, an economy that keys on private profits as an ultimate value, a technological economy. All of these factors tend to create more waste, more pollution, more environmental difficulty.

The pollution that resulted from the infamous oil well blowout off the coast of Santa Barbara, California, ought not to be looked at in isolation as a simple case of corporate negligence. For one thing, Union Oil, the operator of the well, and its three partners in the well, Gulf, Mobil, and Texaco, were granted the lease to drill off the coast against recommendations of geologists. Secretary of the Interior Udall knew there were geologic problems associated with drilling in the area, largely from earthquakes. But, as discussed earlier, the special privileges in the oil industry that reduce taxes and stabilize prices have generated a terrific pressure to explore for oil domestically that would not exist under normal conditions, in a rational economy. So the oil industry keeps the pressure on to drill in areas like Santa Barbara, where it knows that local citizens oppose the drilling and that the industry will face public relations problems, where it knows that the ecology of the area is unique; where it knows that earthquakes will present special safety problems.

Things are even more complicated, in fact. As William M. Blair explained in a copyrighted article for *The New York Times* News Service shortly after the blowout in Santa Barbara, much of the pressure to allow the drilling came, not from the industry, but from the U.S. Bureau of the Budget. The Johnson

Administration was well aware that the government had reaped nearly $2 billion from leasing the continental shelf to oil companies in the Gulf of Mexico, and it felt it needed more money, as governments are wont. Mr. Blair quoted Interior Secretary Udall as having second thoughts about allowing the drilling, and quoted a Stanley A. Cain, assistant secretary for fish, wildlife and parks, regarding the existence of this pressure on Udall from the Budget Bureau, as well as the oil companies.

Major catastrophes, like the Santa Barbara slick that covered 400 square miles of ocean and fouled 40 miles of incomparable beach, get extensive coverage in the press. Similarly, spot news coverage of events like the 40,000 gallons that spilled into Chesapeake Bay in 1970 when oil was being pumped from a tanker into a barge, or the 10,000 gallons of oil that were dumped into Tampa Bay in the same year when a Panamanian tanker ran aground, is commonplace. But the coverage makes each accident seem like an isolated catastrophe, largely unexplainable and caused by misfortune or negligence. The oil industry sticks together and uses all of its power to make it seem as if this is so, of course. As *Time* magazine explained in its feature on Santa Barbara (February 14, 1969), "While known in Souther California as 'the go-go company,' Union also has picked up something of a reputation as a polluter. Only two weeks ago, the company was accused of dumping 1,500 barrels of crude into the Santa Ana River after a mud slide broke a pipeline. Twice in 1967, the company was brought up on violations of California fish and game statutes for polluting Los Angeles harbor ... After the disaster, representatives of oil companies operating rigs off Santa Barbara met quietly to decide, as one participant put it, whether 'to take the drop of the gallows together.' Reluctantly, they agreed to back Union—at least for the time being."

Actually, there is a very real pattern of pollution, not just by Union but by the whole industry—the kind of neglect of the environment that is conscious and profit-motivated. Both *Time* and the *Wall Street Journal* quoted Fred Hartley, Union Oil Co. president, as telling the Senate Public Works subcommittee hearings, "I'm amazed at the publicity for the loss of a few birds." (The Santa Barbara Channel Islands are home not only for an amazing variety of birds from cormorants and grebes to loons and ruddy ducks, but also contain rookeries for the sea elephant, the Guadalupe fur seal—once thought extinct—and the rare sea otter.)

The industry pattern and its base in a selfish, even greedy attitude were perhaps best exposed not by the carelessness of Hartley's remarks or Union's failure to use the proper equipment on its Santa Barbara Platform A, but by the attempts of the California State Attorney General to get academic experts in oil drilling in California universities to help his office to prepare for legal action against the companies owning the Santa Barbara well. He was unable to secure any help. Said Charles A. O'Brien, California chief deputy attorney general, "I find this industry domination of university researchers to be deplorable. It is my hope that the industry itself—presuming it has nothing to hide—will tell the university experts that they may cooperate with us, that their cooperation will not result in the withdrawal of research funds, and that the cooperation will not end their employment as oil industry consultants." Lyman Handy, chairman of the petroleum engineering department at the University of Southern California, the leading department in the state, conceded that it would be "a real ticklish thing" for engineers to work with the state on the case because they get most of their consulting jobs from oil concerns. "It's their bread and butter," he said. He further maintained that engineers in the department "wouldn't be as impartial as we would like to be for fear of alienating our support." The USC department, when it turned down the request to help the state, had already received a $150,000 grant from Western Oil and Gas Association, an industry trade group, to study the effects of the Santa Barbara oil spill on the ecology of the channel. The petroleum industry is also a substantial source of other research grants, Mr. Handy told the press.

Occasionally, someone in the press will try to pull the whole story together and talk about the pattern that exists and the way things work, instead of just about the specific instance. Such was a story by Glenn Mapes in the *Wall Street Journal*[6] in which he simply states that, "world-wide oil pollution—even diluted by the ocean's vastness—is nearing crisis proportions." Mr. Mapes goes on to say that, "In recent years, a few widely publicized disasters—like the grounding of the supertanker Torrey Canyon off Britain and the blowout of a well in the Santa Barbara Channel—have focused public attention on oil spills. Yet, damaging as these occasional catastrophes can be, they're only one part of a far larger problem, the experts say.

" 'It's the day-to-day stuff that's killing us—the chronic oil pollution that nobody reads about in the headlines,' says Lieutenant Commander Paul Sova, a Coast Guard law enforcement officer in New York. Adds a biologist for the U.S. Fish and Wildlife Service: 'A great deal of oil is washing ashore all along our coasts. What's its cumulative effect on our environment? That's what we ought to start worrying about.' "

An intensive scientific survey by scientists at the Woods Hole, Massachusettts Oceanographic Institution on a series of oil spills at Falmouth, Mass., including an oil barge that ran onto rocks there and dumped some 170,000 gallons of heating oil into the water, found that "The impact of oil on marine life has been seriously underestimated," according to Dr. Howard Sanders of Woods Hole. The "kill" from the spills was virtually 100 percent, including some 24 species of fish as well as crabs, lobsters and scallops. Even weeks after the spill there were subtle effects on the sea life at Falmouth. Divers from Woods Hole found fish and crabs whose natural instincts were strangely altered. Flounders allowed themselves to be handled and fiddler crabs boldly stood their ground instead of skittering away.

Mr. Mapes says, "Max Blumer, a noted organic chemist at Woods Hole, observes that many marine animals produce minute quantities of chemicals that perform functions essential to maintaining the cycle of life. These chemicals act as attractants during the mating process. They also aid predators in locating their prey and, conversely, give warning to potential victims that they're being stalked by predators. Oil—whether from a single big spill or a buildup of repeated small doses—may well upset these vital, chemically triggered processes, Mr. Blumer theorizes, and thus could have a disastrous effect on the survival of many species, including those that are commercially important.

"Dumping of oil in the sea may also be creating a new risk of cancer in man. Some crude oils contain compounds that tend to produce cancer in animals. (Researchers, for example, have already found a high incidence of cancerous tissue in certain types of fish taken from the oily waters of Los Angeles Harbor.) Fish and shellfish that are eaten by man can ingest these oils. Hence, Mr. Blumer and other scientists speculate that chronic oil pollution may be leading to accumulation of cancer causing agents in human food."

Mr. Mapes also explains how difficult it is to trace the source of many large oil slicks. He describes a trip he took with a Coast Guard spotter above New York Harbor in which six oil slicks were identified, but the source of none of the six could be traced. Ships often deliberately discharge oil at night or during periods of low visibility. The Coast Guard only patrols within the three-mile limit, and many ships routinely discharge oil wastes on the high seas, and these drift toward shore. Oil tankers regularly wash out their cargo tanks with salt water and dump the residue overboard. Moreover, other types of ships often fill their fuel tanks with water for ballasting purposes and then dump the contaminated mixture overboard before refueling. Manufacturing plants, refineries, and oil terminals often dump oil into nearby water. (In Boston Harbor alone, a spill of several tons of oil can be expected every three weeks, according to officials of the Massachusetts Division of Natural Resources.) The Coast Guard lists 714 major oil spills in U.S. coastal waters in 1968, up from 371 two years before. The larger oil tankers being built, growing oil production in Alaska and the increased amount of offshore drilling all over the world are sure to add to the problem. Strengthening of international conventions on dumping oil in the high seas, radar systems to detect oil leaks and their sources and laws that hold sources monetarily accountable for cleaning up the spills are all required, as a start, but oil companies and shippers fight them.

Former Secretary of the Interior Walter Hickel bravely ordered polluters held liable for the full cleanup costs at Santa Barbara.

And a year later, after another spill off Louisiana, Hickel pressed for prosecution against oil companies that had violated safety regulations and won $1 million in fines. But President Nixon fired Hickel. White House insiders felt he was not a "team player," the Washington press reported. After all, look at those large contributions the "team" gets from the oil industry. (Meanwhile, while capitulating, Nixon tries to make the "team" look good. He proposes a revolving fund to clean up slicks and asks Congress to ratify international amendments on oil pollution. In late 1970, faced with mounting inflation and an increase in oil prices, he ordered that production from offshore wells on federal leases not come under state prorationing, so supply might go up and prices down a little. But the more significant Import Quota system went untouched, at his order.)

While over-investment in the oil business encourages pollution by encouraging drilling in areas like the Santa Barbara Channel, there is another area of the oil business where pollution is directly related to the economics of the industry. This is the visual pollution that exists as a result of the unnecessary proliferation of gasoline service stations all over the country. It is not simply the proliferation of new stations that causes the junky, littered landscape, but also the abandonment of hundreds of old stations that dot our cities and countryside, ugly and deteriorating. The old service station lots are often too small to be useful for a big new station that can handle the gallonage that the oil companies now require, so instead of using their old station sites, the majors simply close them up and let them sit idle. Often, the stations aren't torn down, and not many other businesses want or require the same locations. Similarly, not many businesses can use the type of building that the oil companies construct.

In Portland, Oregon, a city council candidate in the 1970 elections, Neil Goldschmidt, used as a major issue in his campaign the fact that in that city of some 375,000 people there were over 100 abandoned gas stations sitting idle and deteriorating, yet the city government neither required the eyesores to be torn down nor stopped granting gasoline stations the right to build new stations (and sometimes right across the street from the old abandoned stations). This pattern is not uncommon in cities all across the country. If it's not too hard for the big oil companies to get their way in Congress, it's sometimes easier for them to deal with local planning commissions and city councils.

It was interesting to note, but not really too unusual, that the local association of independent gasoline station dealers supported candidate Goldschmidt in his position. The independent dealers (most of the nation's 220,000 station operators are "independent" in that they are not hired by the oil companies and they own their own inventories, if not the land or the station buildings) said, in essence, that the oil companies often try to force them out of business. The majors are interested only in how much gallonage they can get from these proliferating stations, not how the dealers nearby the new stations are able to fare, they maintain.

The major oil companies are fantastically large and fantastically profitable. Of the twenty largest firms in the *Fortune* 500, seven are oil companies and their profits, when added together, frequently equal the profits of the other thirteen companies. The 33 oil companies in *The New York Times* listing of 500 often have one third of the total profit for the 500. How does this size and bulkiness of profit transfer down the line to the thousands of service station operators? The answer to that is that half the nation's dealers make less than $6,000 of take-home profit a year.[7] Well over 50 percent of the men who enter the business each year fail. And more and more men don't fail but give up anyway because their return is so small for the hours they put in. One out of four gas stations now changes hands every year.

It is exploitation, clear and simple. The two main ways in which the exploitation occurs are in the setting of prices and the setting of hours. What the oil companies want is high volume to make their huge capital investments (overinvestment again) pay off.

Gallonage or volume is only partially related to income, of course, and that is through the price mechanism. So the higher the prices, the more income. But there is *some* competition, given the supply of oil available. That is, while prices are usually the same throughout a community for the major oil companies' dealers, there are usually a few independents who sell a few cents below the major company dealers. If the major companies' station prices get too far out of line, they start losing gallonage. So the majors control prices. The problem is then, that the dealers have no union to bargain for them, to see that they get a fair portion of the price they can't control. Since there are always a few people anywhere who are willing to work for less (that is why there are such things as union shops in which everyone must belong to a union) in the oil industry, these people allow some oil companies to give them a very small margin, and this small margin allows those companies to set their prices low, and others must follow suit, or be out of line with the competition. As a story in the *Wall Street Journal*[8] recently put it, "Oil companies have told Congressional committees they would fire any sales representatives found pressuring dealers on matters like prices ... But in practice it often doesn't work that way. 'I'll take a dealer right up the courthouse steps with a threat to break his lease. My job is to see that he follows policy,' says a Midwest sales representative for one big oil company. And a former executive at another company says, 'Oh, yes, we'd set hours and prices and procedures.' And he asks, 'If nobody is setting the prices, how come they're all the same.' "

As the *Journal* story said, ". . . pricing is the operator's biggest complaint. The operators have to buy their gasoline from the big oil companies, and then, they claim, they are told at what price to resell it to the customer. Donald R. Geary, a former Gulf dealer in Pittsburgh, says Gulf Oil insisted he sell at a four-cent margin, which he maintains is not enough to make a living. He says Gulf canceled his lease when he began selling at six cents to seven cents above his cost. He is suing Gulf under the antitrust laws; Gulf denies the allegation."

Being asked to maintain long hours or be open all night is the other matter which irritates service station owners. Often the costs of staying open late (costs increased by frequent robberies) are not even covered by the receipts, let alone the profits, during those hours. But those costs (labor, for example) are absorbed by the dealer, not the oil company. And it means more gallonage for the oil company. So the majors insist, threatening to break the lease, and the dealers capitulate.

In short, whether you want to talk about exploitation of station operators, pollution of our air and water, unbalancing of our economy by the misallocation of resources and the protection of unreasonable prices, or the corruption of our political system, the oil industry is there. Its actions are another price we pay for our automotive culture.

NOTES

[1]August Gribbin, Michael Malloy, Patrick Young and Edwin A. Roberts, Jr., "How High-Priced Oil Gets That Way," *National Observer* (May 12, 1969), p. 14.

[2]August Gribbin, Michael Malloy, Patrick Young and Edwin A. Roberts, Jr., "How Tax Breaks Have Nourished the Oil Business," *National Observer* (May 26, 1969), p. 12.

[3]*Ibid.*

[4]Dan Dorfman, "Heard on the Street," *Wall Street Journal* (November 4, 1969).

[5]James C. Tanner, "Drilling Funds Multiply But Draw Fire for Bid to Lure Less Affluent," *Wall Street Journal* (October 27, 1969), p. 1.

[6]Glynn Mapes, "Pollution of the Seas, Beaches by Oil Poses Major Global Problem," *Wall Street Journal* (November 26, 1969), p. 1.

[7]Jim Hyatt, "Service Station Men Say Big Oil Companies Keep Them in Bondage," *Wall Street Journal* (October 7, 1969), p. 1.

[8]*Ibid.*

CHAPTER **7** SOCIAL
JUSTICE
AND THE
AUTO

We are a nation of people, who, during the decade of the 1960s bought 22 million electric carving knives and 47 million home hair dryers. About one-third of our families now own not one car, but two. More of our families (95 percent) have television sets than have indoor toilets, and the average U.S. family now owns five (count 'em—five) radios.[1]

Yet in the midst of this fantastic affluence we still have roughly ten percent of our population, some 20 million people according to the 1970 census, living in poverty, generally considered to be $3,000 a year income or below for a family of four.

The poor are disproportionately the aged, the infirm, and mothers with dependent children. People in these family units make up from 12 million to 17 million of those in poverty, depending on who is doing the figuring and what the state of the economy is. Much of the poverty in this country is thus ineradicable by training or employment programs. Cripples, six-year-olds and 80-year-olds are not benefited by job training. And it is to our everlasting discredit that we Americans do not care enough for our fellow human beings to distribute the wealth of our nation from electric carving knives and second automobiles into adequate food, clothing, and shelter for those unable to alter their state of poverty.

But for the purposes of this book, I wish to consider, not how this uncaring nation refuses to provide for the people's welfare, but instead, how our transportation system makes people stay poor when they might otherwise escape poverty. As an income distribution tool, our urban transportation system decidedly favors the rich at the expense of the poor. And, income distribution aside, the many undesirable effects of the automobile fall hardest upon the poor. Consider:

● If air pollution is at its vilest in our central cities, where autos congest, oil burners are numerous, and old manufacturing plants smoke away, it is the poor who must reside there and pay the cost of the dirty air with higher rates of respiratory disease.

● If auto accidents are more likely to strike those with older vehicles, out of repair and unsafe to drive, it is the poor who must buy these old jalopies—and then can't afford to repair them.

● If our cities are no longer safe, civilized, vital places to live in, and if automobiles work to erode the few decent urban neighborhoods we have left, it is the poor who must bear the burden of living in the dangerous and dull communities that remain.

● If the auto industry's production lines and marketing techniques make work that is meaningless and fruitless, it is the ambitious man trying to escape poverty who must take the dullest and least worthwhile of the tasks.

● If the automobile as a symbol of masculinity or a symbol of status deceives modern man and distorts his values, it is the poor man who wishes to partake in the supposed benefits but can't afford to do so who pays for it most—not only with the distortion of his values, but with a sense of loss for being unable to share in the benefits that he can't even discover are illusory.

Worth special attention are the relocation and removal of the urban poor by highways, and the victimizing of the poor by those who sell, finance, repair, and insure automobiles.

Laws requiring sticker prices posted on new cars and the new truth-in-lending act have helped to curb some of the standard abuses that new and used car dealers had long perpetuated, principally against the poor. But there are still many dealers who will charge whatever they can for a car and who will arrange financing at illegal interest rates.

Even without dishonest and unethical dealers and finance companies, the automobile pricing system works against the poor. For no American car company yet makes a cheap, safe car that requires little maintenance, lasts long, and gets good gas mileage. Volkswagen comes close to accomplishing this, as do other imports such as Datsun and Toyota and Volvo. And it must be admitted that recent attempts of American car companies to produce small autos like the Vega and Pinto are steps in that direction. But, partially because of American car advertising, the Volkswagen and the other small cars do not provide the status nor the appeal to masculinity of the American-make cars, and consequently VWs are not appealing to many poor people. American-make cars are not cheap to run, nor are they cheap to keep in repair. Further, their original cost is ballooned by frequent styling changes and excessive gimmickry. So, the man who can't afford to pay high prices for a new car or high prices to operate and maintain a car is simply priced out of the market. It is for this reason that over 40 percent of families below the poverty level and over 40 percent of black families have no automobiles. And these ownership figures are highly deceiving, for almost two-thirds of the cars owned by poor families are over six years old and many are either completely unusable or very undependable.

One Los Angeles survey found that of 530 male ghetto residents, only 246 had access to a car. Only 200 of these cars were judged to be suitable for freeway driving and only 153 were insured.[2]

But it is not simply that the poor are priced out of automobile ownership and the mobility that means. Obviously, many do buy cars. But, when they do, because of their circumstances, they are more susceptible to being taken by the system, first because high prices represent a greater portion of the poor's income, and secondly, because poor people often extend themselves financially to buy a car and as a result frequently must default on their auto loan payments. Such defaulting is widespread. Estimates of defaulted auto installment debt ranges from $700 million to more than $1 billion in a typical year. General Motors Acceptance Corp. alone repossessed 138,000 cars in 1969 because of these defaults.

What happens to the poor man when he defaults is particularly vicious. He is hit with a "deficiency judgment." This is because in almost every case, over 99 percent of the time, the car, when it is repossessed by the creditor and resold, does not bring enough money to pay the entire balance outstanding on the loan. So state laws in all 50 states say that *the debtor* must pay the cash difference between the amount the car brings on its first resale by the creditor and what the debtor owes. The poor debtor not only has no car, but he still has a good portion of the car loan to pay off.

Under this deficiency judgment system, creditors are encouraged to take the car away from the owner, often stealthily in the dark of night, and then sell it off quickly (because the sale must be quick, to avoid legal remedies by the debtor to reclaim the car) below its fair market value. Philip Shuchman, a law professor at the University of Connecticut, studied 150 Connecticut repossession cases[3] in which he found that first resale prices for repossessed autos averaged only 71 percent of wholesale value and only 51 percent of retail value. By contrast, he found dealers paid 98 percent of "book" price for nonrepossessed cars they bought at auction. Critics of the deficiency judgment say that creditors could recoup their money when a buyer defaults by simply selling the repossessed autos at fair market price.

This change in the law to outlaw deficiency judgments might result in tighter screening of loans for autos and perhaps would reduce auto sales to the poor, but the poor are certainly not helped by the present system and the government ought to become more deeply involved in seeing that they have transportation anyway.

It ought to be noted that the State of California has done away with deficiency judgments on all major appliances. Similar

California legislation for autos has been fought by those well-known progressive souls—bankers and auto dealers.

The poor are also more susceptible to illegal types of consumer fraud, partially because they lack education, and partially because they are known to have little or no access to our expensive legal system for remedies, so they become logical targets for this fraud. One good example is the auto repair racket. Sam Crowther and Irwin Winehouse, for their book *Highway Robbery*, extensively questioned federal, state, and local law enforcement authorities and then put the estimated cost to the American consumer at $100,000,000 a year for excessive and fraudulent charges for auto repairs. Because we are baffled by and superstitious of our technology, we are in the hands of the dishonest repairman. And the poor pay proportionately more for their repairs. Partially at fault here are state laws that allow mechanics liens, which enable the mechanic to charge nearly whatever he wants and then *hold your car until you pay*. The alternative to such laws are appeals boards with knowledge of the technology involved and the right to investigate and correct grievances. Licensing of mechanics might also help. Some reformers have suggested that extensive programs to teach the poor how to repair their own cars be coupled with programs to help them finance the purchase and make wise purchases. But more about that later.

Our auto insurance system also unfairly victimizes the poor. Because they are more likely to own unsafe cars, the poor have more accidents than persons of higher incomes. Consequently, insurance companies often charge different rates, sometimes depending on residential patterns, to determine who is a bad risk. So, if you live in a poor neighborhood, whatever your income and whatever your driving record, many insurance companies are likely to charge you higher rates. And when discrimination doesn't occur in such a blanket fashion, it often does occur directly on the basis of income.

"White highways through black bedrooms," has become a rallying cry for militant groups in such cities as Nashville, Baltimore, and Washington, D.C. in recent years, and in an earlier chapter we talked at some length about the effect of the proposed freeway in Nashville's ghetto. But it is worth taking some extra time to explain why, both quantitatively and qualitatively, our urban freeway system strikes hardest at the already disadvantaged urban dweller.

There are three basic reasons why urban freeways are more likely to relocate the black and the poor. The main reason is probably political. Persons outside the highway bureaucracy have been able to affect the decisions of the bureacracy almost solely by imposing "negative limits" on where a freeway could go. That is, local residents and the political persons and groups who represent them have not been able, generally speaking, to dictate to the highway bureaucracy what freeway routes will be considered. But they *have* been able to say, in effect, "you can't build a freeway through that neighborhood." Those persons best able to manipulate the political system to this end are those who already have political power—the well-to-do. Nobody wants an eight-lane monstrosity through their neighborhood, and the poor have been least able to mobilize the muscle to stop the highway builders, least able to manipulate the highway bureaucracy.

The second reason is simple cost. On the surface, it costs less to reimburse for loss of the homes of the poor than the homes of the rich, and this fact can weigh heavily in the cost-benefit analyses of the highway engineers.

The third reason is geographical. If freeways are to serve the central business districts where the rich are employed, they must always pass through the neighborhoods most immediately adjacent to that district. Those neighborhoods almost invariably hold our urban poor.

These are all reasons why, speaking in terms of number of persons displaced and numbers of neighborhoods disrupted and divided, the poor have suffered most from our urban highway system. But there is also a difference in the quality of the suffering, and Marc Fried, a professor of human sciences at Boston College, has explained some of this in an article in *The Urban Condition*.[4] Mr. Fried reported on what is perhaps the only independently-collected body of information on what happens to people before and after relocation, both in terms of factual and emotional changes. The study was of an urban renewal project that removed what was largely a lower-middle class or working class population from the West End in Boston to make room for a high-income apartment project. While relocation for urban renewal is not exactly the same as relocation for purposes of a freeway, Mr. Fried pointed out in a letter to the author that, "the problems of highway displacement are quite similar, but, if anything, somewhat worse because (a) relocation payments are probably less adequate, and (b) it is more massive in its effects," than displacement for urban renewal.

Mr. Fried, in describing the feelings about relocation given interviewers by the majority of the people removed from the West End found it "quite precise to speak of their reactions as expressions of *grief*. These are manifest in the feelings of painful loss, the continued longing, the general depressive tone, frequent symptoms of psychological or social or somatic distress, the active work required in adapting to the altered situation, the sense of helplessness, the occasional expressions of both direct and displaced anger, and tendencies to idealize the lost place."

The study found that the source of this grief came not only from the loss and disruption of affiliations with friends and relatives who lived in the area, but also the loss of "a sense of spatial identity" that was partially the result of the fact that people who lived in the West End viewed their "home" as more than just their place of residence, but also as the familiar places surrounding that residence. Mr. Fried notes that, "there is a marked relationship between class status and depth of grief: the higher the status, by any of several indices, the smaller the proportions of severe grief." This is so largely because poorer and working-class people take their friends from a smaller geographical area because that is generally all they have access to, and because, as Mr. Fried says, "of the importance of external stability" found by lower-income persons in this identification with familiar places. He also points out that "a predisposition to depression markedly accentuates the depth of grief in response to the loss of one's residential area."

In short, the poor, who draw their friends from a small geographical area, who require the external stability of familiar places, and who are more likely already to be depressed, are likely to suffer more emotional distress when they are forcibly removed from their homes and from familiar neighborhoods. The amount of emotional distress suffered by relocatees can be lessened by helping them to remain in the old neighborhoods, or as near as possible, and by supplying them with truly adequate relocation assistance. Our freeway removal programs have generally failed to accomplish either objective in any meaningful way.

But it is not only emotionally that the poor suffer more from being relocated. They also suffer because of the lack of decent low-income housing in our society. Chester Hartman writes about the study of Boston's West End and 33 other (not-so-independent) studies of the effect of relocation from urban renewal projects. He compiled the results, then wrote in the *Journal of the American Institute of Planners* that, "the vast majority of displaced families incur increased housing costs, often of substantial proportions and irrespective of housing improvement or the family's financial capabilities."[5]

Mr. Hartman particularly noted a large Chicago study in which displaced families reported that, overall, rent as a proportion of the families' income rose following relocation from 16.6 to 26.3 percent. He noted that "this same study indicates the degree to which poorer families suffer most from these increases: among those earning less than $3,000 per year (35 percent of all households) median rent/income ratios rose from 35.3 percent before relocation to 45.9 percent after relocation; among those in the $3,000 to $3,999 bracket, the median ratio increased from 18.3 to 25.4 percent; and among those earning over $5,000, the median ratio increased from 9.1 to 17.4 percent." Mr. Hartman's compilation of the 33 studies also showed that overcrowdedness was often increased by relocation. He also casts severe doubt on the finding of some of the studies that the structural quality of the homes the relocatees moved into was improved over the ones torn down. He notes that in the case of the West End in Boston, the independent study found that 25 percent of the persons had moved into structurally deficient or unsound dwellings, while a study by the urban renewal agency found only two percent had done so. Mr. Hartman suggests that the agencies doing the relocating often tried to "look good" in the studies they do of their renewal projects.

It is also important to note that Mr. Hartman found that racial factors were particularly important in determining the effect of a forced relocation upon a family. He says that "every study" shows that "the effects of discrimination make decent relocation housing more difficult and expensive to obtain for nonwhites and force them to pay high rents, even for poor housing." He points out that a study in Akron showed it took seven weeks for an average white family to find housing and white families often needed only the newspaper to do so. But Negro families took an average of twenty weeks and were forced to rely primarily on informal sources, such as friends and relatives. Then, speaking of racial segregation, he adds that, "From the few studies in which these broader questions are discussed it would appear that relocation efforts have gone no further than dealing with the individual family and its housing problems, with the result that existing patterns of racial segregation have either continued or become intensified."

Mr. Hartman also found that many displaced families moved directly into areas that were planned for redevelopment as housing or highways in the near future. He notes that one New York City study of 709 tenants moving from urban renewal sites into new addresses, 49 percent moved into housing in areas mapped for future redevelopment.

Three conclusions come out of the works of Mr. Fried, Mr. Hartman, and others on relocation: much of the result of displacing families has been for the rich to get richer and the poor to get poorer, economically, socially, and psychologically. To reverse this trend, there must be a sufficient number of vacant units in sound condition, available at prices the poor can afford, open to nonwhite occupancy, and suitably located for the social as well as the economical needs of the displaced people. Finally, it would be preferable to avoid displacing the poor altogether.

I have still left untouched several effects of our urban transportation network upon our urban poor. The massive government financing of interstate highways is worth a mention. Auto use, once an auto is owned, is not related to income, at least not in a very direct way. If a poor man does obtain an auto, he still pays the same taxes on his gasoline as a rich man. And financing of rapid transit, quite often from local property taxes or other regressive forms of taxation, also tends to transfer income from poor to rich. Too, the inner city and short-haul transit lines used by the poor more frequently pay for themselves because of heavy use and thereby provide a subsidy for the long-haul suburban-to-city lines that are little used and serve a higher income clientele.

In fact, one must be very careful about assuming that rapid transit subsidization helps the immobile poor. If regressive taxes like property or sales taxes are used for the transit subsidy, the subsidy will normally result in the poor financing transit for the rich. Martin Wohl's study of who is served by rapid transit shows, for example, that the 1964 opening of the Skokie Swift rail transit line in Chicago that connects the village of Skokie with downtown Chicago resulted in subsidizing transit (by the federal government and the Chicago Transit Authority) that serves a ridership consisting of households 86 percent of which own a car and 33 percent of which own two or more cars (compared to similar percentages of 72 percent and 15.3 percent for the entire Chicago area). Mr. Wohl also points to taxpayer subsidy of such suburban commuter lines as the Long Island and New Haven lines in New York and the Highland Branch road in Boston that he demonstrates involve perverse income distribution from poor to rich. He cites, as well, the plans for new transit systems in Washington, D.C., and the San Francisco bay area which are being built largely to serve high-income families,[6] but more about that later.

The loss of mobility the poor suffer from the over-reliance our society places on the automobile that is beyond their financial grasp is not very well understood in its full effects, income-distributional or otherwise. There is some question as to exactly what the poor give up. To really study this thoroughly one would have to look at trips not consummated or compromised. Trips that the poor want to make, but cannot. But there has been little or no effort at research along these lines by scholars or the government. Metropolitan transportation studies of the kind required by the government to justify highway construction do tabulate the number of trips per household, but such studies don't include walking trips, and there is considerable evidence that the residential densities of the poor as well as their life style tend to encourage trips to be made on foot, whether or not an automobile is owned. So judgments about the mobility of the poor made from these studies are questionable. But it seems logical to assume that many of the urban poor pay high prices at ghetto stores because they can't get out to shop elsewhere. The selective looting and burning that occurred during ghetto riots indicates they know where they are being fleeced, and by whom, but are frustrated by their inability to do anything about it. Similarly, it seems logical that community-wide cultural and recreational facilities are denied the poor when such facilities are located outside the ghetto, although there is some question here as to whether the poor could afford to partake of some of these benefits (or would want to) even if they could reach them easily.

The one clear and substantial effect of the immobility of the poor is a reduction in ability to find and maintain employment. There are three factors that work alongside the absence of a reliable automobile to make this an increasingly serious problem for the poor. First, the poor, particularly blacks, are segregated residentially in the urban core. Second, the job opportunities (openings as opposed to existing jobs), particularly the opportunities for manual and blue-collar work that are likely to be accessible to the poor, are more and more being found in the suburbs, as industry decentralizes to avoid high land costs (and taxes) and as industrial reliance on centralized rail freight transportation is reduced. Finally, the trips to these highly dispersed suburban working places are not well served by current bus and rail transit routes and it would require heavy expense to expand coverage enough to serve them.

As a result of these circumstances, first spelled out and dramatized by the 1965 McCone Commission Report on the causes of the riots in the Watts district of Los Angeles, several experiments have been undertaken to try to deal with the problem. A federally-subsidized bus line was started along Century Boulevard in Los Angeles, running from Watts to the airport and an industrial area nearby, and other routes were tried out in Los Angeles. The Century eventually got up to 17,000 passengers a week. In St. Louis a similar set of routes took ghetto residents to an industrial park in the suburb of Hazelwood. And in Buffalo and on Long Island other experimental ghetto-to-suburb routes were begun.

While these experimental routes did help some people find jobs and evidently also provided some transport to health facilities that were otherwise difficult to reach, three inter-related problems presented themselves.

1. Predictions of vast numbers of jobs being filled just didn't materialize. Thousands of openings existed in St. Louis in the Hazelwood area, for example, and thousands of persons were unemployed in the ghetto. But transportation was not a magic key to unlock the door and match the openings with the people. It is now beyond doubt that there are several other factors involved in the employment problems of the poor. Sometimes the wages offered in the suburbs are no higher than the poor can make downtown at menial tasks that they refuse to take in the first place. Sometimes employers simply use the lack of transportation as an excuse and don't intend to hire black men even if they can get to work. Sometimes the skills of the unemployed are not adequate, no training programs exist, and the employer is unwilling to fund on-the-job-training. Sometimes the unemployed man is held back by lethargy, a lack of motivation or poor work habits and therefore can't keep the job he is given. Sometimes the poor simply can't obtain information about job openings in the suburbs and so don't know where to go to look. As John F. Kain put it in an

article in the *Journal of the American Institute of Planners*, "Typically workers learn about jobs from friends, neighbors, and relatives or by seeing a help-wanted sign in the window. These informal mechanisms are almost completely absent for ghetto Negroes in the case of suburban jobs. If all of your friends live in the ghetto, if few of them are employed in the rapidly growing suburban parts of the metropolis, and if you seldom visit the suburbs, there is only the remotest chance of your learning about jobs available there."[7] In short, lack of transportation is only one factor among many that cause unemployment. Providing transportation may be necessary, but it is seldom sufficient in itself.

2. With full-size buses, the cost of operating numerous lines to the suburban working sites from the ghetto is considerable and in *no* case has the revenue from a line paid for operating costs within a short time after start-up. The demand may sometimes exist for such a route, but there is also the problem of informing people that the new route exists. The time lapse involved is expensive.

3. The experiments with ghetto-to-suburb bus routes discovered that the buses were eventually not needed or wanted in most cases. The man who found a job and survived the probationary period either got in a car pool or bought a car. He eventually stopped using the bus service and this was disastrous for the service. Customers turned out to be only temporary customers and when they left, they had to be replaced by other customers or the bus line couldn't even come close to covering the cost of its operations. The most reliable users of transit from home to work among the poor are not the married men who most desperately need the transportation assistance to find the job. Instead, they are married women working part or full time, the very old, or the very young who cannot drive. In short, many of the most reliable users of transit are marginal members of the labor force. For a poverty-level family, their employment may be the difference between eating and going hungry. But they are also less likely to stick with a job over a long period of time than a married man, and that, too, is a factor in providing transit service that has a guaranteed ridership.

While the fact that the married man often does not continue to use transit after the end of the probationary period on his job may adversely affect the provision of non-subsidized ghetto-to-suburb bus lines, this does not mean that the provision of transportation to enable the poor to find a job and keep it in its initial stages is not crucial. The transportation problems in finding work are many and various. Many plants ask job-seekers to take application forms home to fill them out, thereby using the willingness to make a return trip the next day as an indication of interest in the job, even though the return trip may be difficult or expensive, considering that no job is promised. Or the transportation to a suburban plant may be highly time-consuming, so that job applicants arrive late in the morning at plants where personnel officers regard early arrival as proof of the proper work attitude. Sometimes employers will even restrict new employees to those with an automobile or with guaranteed access to a car pool. Or when a worker finds a job, he may not be able to finance purchase of an auto immediately, instead relying on inadequate public transit or unreliable car pools, with the result of tardiness or absence from work that causes him to lose his job. Or, his car may break down. In interviews, Watts residents frequently cited car maintenance problems as the reason for a lost job.

It is inappropriate to discuss in detail "solutions" to the problems of the immobility of the poor in an isolated context and I shall try to deal with the alternatives to our present urban transportation systems and their ramifications in an ensuing chapter. Suffice it to say that experts in the field of transportation and poverty generally lean toward one or a combination of three different "solutions"—

1. Elimination or reduction of impediments to enter the taxicab and "jitney" business. (It's interesting to note that in most cities the poor use taxicabs out of all proportion to their numbers, despite the high costs.)

2. Provision of more ubiquitous, flexible, speedier, and convenient public transit. It's generally agreed that to reduce fares would give less benefit to the poor than to

increase coverage, frequency, speed, and directness of transit.

3. Subsidies to allow extension of private ownership of autos to the poor or to provide for auto-renting or organized car pooling.

This last proposal is worth some consideration here as it won't be discussed later and it presents an interesting dilemma. Sumner Myers, Director of Techno-Urban Studies with the Institute of Public Administration, and others, have pointed out that if Volkswagens were to be purchased in large groups they could be rented out to the poor for seven or eight cents per passenger mile, which would be below the cost of providing transit in many cases. (The same is true of American-make used cars three years old but still in good shape.) The car also can be used for other than trips to work, and if accompanied by a program to teach the poor how to buy wisely and do much of their own maintenance, would provide other benefits as well. It is also much more flexible than anything short of a taxicab-type transit system. It also gives the poor something of a "stake" in society if the car is really theirs. All of these points are perfectly valid. But the argument ignores the gross effects that our entire culture obtains from the automobile, which I am trying to show are substantially negative and extremely pervasive. It is for this reason that I feel, and I want to emphasize this, that the provision of private automobiles for the poor at government expense ought to be *a last resort*. However, I cannot justify the current immobility of the poor, particularly in terms of finding and keeping employment. And I admit it is *not* fair to make the poor pay for the sins of our entire society by telling them that we won't provide them with something that is now, unfortunately, practically a necessity for survival in our society—the automobile. But this does not relieve us from our obligation to provide decent alternatives to deal with the problems the auto presents. And wherever possible, the provision of these alternatives ought to include service for the poor.

In fact, it is vitally important that planning for transportation begin to consider social and income characteristics of the people to be served. In June of 1968, Thomas H. Floyd, Jr., th acting director of the Division of Demonstration Programs ar Studies in the Urban Transportation Administration of the U. Department of Housing and Urban Development, said, "Thei appears to be a great reluctance by transit and transportatio planners to become active community catalysts who call th city's attention to transportation problems, like the immobility of the poor, and help it sort out the costs and benefits of various solutions." Planners do need to develop new bases for their decisions. They have a responsibility to begin to respond to the needs of the poor and to stop pretending, for example, that all transit proposals will do so, or that highway location, with all its ramifications, is not closely related to the distribution of income among various segments of our society.

NOTES

[1]Jack Rosenthal, *The New York Times* News Service (December 12, 1970).

[2]Martin Wohl, "Users of Transportation Services and Their Income Circumstances," paper to Transportation and Poverty Conference, American Academy of Arts & Sciences (June 7-8, 1968).

[3]A. Richard Immel, "Repossession Practices for Cars Called Unfair to Defaulting Buyers," *Wall Street Journal*, p. 1.

[4]Marc Fried, "Grieving for a Lost Home," *The Urban Condition: New York*, Basic Books, pp. 151-171.

[5]Chester Hartman, "The Housing of Relocated Families," *Journal of the American Institute of Planners* (November 1964), pp. 266-286.

[6]John F. Kain, "Coping With Ghetto Unemployment," *Journal of the American Institute of Planners* (March 1969), pp. 80-83.

CHAPTER  ALTERNATIVES
TO THE
AUTOMOBILE

I have purposefully left until last what I feel to be the strongest,
yet the least often acknowledged, or least clearly understood,
argument against our current direction toward greater and greater dependence on the automobile. That is the automobile's
effect on our urban form, both physical and social. Its effect on
how we interact, how frequently and in what ways we come
into contact with others who are different and, in fact, to what
degree groups within our society are allowed or enabled to be
different and yet live together.

Let me here offer something of a caveat. Simply because I am
concerning myself with our transportation system and its effects does *not* mean that I believe it is *the* most important
determinant of our urban form. I do *not* believe that the
automobile is somehow at the root of all of our urban social
problems. The system of transportation we choose can only do
so much. What it does is to affect how we organize our dwellings and use our lands in urban areas. Around the turn of the
century, before the automobile, for every thousand who were
added to a city's population, the city's size expanded by about
ten additional acres of land. In 1930, cities required about 30
new acres per thousand people, and they now use more than
200 acres for each additional thousand. This could not have
taken place without the automobile's growth. (That growth
continues—the number of cars on our highways is growing faster

than our population. As noted earlier, the number of two car families in the U.S. increased from under 15 percent to over 30 percent in the last decade.)

But it is silly to pretend that the accumulated choice of means of transportation by our society is the single cause of the way people have decided to live (and is thus the cause of the suburban life style, for instance). The desire and ability of each family to own its own single-family home, for example, has probably been a larger factor than choice of transportation.

I realize that to belittle the role of transportation as a cause of our physical (and thus our social) organization is to admit that basic changes in transportation don't necessarily achieve basic changes in our society.

But if we can understand how transportation does work to shape our physical and social organization, exactly what role it does play, then we can use it as a means to an end. If we can decide on the direction we must go, as a society, then we can decide what we need, in the way of transportation, to achieve that end.

This business of deciding on a desirable direction for our urban physical and social form (often called planning), and then using our government policies on transportation (as one example) to move us in that direction, clashes head-on with some very strong attitudes. Particularly when the chosen direction would move us away from our dependence on the automobile. One conflicting attitude is that people "prefer" the automobile, and since ours is a democratic society, people should be allowed to have what they "prefer." Let me try to deal with this argument in its fullest complexity.

First, is it factually accurate to say that "people prefer the auto"? It is true that the number of our autos has increased rapidly and the number of riders on our *current* mass transit facilities has decreased rapidly. So, superficially, the statement appears correct. There has been a great deal written and said about our democratic free market system and how people are choosing the auto through it. The mythology is supported by a wide range of experts. Even John Meyer, one of the most knowledgeable writers about transportation, besides being a professor at Yale, writes in an otherwise outstanding article in "The Metropolitan Enigma"[1] that, ". . . if we had a free market in the provision of urban highway commuter facilities, some considerable expansion of such facilities would probably take place." This free market argument is most frequently stated in income terms—that is, if everyone could afford to drive an automobile, everyone would. George W. Hilton, a professor of economics at UCLA, in a speech widely distributed by the California State Chamber of Commerce's freeway support committee, says, ". . . an increase of one percent in family income will typically reduce the family's use of rail passenger service by 0.6 percent. Thus, rail passenger trains provide an inferior service with respect to income, analogous to potatoes, farinacious foods, and other inferior goods, consumption of which decreases with increments in income. In contrast, Walter Oi and Paul W. Shuldiner have estimated the income elasticity of demand for the services of automobiles at +1.2. This figure is a quantification of a strong normality of the automobile in consumption patterns, as manifested in the tendency to use automobiles increasingly in place of public transportation of all sorts (except air), to buy successively more expensive automobiles over time, and to buy second and third automobiles for families as their incomes increase."[2]

Sometimes the free market argument isn't an economic one made with respect to income, but is more ideological and overemotional, as in statements by Karl Moskowitz, an engineer of Sacramento, California, in a paper presented to a symposium of the Automobile Manufacturers Association in Detroit, Michigan.[3] Mr. Moskowitz said that some people claim the social viewpoint favors transit over automobiles, but he adds, "unless social is spelled with a capital "S" as in 'Social Notes from Newport and Park Avenue' (where transit may be preferred—for the masses) or as in U.S.S.R. (where transit is also preferred, for reasons of their own), the social viewpoint must be considered equivalent, not opposite, to the viewpoint of most individuals—the individuals to whom the automobile is superior, convenient, flexible, taking them where they want to go, when they want to go, comfortably and in privacy."

But wait a minute. If the automobile is so superior, why is it a fact that more than 50 percent of U.S. citizens age 18 and older either can't or don't choose to drive? This "most individuals" business is a little tricky, all right. In the mid-1950s *Fortune* magazine interviewed 840 auto commuters in Los Angeles, 370 in San Francisco and 1,395 in Washington, D.C. The magazine found that, in all three cities, more people said they didn't enjoy driving and "would almost certainly switch" to transit if it met their requirements of time, than said they "couldn't imagine switching." If transit travel time matched their current driving time, some 64 percent in L.A., 68 percent in S.F. and 60 percent in Washington said they would switch to transit.

Also enlightening is a much more recent study conducted by the American Association of State Highway Officials in cooperation with the federal Bureau of Public Roads. In 1967, two research firms were hired to conduct hour-long interviews with identical questionnaires of 2,500 persons, selected nationally by a random sample. The study emphasizes, by the way the questions were chosen and worded as well as by the presentation of results, that "The automobile is by far the most important mode of travel to the American household . . . attitudes toward the automobile are generally positive and the value placed on the automobile is extremely high . . . the attitudes toward present public transportation services and facilities tend to be generally negative rather than positive." But, there is a surprise buried in one of the tables: more than twice as many people felt that "The real answer to our passenger transportation problem is more and better public transportation" than felt the "real answer" is the auto. And more than three times as many people were in the "most agree" category with respect to that particular statement concerning public transportation than with respect to that statement concerning the auto.

But whether auto enthusiasts or transit enthusiasts are correct about the preferences of people for one form of transportation or another is beside the point. For there is no democratic free market system in which "the people" get what they want. The major decisions about urban transportation are made by very large institutions, industrial, financial, and governmental. And all these institutions are influenced and managed by the industrial system. Certainly, people are "free" to stop buying or driving automobiles tomorrow, if they want to. But many would then have no way to shop or get to work, no way to survive. Only fourteen cities have electric railway systems (not counting standard passenger railroad travel), and many bus systems have deteriorated to a point where they are simply inadequate. In short, for most people to give up their autos at this point would constitute a major economic sacrifice. People are not really "free to choose" unless there are viable alternatives. The state highway officials' survey revealed, for example, that of the 5,000 persons interviewed, less than four percent had used any form of transit the day before the interview, whereas 85 percent had used the auto. The interviewers were talking to a group of people, however typical in other ways, who had already decided that the auto was best for their own use, not transit, so naturally they would consider the auto "important" and would have "generally positive" attitudes about it.

The automobile system functions because it is profitable for millions of automobiles to be built and sold; because it is profitable to sell billions of gallons of gasoline for them; and profitable to repair and maintain them. In earlier chapters I have tried to deal with the notion that these huge industries function the way they do because that is how people want them to function. This is simply no longer the case. It takes hundreds of millions of dollars every year to persuade people to purchase the variety of autos now being produced, to influence and manage their decisions to buy. The concept of a "free market" is fiction, perpetuated by the corporations because it serves their ends. (And even if the current auto system is what people want, we must, of necessity, also be concerned with what people should do, individually and collectively.)

But even if I were to lose this argument, even if there is a free market for automobiles, there is still a flaw in the notion that people really have had the option to choose between the automobile and other forms of transit in recent years. This flaw becomes apparent when you look closely at government's role in providing facilities for the automobile, particularly streets and highways, as opposed to its role in providing public transit facilities. If people were really to be given a choice, then equal provision of facilities by government would be indicated. This has hardly been the case. The U.S. government has set up a multi-billion-dollar highway trust fund, financed from "highway-user" taxes, such as gasoline taxes. Using these monies, the federal government provides 90 percent of the costs of building freeways, requiring that local and state governments put up only ten percent. The trust fund has been disbursing about $4 billion a year. Meanwhile the federal government had been providing less than $175 million a year for public transit, until recent passage of mass transit legislation, which now provides about $1 billion a year, beginning in 1971. But this transit money, for capital equipment and construction only, not operations, provides two-thirds financing, requiring local governments to put up fully one-third—not ten percent. And the federal government programs are only half the story. Property taxes and other state and local taxes and fees have also been used to provide bridges, parking, local streets, traffic signals, traffic policemen, traffic courts, etc. Meanwhile, public transit systems that are privately owned—still 90 percent of the 1,100-plus systems if you include buses—have to pay property taxes, license fees, federal income taxes, and all sorts of other payments to governments.

It is possible to argue, as many in the automobile and highway industries seem to, that government policies are a perfect expression of the public's preference. For, they say, we have a democracy. They also point to the fact that the federal highway trust fund, and most state monies for highways, are provided by "highway-user" taxes. They say that this method of financing means that any freeways built are only an expression of the current demand for highways, since the taxes provided are directly related to current highway usage, and since usage is directly related to demand.

Let's examine both of these arguments. Are government policies a pure expression of the people's desire for expanded auto usage? This may, at one time early in this century, have been the case. Historically, people wanted roads for their autos. But that is history. And as we have seen, the world has changed around the automobile, and the auto itself is no longer, comparatively speaking, a simple, practical, tough, economical, safe, non-polluting means of transportation well suited to the times. For even if you grant that at one time in history the automobile and highway system grew because of pure demand for it, this does not mean that government policies since World War II, for example, have been an expression of that kind of demand. The role of the auto, oil, trucking, and highway construction industries in getting candidates of their choice elected, and then influencing decisions after election, is easy to document, and I will do so later. At this point, it is sufficient to say that action by state, local, or federal government favoring highways and the auto hardly has represented the purest form of democracy. One should also add that where such action has been democratic, or where such decisions have been endorsed by the democratic process, and the management of that process by the industrial system has *not* been the deciding factor, people have seldom been given practical and obvious alternatives to expanding the auto system. With current technology what it is, and with the current complexity of our urban society, the development and presentation of real alternatives to the auto requires a high level of technical skill (and no little political courage). The automobile industry and the industries related to it, have had a secure hammerlock on such skills. Engineers who are getting the bulk of their income from highway construction are not likely to actively advance and promote alternatives that would make the auto far less necessary. Piecemeal alternatives, perhaps, but not real ones. For all of these reasons, it is not accurate to say that government favoritism toward the automobile is currently based on public preference.

Nor is it accurate to say that the financing of highway construction by "highway-user" taxes is an expression of popular demand for more highways. To assume that because one uses highways (often because it is the only way one can get around) means that he wants to be taxed to make that highway system grow, is not logical. When I pay my gasoline tax, I would rather see it go to mass transit. The gas tax is *not* an expression of my demand for more highways.

There is also, incidentally, a considerable amount of basic dishonesty in saying or implying, as the above argument does, that "highway-user" taxes pay for all the costs of highway construction. As we have seen there are considerable costs from highways, such as unfavorable community impact, family dislocation, removal of property from its previously higher economic use, etc., that are currently *in no way paid for*, let alone by "highway-user" taxes.

Our conclusion must be that "public preference" for the auto, whether expressed in the marketplace or in Congress, is conditioned by those who make, sell, repair, and fuel it, and other corporate interests to whom the construction of highways means direct economic benefit. This is an important conclusion, for it means that if the industrial system now determines the direction we take in providing urban transportation systems, we are philosophically much freer to talk about changing that direction than if the direction were somehow derived from "the will of the American people," or even "the individual choices of most people."

So, on to discussion of the directions our physical and social form ought to be taking in our cities. This is obviously an extremely complex subject and anyone who tackles it immediately risks the danger of over-simplification, unless he is able to devote more space to it than I have to give. In order to narrow the subject down to manageable size, let me deal only with matters of social structure that are more easily related to, or seen as determined by, the physical form our cities take. For our transportation system's influence on physical form cannot easily be disputed.

It seems to me that many of our problems as a society stem directly from the fact that a large portion of our populace maintains attitudes that are both narrow and self-interested. Paul Goodman has pointed out, for example, that what we typically call racism in America is really a combination of narrowness and self-interest; it does not distinguish among the objects of its repugnance as genuine racism does. Most Americans whom one might originally label racists, particularly urban Northerners, do not, for instance, take action against blacks because they are black, although the actions are often similar to those taken by people who really are racist (in that they feel anyone black is inherently inferior, because of his blackness, his hair, or his features). Edgar Z. Friedenberg recently called this narrowness and self-interest by another name: "squeamishness." And it obviously does stem in many cases from a desire to avoid real human contact with people in other ethnic and racial groups. The result of lack of such contact is an inability to place yourself in the other person's shoes.

Our American tendency toward violence can also be attributed to this, at least in part. If one avoids contact with (and thus understanding of) others who appear in some way "different," it is obviously much easier to deny their humanity and do them violence, whether they are Viet Cong, or American Negroes, or long-haired hippies. Man can be seen as uniquely lethal in lacking natural limits to his aggressiveness against his own kind. And if our technological weapons permit us to kill or injure without recognizing our victims as human, and if our society encourages isolation from human interactions, and thus isolation from conflict and disorder, there is a tendency for conflict to become more lethal when it does occur. As Friedenberg says, when conflict does come to narrow people, "It is more frightening because unfamiliar, and one's adversary is perceived as a devil who might do anything, unless one is prudent enough to do it to him first."[4]

As our urban society seems to reduce itself more and more to a set of warring enclaves, material abundance can sometimes make things worse. A community that contains narrow-minded people, and also has the resources, can materially control its boundaries and internal composition, as Richard Sennett has pointed out. Also, by duplicating facilities that, normally, a poorer community would share, it reduces the occasion for interaction.

We are, indeed, in a society in which many people try harder to avoid conflict and disorder than to achieve any positive goal. On the other hand, we may need, in our very complex society, islands of quiet and security where people don't have to feel threatened. But in order to attain that security, we must remember that we can only stay the same by being willing to change, by confronting and therefore understanding other people, thus knowing how and where we are truly threatened by other people and other ideas.

So our need at this time is for people to encounter one another, for true reaching out, for interaction in which it is possible to understand the humanity of other people without necessarily agreeing with them. This requires a broad set of casual contacts with a diverse range of people. It is not encouraged by tract homes in the suburbs in which people can hide and fail to learn how to cope with challenges and external threats. We cannot any longer encourage people to limit themselves to patterns of life that insist that everything of value is included in those patterns.

And this is really what Jane Jacobs' work is about. For she loves cities in which there is real diversity, in which there is vitality and interaction, even (non-violent) conflict, in the street life. She is careful to distinguish among different kinds of relationships between people. There are private social relationships among friends in which much is shared. People have a need for these kinds of relationships, and they generally develop best among people who have a great deal in common. These private friendships are not likely to wither simply because two friends have to travel a distance to get together. But, she points out, the *other kinds* of social relationships, those often transactional but always limited sorts of relationships in which the two people do not feel a personal responsibility about each other's private affairs, tend to develop only in certain types of settings. In a city neighborhood in which there is much walking and much street life, it is possible to know all kinds of people without unwelcome entanglements, without boredom, without obligations beyond the limited relationship. My favorite example is the shopkeeper in Jane Jacobs' old neighborhood who keeps keys to peoples' apartments for them when they go out of town, a custom once common in certain New York neighborhoods. Then friends or relatives who want to use the apartment for a weekend, or who are going to be arriving late at night, are told they can pick up the key from the shopkeeper. This is not a service that is easily formalized, for the shopkeeper must be the sort of person who is trustworthy, but who does not develop a strong sense of responsibility for the private affairs of those whose keys he keeps. It is Jane Jacobs' contention, and one with which I agree, that a complex web of such limited relationships are the sort of thing that mark a high order of civilization. And it goes without saying that such relationships endure over a period of time and help to develop understanding for people unlike oneself.

Mrs. Jacobs also notes that a "street life" and "sidewalk contacts" make for safety in a neighborhood, because the people who spend time on the streets and sidewalks going about their normal business have watchful eyes, and their limited relationships do make them interested enough to feel responsible for the physical safety of others. Most importantly, the tolerance, the room for great differences among neighbors which are possible and normal in intensely urban life, but which are foreign to the suburbs, depend, for their very existence, on physical characteristics of our cities that encourage and allow "lowly, unpurposeful and random sidewalk contacts," that she says are "the small change from which a city's wealth of public life may grow."

She sees four basic generators of this diversity and vitality. I have listed them in an earlier chapter. They are worth repeating: 1) the need for a mixture of primary uses in a neighborhood—work, residence, and commercial, so that there are many people who go outdoors on different schedules for different purposes, but use the same facilities. 2) short blocks and frequent streets so there are opportunities to take many routes in going to the same place and thus widen the range of sidewalk contacts. 3) high residential density, enough to support a range of specialized shops and activities. 4) a mix of buildings of varied age and condition, so that there are old buildings which can shelter undertakings that are economically marginal.

The automobile is destroying, not building, these four basic generators of diversity. Where a mixture of primary uses might develop, or where neighborhood would be dense, the automobile quickly becomes overpowering. If, in these neighborhoods, each person drives, the congestion of autos is overwhelming and the space required for them works against the density and eventually eliminates or reduces it. Short blocks are for people, long blocks for the auto. And old buildings are torn down to make way for new highways.

Los Angeles is the epitome of the city that has almost none of this intricate and intense urban life, and its copiers in the West are becoming more numerous every year. As a one-time resident of Los Angeles, I absolutely agree with Jane Jacobs—it has virtually no street life, no public life to speak of. There are blacks and Chicanos by the hundreds of thousands. There is the Hollywood film colony, and the futuristic aerospace industry, and the groves of academe at USC and UCLA. But there is no mixture of any of these groups, no basis for understanding or interweaving of cultures. It was not an accident that the firs major urban riot occurred in Watts, for the frustration and alienation that stems from the isolation of persons in that city is immense. Los Angeles, the largest of our cities to be built after the advent of the automobile, and the city most completely dependent upon the auto, holds little or no hope for bringing together the polarized and warring groups of our society. Where there is no contact, there is no basis for understanding and tolerance.

And unfortunately, because of the very nature of the automobile system, almost all of the major cities in the West are going the way of Los Angeles, and many in the East are well along that path too. For, as Jane Jacobs has pointed out, positive feedback is at work. Freeways create the need for parking lots. And more parking lots allow more freeways. Each action produces a reaction which intensifies the condition responsible for the first action.

This positive feedback system is most obvious with regard to the amount of land now used by our cities. As we spread out, we have more need for the automobile. And the more dependent we are on the automobile, the less likely we are to be able to reverse our tendency to sprawl all over our land.

It is probably wise to take a detour here to re-emphasize the point that the automobile's effect on land-use patterns is important in a variety of ways. Most important is the impact on our social structure which I have tried to outline. But we ought not to disregard the economic fall-out. There is the whole question of economic efficiency of a widespread city, as opposed to a compact city. For example, the utilization of our huge investment in an automobile transportation system is unbelievably low. Investment in the auto fleet itself, in garages, carports, parking buildings, parking lots, roads, bridges, and tunnels is enormous. There is also the cost of the facilities needed to make, sell, and repair the auto, and those needed to junk it too. Yet, with all this investment, the auto is used, on the average, only one to two hours a day, or less than 10 percent of the time. When this utilization is multiplied by the low utilization of the space in the car, we find that the huge investment has a utilization of less than two percent. Roads and streets are sometimes utilized at a higher rate. But the parking spaces on streets, at grocery stores and shopping centers, at our churches and schools, at our football stadiums and auditoriums, are probably utilized at a lesser rate. For all that concrete and all that land to sit idle so much of the time is inexcusable.

Another type of economic waste that results from sprawl is the cost of delivering mail, milk, sewage treatment facilities, water, electricity, phone service, garbage collection service and home repair services to the sprawling suburb. This includes the added expense of pipes and wires and the additional cost of traveling time for laborers. Too, the greater time required by the residents of the suburb to travel from home to work, to school, to recreational or cultural facilities, or to shopping centers, must be given some value. Earlier, I mentioned the loss of good farmland, and land that is valuable for other than agricultural reasons, to the highway itself. But there is also the loss of land from the much sparser, much less dense residential tracts that the auto encourages.

The mushrooming sprawl in our urban fringes is converting over 1,500,000 acres of U.S. farmland to non-farm uses every year, 50 percent more than the rate of the 1950s. "The urbanization of prime farmland is one of the most serious problems facing us in agriculture," says Maurice Peterson, Dean of Agriculture for all campuses of the University of California.[5] One reason is that urban expansion occurs almost entirely on the very finest agricultural land, because it is flat and easy to develop. In California, where during the 1960s, 140,000 acres of farmland were lost to urban sprawl every year, more than half of the loss occurred in land so rich in soil, climate, and other growing conditions, that it was officially rated as "prime" by the U.S. Soil Conservation Service.

Prime farmland disappeared most rapidly in Santa Clara County where San Jose's industrialization boosted county population to one million by 1970 from 288,000 in 1950, in the process taking half of the county's 140,000 acres of prime farmland. Farmers selling land in the Santa Clara Valley usually moved to Central California, so statewide production of the fruits grown in the Santa Clara Valley didn't drop. But the quality of the fruit being produced in the central valley just doesn't measure up to what was produced in the Santa Clara Valley, say packers and farmers.

Indeed, prunes and apricots grown in the Santa Clara Valley traditionally brought one half cent a pound (from five percent to ten percent) more on the wholesale market because of higher quality. The difference has disappeared because so little of the top-grade fruit is produced now. As one farmer converting his apricot orchard into a suburban shopping center told me, "the average supermarket shopper will never notice the loss in quality." Similar situations have occurred in California with regard to strawberries, Valencia oranges, and asparagus, where there have been actual acreage reductions.

There are, of course, crop surpluses, and more than 220 million acres of prime cropland still remain in the U.S. Too, there are steady advances in output per acre and the Department of Agriculture remains committed to a policy favoring conversion of farmland to other uses. But our future needs for food production will be great. The Department of Agriculture says that we will have to produce about 42 billion pounds of red meat by 1975, about 14 billion more than we produced in 1960; 57 million tons of fruit and vegetables, or roughly 17 million more than in 1960; and 172 billion pounds of milk, or 42 billion more than in 1960. For eggs, our requirements will increase by 14 billion to a total of 84 billion by 1975.[6] One wonders about the long-range benefits of the way we are using our land, in terms of our ability to feed our own nation, let alone a hungry world.

It is worth a footnote here to the effect that all of this sprawling growth in the suburban fringes of our cities does not come from our inner cities. Many of our inner cities are nearly stable in residential population. What looks like dispersion has largely been new growth in our urban areas—people coming in from rural areas coupled with increased birth rates. When you realize that the daytime use of our inner cities (still largely retail use) has declined even less than has residential use, and that the "high employment per square foot" uses like office buildings continue to go downtown in most cities, you begin to realize why the suburban industrial and residential growth hasn't made an even larger impact on our downtown traffic and usage patterns.

If we really want to reverse the sprawling growth of our cities, with the constant accommodation to the automobile, and begin to develop healthy cities with rich and vital public lives, how, exactly, can we begin? The logical place to start would be with our politics, of course. But let me put off that discussion for now, and let's make the assumption that we can do what we want to do politically. It's not possible to absolutely eliminate political considerations, of course. For example, there is the given political context—consumers of transportation will undoubtedly continue to have certain freedoms in the United States. The freedom of an individual to substitute one type of transport for another when it pleases him and where there are alternatives, the freedom to choose one route over another, the freedom to choose place of residence. Or the freedom of businessmen to locate their businesses where they see fit, or not to do business in a given locale altogether. (This, incidentally, is a circumstance often ignored—the demand for transportation is not perfectly inelastic when businesses and citizens can move their homes or places of employment.)

In the second place, within the given political context, it is not now reasonable to assume that it will be possible to institute rapidly entire new systems of transportation—systems that will completely and immediately eliminate the automobile as we know it. The automobile assumed its dominance in a piece-meal fashion, and it ought to be phased out in the same way. This is not only necessary, but probably desirable. It means that we will have to take the steps necessary to bring about the attrition of the automobile wherever we can find them. The steps ought to be conscious and planned, where possible. But it is not reasonable to expect our planners and politicians to supply such an enormous and complex undertaking that would happen all at once. This is why it is necessary that our politicians and planners and any interested do-gooders have a good understanding of the range of techniques possible, and their likely effects. We ought to understand by now, for example, that building more freeways does not alleviate traffic problems, and building more parking lots downtown does not alleviate parking problems. But just what are the logical and immediate steps to take?

In each case, *how* the steps are taken is more important than the steps themselves. But the strategies can roughly be broken down into six categories:

1. Revitalize old, or start new rapid transit systems.

2. Encourage non-auto and non-transit modes—walking, bicycles, golf carts, and conveyor sidewalks are examples.

3. Favor buses (and trucks) at the expense of private passenger cars.

4. Encourage expansion of taxis and jitney fleets, car pooling, and "sharing the ride."

5. Adapt private passenger cars (and buses) for dual-mode use, on rail trucks or on rail cars, or for automated freeways.

6. Penalize private automobiles by creating congestion, using pricing systems for highways or instituting other restrictions to discourage the use of autos.

Before discussing in detail some of the specific actions that should and should not be taken within each of these categories, perhaps we ought to consider first how a community that wanted to adopt the "best" combination of these strategies might proceed. It would start by defining "best." That is, by having general goals or "high level criteria" as engineers might say, so that it could judge its low-level criteria, or operating and construction standards, by these goals. I have tried to give some indication of what I think those goals should be. The list of six specific strategies could move a city toward desirable goals. The problem, generally, is that a city, or a region, develops specific strategies without ever relating them to the larger goals. The strategies, the low-level criteria, are based on very poorly understood and highly inadequate cost-benefit evaluations, or based on no evaluations at all. And the specific strategies are often inconsistent with one another and with any reasonable or desirable goals. The prevailing practice has been to accept the strategies that are implicit or explicit in the use of highways or rapid transit or buses and to carry out investment analyses with these as givens. Without the larger goal-setting process, and without any attempt to relate the specific strategies to the goals, administrators, engineers, planners, and other technicians will frequently decide that a particular alternative is unacceptable for political reasons. Yet, in a democratic society, a true process of goal-setting and policy-making with citizen participation should take such decisions out of the hands of the technicians. It should also end the sort of planning we now get in which there is extensive analysis of predetermined solutions, mere attempts to justify the decisions made by the technicians, usually, in the case of transportation, consultant firms hired to produce "a plan" that invariably is a narrow engineering document or a simple public relations effort.

Once the goals are set, if they are the right kind of goals, they will require that information be put into the planning process that is not now available in most cities, and thus must be developed. In the case of transportation, current and desired patterns of use, called origin-destination studies, are now usually available, and are necessary, but are not sufficient. When trying to decide what strategies to use, and at what level to employ each type of transportation, there must also be complete information on current and prospective operating service and price levels, on the social and income characteristics of the current and prospective users at each of those levels for each strategy, and on the *social and economic* costs of each level of each strategy. Ideally, in addition to income distribution effects, the cost-benefit studies would include some quantification of such community values as aesthetics, ecological effects, and effects on Jane Jacobs' four basic generators of neighborhood diversity, for example.

This planning ought to deal primarily with immediate decisions and optimization of all immediate alternatives before it worries too much about the long-range effects. It must also carefully avoid looking only at system-wide effects. Highway planners, because of their fixation with total systems, frequently lump together parts of a system that have favorable cost-benefit ratios with parts of a system that do not. One cannot use a system-wide evaluation of benefits and costs to justify the elimination of congestion or the construction of additional capacity at particular times and places.

I want to emphasize that an extensive search for American cities where this type of *metropolitan*, region-wide transportation planning is going on has been fruitless, without exception.

Let's take a close look at the dramatic examples of large new U.S. investment in urban transportation outside of the highway, for those should have produced the most sophisticated planning. There are really only two major examples of new systems: San Francisco and Washington, D.C. I am most familiar with San Francisco, but know enough about the Washington, D.C. system to know that some of the problems in San Francisco are duplicated there.

The San Francisco Bay Area Rapid Transit (BART) system, consists of a 75-mile electric railway that will connect such major East Bay cities as Oakland, Fremont, Walnut Creek, Berkeley, and Richmond with San Francisco by way of a tube running under the bay. Originally planned for completion by 1971 and a startup date for its first section by 1967, the system completion has been delayed by about two years and startup of the first phase by some four years. The delays, outlandish engineering fees, and unexpectedly high inflation have pushed costs up to over $2 billion (including interest costs of over $650 million, rolling stock costs, costs of the tube, and costs of engineering fees.) The costs of a $792 million general obligation bond issue passed in 1962 alone added some $20 a year to the average property taxpayer's load in the three counties. It is an indication of the desire to find alternatives to the auto that such bond measures passed by over 60 percent in both San Francisco and Washington, D.C. Other cities have had less luck, but there are reasons.

BART, like our giant freeways, was not designed with a wide range of citizen participation. It was put together, promoted, and sold by corporations who would eventually profit from it. Burton Wolfe documented this quite well in an article in the "Bay Guardian," chiefly through a deposition taken from Carl F. Wente, former chairman of the board of Bank of America and chairman of the finance committee for the group that promoted BART, Citizens for Rapid Transit. Wente explained in the deposition, taken by an attorney in a taxpayer's suit against BART, how he *solicited and received* substantial funds from firms eventually to reap heavy benefits from BART. Among them were Westinghouse Electric Co., which received a $26 million contract to install BART's automatic controls; Bethlehem Steel Corp., which received the $23 million contract to build steel structures for the transBay tube; Kaiser Industries, Inc., subsidiaries of which received a $16 million contract for tunnel liners, the bulk of a 35-million barrel cement business and a good portion of a $31 million contract to dig a tunnel through hills in the East Bay; the Perini Corp., which after forming a joint venture with a possible competitor, Morrison-Knudsen Inc., received two subway contracts totalling $37.1 million; the three engineering firms who formed a joint venture and received over $100 million in fees—Parsons, Brinckerhoff, Quade & Douglas, Tudor Engineering Co. and Bechtel Corp.; and the three major San Francisco banks, Wells Fargo, Bank of America, and Crocker-Citizens, all of whom have heavy investments in downtown buildings in San Francisco. The key station on Montgomery St. for BART will come up in the Wells Fargo building and there will be a connecting tunnel underground to the new Crocker-Citizens Building.

Altogether, Wente and the committee raised $203,218 plus considerable advertising and services that were donated. Listen to Wente tell how it works: ". . . I solicited Kaiser (Edgar Kaiser of Kaiser Industries) and I told him at the time: 'You are interested in this for several reasons. First place you are interested from a civic standpoint; it is a good thing for the city. You have your office here. You are in the cement business, you are in the aluminum business, you are in the engineering business, you are in all kinds of—your outfit ought to be interested in this from every conceivable angle.'

"He asked me what I thought, and I told him the same as I told the other fellows: 'Now, as a group, you ought to give 25,000 bucks.' He says; 'Criminy sakes, that's too much money.'

"I said: "Relatively, that is small considering the size of the billion dollars' worth of work—let's be frank—you fellows are going . . . (he stopped there, realizing what he was about to say) . . . There is potential there.' "[7]

But the key decisions about BART have been made by those ever-present emissaries of the establishment—engineers. And San Francisco's establishment made sure that it got people it could trust to do what it wanted. The Bechtel Corp., for example, is dominant in the joint venture. It is owned solely by the Bechtel family. Director Kenneth Bechtel has been one of the top ten stockholders of the Wells Fargo Bank. Stephen D. Bechtel, Jr., president of Bechtel, sits on the Crocker-Citizens board of directors. Both have had long relationships with Kaiser Industries in joint venture contracts and other sorts of projects. Burton Wolfe asked George MacDonald, BART's public relations director, and formerly public relations chief of Kaiser Engineering Services, "Which of the Bechtels really runs BART —Steve Bechtel Senior or Steve Bechtel Junior?"

"Both of them," MacDonald replied. "Both of them have sunk their lives and fortunes in this thing." It is probably unnecessary to point out that Bechtel continues to do considerable engineering on downtown building projects in San Francisco, spurred by BART.

The engineers really have run BART. Theoretically the power is in a Board of Directors (not democratically selected, but established by BART to represent cities and counties in its area.) But anyone who ever went to a BART directors' meeting understands how completely the engineers controlled everything. During BART's first three years, from 1962 to 1965, the BART board of directors, for all practical purposes, did not check how the joint venture was disbursing funds. Contracts were examined by a staff headed by a chief engineer. The first chief engineer was Kenneth M. Hoover. He was a paid consultant with the Parsons Brinckerhoff portion of PBTB until BART hired him as the chief engineer. As BART's first chief engineer, he was asked by directors who BART should hire to manage its engineering. He recommended the joint venture that included the firm he just left. As Wolfe points out, several BART directors have said they voted for the engineering contract with the PBTB joint venture because of letters of recommendation from three prominent outside engineering firms. He then notes that the three have been awarded subcontracts from the joint venture for $539,912.

Hoover was eventually retired as chief engineer in February, 1965, amidst controversy in the press over his lack of an engineering degree and criticism of BART engineering, but he was retained as a consultant. He was replaced as chief engineer by Stanley Forsythe, who was senior transportation consultant with Bechtel until June 30, 1963, when he went on the PBTB joint venture payroll. Again, the chief of staff checking the engineers came directly from the firms being checked. By the time Dave Hammond was hired as chief engineer in 1966, the first outsider, but an individual who had worked closely with the joint venture firms when with the Army Engineers, most of the BART contracts had been let.

One of the results of this close control by the engineers was that the original estimate of engineering fees—$47 million on a cost-plus-percentage contract in which the more the project costs the more the joint venture gets—more than doubled to over $100 million.

But with the relationships between the engineers and the downtown and corporate interests what they are, it is not hard to understand how much more significant problems could occur than a sharp rise in engineers' fees. For if corporations are interested in increasing their land values, or getting valuable contracts, there will be little concern for income distributional effects, for aesthetics, or for developing a transit system that will make neighborhoods vital and liveable. So BART's routes do not go to the Fillmore or Hunters Point ghettos in San Francisco. The routes, in fact, are distinctly aimed at serving suburb to downtown San Francisco commuter use, the same sort of travel already well served by freeways and autos. The income distributional effects are obviously perverse.

In fact, it is safe to say that little real thought was given to how BART might serve *people* within the Bay Area. A real study of needs and demands would have dictated a look, for example, at how San Francisco and Oakland's extensive bus and streetcar systems were being utilized and where they would logically hook up with BART. Such a study eventually was conducted—long after BART's routes were laid out.

Yet BART knew all along that some two-thirds of its riders would come to its stations by another means of surface transit, where possible. And long after the coordinating plan was completed, there were still no plans for "feeder" service to five key suburban BART stations in Contra Costa County, east of Oakland. The Oakland bus service certainly has no intention of providing that service, and it continues to plan to run "at least ten" of its current 30 bus routes across the Bay Bridge between Oakland and San Francisco, in direct competition with BART. Oakland taxpayers will be in the position of subsidizing two competing services, neither of which has to cooperate with the other except where it happens to feel like it.

BART will just naturally improve and intensify the neighborhoods around its stations. But there is solid evidence that station sites and route decisions were made without such considerations in mind. For example, the only station within anything like a poverty area is on the edge of West Oakland. At last check, instead of using the station to make things happen in that area, BART's laissez-faire planning attitude was allowing Southern Pacific Railroad to buy up all sorts of land from ghetto residents near the station.

BART spokesmen have consistently rationalized their failure to seek and get cooperation from communities in helping to make the stations fit into their surroundings. As one BART spokesman admitted in a paper supposedly answering BART critics, "It is necessary to remember that some of the most annoying experiences for the BART rider are likely to occur before he has reached the BART premises or after he has left them and this seems to have become nobody's serious concern."[8]

In an interview I had with Dave Hammond, then BART's chief engineer, he said, "However desirable it might be, we're not in this thing to redevelop the whole area. Our assignment is just to build a fast, safe, effective rapid transit system." And Bill Stokes, BART's general manager, added that, "We wouldn't have the presumption to be regional master planners. Our money, responsibility and legal authority stop at the right-of-way."

Perhaps the best indication of this freeway-builders' mentality prevailing among BART staff came on a dispute over whether the portion of the line through Berkeley would be built in a subway or on elevated tracks. The elevated line would have cut Berkeley in two. About 90 percent of Berkeley's Negro population would have been "on the wrong side of the tracks." BART insisted that to put the line underground would be too costly and refused to do so, despite strong urgings from a unified Berkeley City Council and other Berkeley citizen groups. BART estimated costs at $20.5 million. But Berkeley said it would only cost $11 million. Berkeley finally put the measure on the ballot and taxpayers voted to tax themselves for whatever the subway would cost. It turned out to be about $11 million. It was only one example of BART's failure to respond to community desires.

Probably the most controversy in the press came with the resignation of consulting architect Donn Emmons, and the consulting landscape architect, nationally-acclaimed urban designer Lawrence Halprin. As Emmons put it, "Engineers are making decisions that should be made by people with a knowledge and interest in urban design." He complained that planning and architectural considerations were continually being disregarded by the engineers, who had the ultimate authority under the BART structure.

Emmons noted that General Manager Stokes told him not to go above the engineers to BART directors. Emmons complained about several instances where his advice was ignored, including one place where a vehicle underpass would have saved customers a mile-and-a-quarter detour around the track. His aerial structures, designed for BART, received wide critical acclaim, but he bitterly complained that any special changes in the structures, such as those to span a long distance, were designed by engineers "with small regard for appearance or effect on adjacent environment."

Halprin produced a long bill of particulars with his resignation:

> On Grove Street our advice was ignored and now the El will run down the middle of Oakland, blighting all along its path. [He had recommended it be placed on one side of the right-of-way and linear parks be built underneath.]

> Many of our recommendations on ways of integrating the East Bay portion of the system with the regional parks were ignored and are now impossible of achievement.

> Our fencing studies have been called the only significant contribution to this subject ever devised. We developed, along with manufacturers, alternate and elegant new fencing types which were to cost no more than the typical cyclone fence with barbed wire top—this too is ignored. . . .

We showed how fencing could be located in positions so that (in the future if necessary) land could be made available for hiking, bicycling, and riding trails. Nothing of this nature is being done. . . .

On parking lots we felt that the impact of vast acreages of asphalt paving for parking areas must be ameliorated by screen plantings so as not to blight neighborhoods, by decent walkways which would bring clients on foot to the station by a handsome environment of lighting, benches, trash cans, plazas, etc., around stations so that they add to rather than detract from the urban scene. The site planning we have seen indicates that none of this is even being considered by your engineering site designers, much less accomplished. I continue to be amazed at the fact that station site planning is *not* being done by architects and landscape architects.

BART has taken remedial action to correct some, but not all of the problems Halprin and Emmons pointed out. And the basic orientation toward engineering continues to this day, proof that it is just as easy to get bad transit planning as it is bad freeway planning.

Some of the problems BART has found are being avoided in Washington, D.C. But it is safe to say that the same basic lack of planning has occurred there. For that system, just as the system now being proposed in St. Louis and ones that have failed at the ballot box in Seattle, Los Angeles, and Atlanta, are all essentially the same. They are very rigid, high-speed, rail transit "corridor" systems running on straight lines from key suburban points to the downtown business section. With the exception of a planned detour taken through the ghetto in the Seattle plan that failed, there seems to have been little or no consideration anywhere of the fact that suburb-to-downtown rail corridors will be used principally by relatively wealthy suburbanites. Nor of the fact that they reinforce the sprawl patterns of the automobile more than other types of transit systems. In every case there seems to be a tendency to think also in terms of "pure technologies," that either you have a high-speed rail system or you have highways. Integrated solutions have received little or no consideration when it comes to large public expenditures. (Milwaukee seems to be headed toward an expensive bus system, however, and in Pittsburgh there is Westinghouse's Skybus, the two notable exceptions.)

Obviously the recent planning that has gone into U.S. transit systems has differed very little from any other urban planning in this country. It has not started with a clear understanding of goals, and the goals that it has achieved are not desirable ones. But let's make the transition into a close look at strategies available, starting first with rapid transit.

If one wanted to make transit work to support the kinds of neighborhoods Jane Jacobs records and envisions, as opposed to making transit serve industrial profit interests, I think one place you would start would be by tossing out the high-speed rail "corridor" concept. Obviously a "grid" system is superior. New York, in the United States, comes the closest to really having an extensive transit "grid," much like the common street "grid" in all of our cities. But there have been plans for "grid" systems that are even more extensive than that in New York. I am thinking particularly of the Babcock plan, named after the engineer who developed it as a public service, which was described at length by Los Angeles architect Robert E. Alexander in the journal *Cry California*. The Babcock plan was designed to cover a central area of about 100 square miles, ten miles by ten miles, or twelve by eight, surrounding Central Los Angeles. The plan would bring every part of that area within ten minutes' walk of a station, and the train frequency at each station would in turn bring every part of the area within a few minutes of it. Points on the perimeter could eventually be linked to surrounding communities with "corridor" lines where and if desirable.

Alexander describes the plan: "The Babcock Plan proposes a series of one-way loops about a mile wide and eight to ten miles long, carrying trains south, then north, in an endless single-tubed circuit, with stations about one mile apart. Superimposed on this series is an east-west series of similar loops, forming a checkerboard of one-mile squares. Every "black" square on the board contains a shuttle making contact with a station on each of the four sides of the square. The shuttle serves the function of allowing the passenger to change direction 90 degrees, 180 degrees, or 270 degrees. Computer control brings a shuttle to the station as doors open on the loop train. This system places a station within a half mile—ten minutes' walking distance—of every point in the area. . . .

"Minimum train frequency is six minutes, capable of increasing to one train every 45 seconds during peak hours. Any station can be reached from the center in 25 minutes and typical trips range from six to 20 minutes."[9]

Obviously, such a system has many advantages. It really provides convenience and frequency, and begins to compete with the automobile, as a result. It would obviously tend to make the area it served a more densely populated area, and could easily encourage a mix of primary uses—residential, commercial, and work. In short, its planning potential for neighborhoods is fantastic.

Just as obviously, its cost would be higher than the typical rail "corridor" system. And its benefits would be limited to a certain group of people who lived, worked, or frequently used the area it covered, just as a rail corridor system is limited to serving people along its lines. Alexander says that when the plan was published in 1950, the central system was estimated to cost about $1 billion, and a study showed that residents within the area served in Los Angeles could have produced revenues of $90 million per year at ten cents per ride, which was then considered to be self-liquidating of the system's construction expense. Costs today would be substantially higher, perhaps double or triple, and a higher fare of 25 cents might be required, and I'm not sure that it is as likely to be self-liquidating at today's costs with that fare, as it might have been prior to the growth of the auto system since 1950.

But there is an obvious way to pay for the system and a logical one, too. That is a tax upon the increased land and property values that occur in the area after the system is built. A study of rapid transit possibilities in Baltimore, for example, projected that for every $1.00 invested in construction of transit, the city would get back $2.90 in increased property taxes. Other studies in Tampa and San Francisco indicate this is a conservative estimate. In Toronto, a 4½ mile system, in use for ten years now, has helped to attract $10 billion of new construction to the area on the line. My contention is that a good new "grid" system would have an even greater pull than a "corridor" system for generating new construction and redevelopment. But more important, for our purposes, the new construction would undoubtedly make the area more dense and close-grained.

If a more extensive system than a "corridor" system might be one alternative that cities are not considering, another that is not looked at often enough is a system that is not quite so high-speed or "rapid," that does not cost quite as much or require grade-separated rights-of-way and therefore does not need particularly high ridership to be economically feasible. Henry D. Quinby, writing in *Traffic Quarterly* in April of 1962, described what he called a "limited tramline." It has particular appeal as a short-term, immediate solution.

Mr. Quinby notes that to purchase right-of-way that is separated from other transportation is often quite expensive. So he talks of buying special right-of-way only where absolutely necessary and using instead any old railroad lines, available open space, and center medians on arterials and freeways (as Chicago has done with its new transit). Outside the central business district the space for the line would be reserved but not necessarily grade separated. He notes that for his "integrated" system you need only 22 feet in the median with 30 to 34 feet at stops. He suggests a train technology that is particularly well suited for trips from eight to twenty miles long with average train speed of from 14 to 30 miles per hour and stops every 1,200 to 2,000 feet. He notes that new electrical systems controls would allow his "tramline" to accelerate and decelerate much faster than the old trains (and he points out that diesel buses could accelerate only two-fifths as fast.) Mr. Quinby's vehicle would be 88 to 95 feet long and nine feet wide, capable of carrying 280 to 330 seated and standing, as compared with 85 in the typical urban diesel bus and 125 in the typical rail transit car. He would couple two together and with frequent headways would be able to carry 34,000 passengers per hour. He suggests that passengers would enter only from the rear and exit only at the front and side, and that a two-man operation would allow tickets to be collected while the tramline was in motion (switching to a one-man operation on light hauls, with car-borne information signs).

It seems to me that Mr. Quinby's basic contribution is to show us how flexible our technology is. With larger cars, slower speeds, ticket-collecting-in-motion and no need for grade-separated rights-of-way, he has developed a less expensive system but one that would provide superior service to old trolley or bus systems. It is not as exciting for engineers to create such an in-between system or to think up rear-entry-side-exit type of solutions to speed up boarding. But Mr. Quinby is well aware that for the typical bus rider, the in-motion time consumes only 41 percent of the trip. Waiting and boarding time take 20.9 percent; loading stops take 12.5 percent; and traffic stops (mostly lights) take 12.2 percent; while 13.6 percent of the time is taken walking to and from the stops. Obviously, any vehicle that can make significant reductions in boarding, loading, and traffic-stop times is going to pick up more speed than new mechanical technology, however exciting it might be. Such analysis seems to be beyond the ken of those building or planning new rail transit systems, just as the potential of a "grid" system has passed them by.

There is also new technology under development that has the potential to deal both with the "grid" system and with the problem of having to wait for other passengers to get on and off. The concept is "personal transit" and it is opposite the concept of "bulk transit." Most new systems conceived and tried on the public have been "bulk transit" systems in which *many* passengers are simultaneously served by a single vehicle. "Personal transit" would consist of small vehicles, each carrying about the same number of persons as an automobile. These vehicles would travel over exclusive rights-of-way, over standard routes, automatically routed individually. Empty vehicles would be recirculated automatically to maintain an inventory at each station. Passengers could be routed past stations without stopping. Propulsion could be in the vehicle or in the guideway itself, electric or other kinds. Each guideway could be extremely narrow—about five feet wide and could be a single lane over much of its length. Privacy and security would be provided (although human interaction is reduced) and automation could make "personal transit" safe. The greatest amount of development work is needed for automatic electronic controls that would maintain safe and reliable headways. The problem is occasional necessity for emergency stops, and such emergencies shouldn't cause accidents.

When describing in such glowing terms a system that has not yet been built or tested anywhere, but that exists, in paper terms, in at least twenty different places, it is necessary to recall our starting point for this discussion. When trying to decide whether or not to develop personal transit, one must look past estimates of operating service and price levels to the income and social characteristics of the prospective users and to the social and economic costs and benefits of building and operating the system. If developed as a true "grid," by sensitive community planning teams, personal transit has enormous possibilities, particularly since it would take so little space. Disruption of communities could be minimized.

Before leaving the subject of rail transit, I want to make it clear that I don't want to seem too hard on rail transit "corridors." I would much rather see our society spend money on rail transit systems than on highways, even if they are as poorly designed as BART, and even if they serve only well-to-do suburbanites. And it is not really fair to claim that such systems are passé, as both auto enthusiasts and transit visionaries do. General decline in mass transit patronage (from 18,981,000,000 revenue passengers per year in 1945 to 13,845,000,000 in 1950, to 6,616,000,000 in 1967) has blinded critics to some rather remarkable "success stories" by rail transit corridor systems. It would be nice to be able to cite the new transit systems in Toronto and Montreal as successes. They are that. But there are several factors that make the two Canadian cities poor comparisons with U.S. cities and poor guides for what could happen here. In Toronto, the Yonge Street subway and its extensions, as well as a new rail system for commuters, have been subsidized by government at a 70 percent of total costs rate, without taxes, and there are few U.S. cities where this even approaches being the case. But more important, population densities in the two Canadian cities far exceed anything in the U.S. In 1961, the last year good figures were available, Montreal had 9,300 persons per square mile, and 26,400 persons per square mile in its central city (of about 1.4 million people). Toronto had 8,200 persons per square mile and 20,580 persons per square mile in its central city (of nearly one million people.) New York was far and away this nation's densest city with 7,462 persons per square mile and 24,697 persons per square mile in its central city. No other U.S. city had more than 6,600 persons per square mile or more than 16,000 per square mile in its central city. Many were far under that. Since 1961, U.S. cities have been decentralizing at a rate far more rapid than Toronto and Montreal, due in large part to the fine transportation systems those two cities have. In 1966, for example, prior to a huge new commuter rail extension, Toronto not only had 870 buses and 334 rapid transit rail cars (fifth on the continent) but it had 845 street cars and trolley coaches, far exceeding any other city on this continent.

Probably the most unqualified U.S. success came shortly after the opening of a new 14.5 mile rail line from Lindenwold, New Jersey-to-Camden-to-Philadelphia. The $92 million line was built by the Delaware River Port Authority along old railroad rights-of-way. Operated by one man, the trains run no longer than twelve minutes apart all day long (four minutes at rush hour) and go up to speeds of 75 miles per hour, making the trip from Lindenwold to downtown Philadelphia in 22.5 minutes. Six new suburban stations were added and 55 new rail cars purchased before the line was opened in February of 1969. With fares between 30 and 60 cents, it began with 17,000 passengers daily, increased to 21,000 passengers daily in May, and by August of that year was up to 24,450 passengers per day. The increases were enough to put it close to break-even by the end of its first year of operation.

Two side effects were impressive. The U.S. Department of Transportation was so surprised at the success of the line that it quickly planned to help it with feeder bus accommodations. And there was a substantial real estate boom along the line, particularly near Lindenwold where Rouse Co., developers of the Columbia, Maryland, New Town, unveiled plans for a 392-acre, $80 million "downtown-in-the-country" development. It was originally to include hotels, offices, four department stores, 150 stores, and some 2,000 apartment and townhouse residences by 1976.

While the Lindenwold economic success is probably unmatched by any other new U.S. lines in recent years, other cities have been proving rail transit isn't dead. In Cleveland, the privately-owned and operated Cleveland Transit System decided to extend one of its lines 4½ miles to the airport (again on old railroad rights-of-way) and add three suburban stations. The extension, completed in November of 1968, made Cleveland the first city in the nation with downtown-to-airport rail service, at a cost of $18.6 million. Within a year after opening, some 12,000 passengers a day were going through the new stations and 3,500 per day were going to the airport station. However, many users of the new stations were using transit before, and the total system in Cleveland picked up only 5,000 passengers per day in the first year, 50 percent below expectations. Too, people using private cars to get to the airport largely continued to do so. Taxicab service, on the other hand, fell sharply. Others considering airport extensions ought to take a close look at Cleveland for another reason, for once again bad coordination of the transit system with the surrounding environment is a problem—in this case, the transit rider getting off at the airport station has a 360-foot walk to baggage check-in counters, across a busy airport roadway, through turnstiles and up an escalator, a difficult trip if the rider has heavy baggage. The transit system has only been able to get one airline to set up baggage check-in counters at the station.

While it is probably a strategical mistake to cite anything connected with the ill-fated Penn Central Railroad as being successful, the new high-speed Metroliner trains between New York and Washington, D.C., instituted in January of 1969, have to fall into that category, at least in economic terms. While we have largely been dealing with intra-urban commutes, the Metroliners are inter-urban, or between cities instead of within them. The distinction, however, is not as clear as one would think, since the entire East Coast is quickly becoming nearly completely urbanized and many passengers, on airlines as well as the Metroliners, have daily "commutes" between cities there. In any case, the Metroliners do demonstrate that rail passenger transportation isn't dead. For, in the first six months of the service of the high-speed trains that reach speeds exceeding 110 miles per hour, there was an 11 percent increase in passengers in the New York-to-Washington rail corridor, the nation's busiest. And non-stop ridership between the two cities jumped 72 percent, largely at the expense of air shuttle service. Nor did the Metroliners simply rob passengers from the regular runs, as some observers had feared they might. In fact, the number of passengers on conventional Penn Central trains on the route rose about one percent in the six-month-period. This, combined with the Metroliner growth, "represents a reversal of a steadily downward trend in passenger service since we first began keeping such records in 1953," a railroad spokesman told reporters.

The Metroliner trains each have six cars, with a total of 308 seats per train. In the first six months, about 250,000 passengers rode the trains, accounting for $2.5 million in revenues. For the 226-mile trip from New York to Washington that takes about 2½ hours on the train, a passenger pays $25. Eastern Airlines' shuttle service was charging $36 when the Metroliner commenced service (and cab fares are much higher from the airports). The planes are still beating the trains in speed, even with the longer cab trips to downtown points included, but food is offered on the trains, music is piped in, and seating is not five across. All three factors have made some luxury-minded passengers favor the trains over the East Coast air shuttles that have no food or music, but do have five across seating.

An experiment in the Chicago area has proven, albeit on a much smaller scale, that high-speed trains aren't necessary to bring the passengers back—comfort and service will do. William Butterworth, who runs a travel agency and likes rail travel, in 1968 persuaded the Rock Island Line to put a club car on its passenger train's daily 180-mile trip from the Quad Cities area on the Iowa-Illinois border to Chicago and back. The trip takes just over three hours each way, about the same as driving time, but slower than the airlines. It leaves the Quad Cities area at 8:45 A.M., gets back at 9:00 P.M. Mr. Butterworth charges $18.80 for a round-trip ticket, about half the air fare of $36, and his price includes breakfast in the morning (usually bacon and eggs) and steak or trout at night. With emphasis on good service, luxurious surroundings, and cleanliness, the club car was breaking even on its expenses—getting about eight paying passengers per day, at last check.

Just like the Penn Central, you can hardly call the overall Chicago Transit Authority operation successful, either. Its fares went up to 40 cents in 1968 and ridership dropped dramatically. But, you do have to give the CTA credit for its innovative service expansions. In 1969 it completed construction of fifteen miles of high-speed rail transit routes built largely in the median strips of the Kennedy and Dan Ryan expressways there. The costs—some $107 million—included $18,750,000 for 150 new air-conditioned, stainless steel cars. But the credit should not go so much to the new rapid transit lines, but the way the Chicago system planned to use them. Knowing that its patronage on bus lines had been declining much faster than on its rapid transit lines, it decided to use the new rail rapid transit lines to duplicate existing, heavily used bus lines. For example, of the 102,000 daily rides it planned to achieve from the new Kennedy rail route, it planned for 67,000 to be continuation of the bus route in that line and 22,000 to come from new bus-transfer rides. With the buses it took off the line it remapped 40 percent of its surface bus routes, meaning 49 different and new bus routes, a very substantial upgrading of its bus service. By carefully choosing the new transit routes it was almost guaranteed a ridership (from previous bus patrons) to make the new routes pay. The expansion ought to serve as a model for how a coordinated bus, rail transit, and freeway system (even if coordinated because of Richard Daley) can be designed to produce dividends.

If we are to use rail transit as an alternative to the automobile and highway system we can't be mesmerized by new systems and new equipment, however. Indeed, such an approach leads to thinking almost solely in technological terms, as illustrated in an article in the February 24, 1969, *New York* magazine by Craig Hodgetts and Lester Walker, two young New York architects. The magazine introduces the article by saying the two young men, "attempted to free their minds—for the purposes of this study—from political, sociological, and economic considerations and concentrate purely on what can be done to make cities manageable. . . ." The authors propose three basic ideas: 1) "a strip city," hardly a new thought, between Boston and Washington, 2) construction of the high-speed "Bos-Wash Landliner" that moves through this strip city, spanning highways and swallowing moving buses, and 3) pre-fabricated, flexible low-cost housing. To reverse "the effects of urban suffocation," as the magazine says the authors propose to do, I suggest we free our minds instead from this technological sophistry and concentrate on political, sociological, and economic considerations. That is what is needed.

The old-fashioned, outdated Cable Car is a beautiful example of just how unimportant our technology is. San Francisco has 39 of them in service and every year they carry 13 million happy passengers over their 10½ miles of track. They are not particularly rapid, and accidents on them are too common, but they are a joy to ride on, and their very existence adds immensely to San Francisco's tourist appeal, making them worth every dollar of the $1.7 million San Francisco loses each year on their operation. Even without considering the added tourist income, the pleasure they give and the charm they add to The City make them worth the money.

Sometimes, of course, our technology could simply be used to make the transit ride pleasanter and more enjoyable, instead of making it faster or more efficient. Then it might make more sense. Richard Howe, a St. Louis commercial artist, has conceived a "no-windowed bus or rail car with a totally controlled environment." The driver can't be seen and the riders face sideways. There are movie screens on the side walls and earphones for "personalized sound." The medium could educate, entertain, or provide information. Howe thinks shopping centers should develop such vehicles to bring people to their centers. The shops in the center could be certain of reaching the buyer with advertisements just prior to his arrival. I'm not sure I favor this last idea, but the idea of using new technology to make the trip more pleasant is an appealing one, and transit shouldn't leave it solely to the airlines.

To some people, it makes sense to divide urban transportation into motorized vehicles—buses, taxis, trucks, and private cars being the primary examples—and non-motorized transit—railroads being the prime example. But there are many other ways of traveling within a city that aren't "automotive" and yet are not railroads either. And as their potential is optimized, the automotive types of transportation are needed less. Here are four that come easily to mind:

1. Bicycles. In Amsterdam, 150,000 people ride bikes to work every day. Thousands more commute by bicycle in other European cities, and in Asia and Africa. The cost is roughly one percent of driving the automobile. Climatic conditions can cause problems, but bicycling, in whatever weather, is good for the health. Even today, in many of our larger cities, during the rush hour it is faster to get downtown, from ten miles or less, by bicycle than automobile. The most serious hazard for a cyclist is venturing into traffic, and as a result, many cities, recognizing that bikes pollute less, are quieter, and take up less space than autos, have begun to set aside "bikeways." Chicago now has 36 regularly traveled bike routes. You can cycle from downtown Boston to Cambridge on a bicycle path along the Charles River. Milwaukee has 64 miles of marked bikeways. Cities all over Florida have designated bike routes from suburbs to downtown, and one Florida bank has even established pedal-in teller windows.

2. Conveyor belts and moving sidewalks. At the time of writing, San Jose, California, was considering a conveyor belt, actually a futuristic system of endless bins, vehicles without wheels moving down a belt made up of powered

rollers contained in a fixed track. If San Jose decides to buy the system, it would pay $5 million for an 8,800 foot system, 4,400 feet running each way from periphery garages into the heart of downtown. The system has two speeds and couples with a moving sidewalk for entry and exit. The speed of the moving sidewalk at entry is 1.5 miles per hour and the "bins" move alongside the walk, also going at 1.5 miles per hour in the loading area. Then when the "bins" leave the station with passengers, they speed up to 15 miles per hour.

Most moving sidewalks presently in use are slower than walking speed: 90 to 180 feet per minute versus 290 feet per minute walking speed. In the future, however, accelerated conveyor belts will operate at speeds of six to eight miles per hour, and will save passengers ten minutes per mile traveled. These high volume, continuous systems that can carry up to 36,000 passengers per hour are not yet in use, but designs for them promise they will be reliable, silent, and economical. The longest moving sidewalk in use in the U.S. is one of 420 feet at the Los Angeles International Airport. In a Paris Metro station, three 600-foot-long belts parallel each other. Made of tempered spring steel and moving at 150 feet per minute, together they can carry 12,000 people per hour.

3. Electric golf carts. Over 42,000 electric-powered golf carts are made in this country every year. Selling for up to $1,800, they require a battery charge once a week or so if used regularly. Westinghouse makes a model that will go 25 miles per hour, but the vast majority of the carts now made will travel only from 10 to 12 miles per hour. California has legalized their use on streets where speed limits are below 25 miles per hour. The obvious advantages are small size and no air pollution. Low speed also means increased safety.

4. Walking. This most ancient and honored means of travel is now being encouraged around the world, sometimes even at the expense of automotive travel. Pedestrian malls are increasingly a "modern" sign of urban planning (one should note that Jane Jacobs disapproves of them, feeling that they are often lifeless places. She would encourage walking where the action is, and that is *usually* on streets used by autos.) In Minneapolis, downtown Nicollet Street was recently

closed to all but pedestrians, buses, and delivery vehicles. Too, in Washington, D.C., vehicular traffic was recently banned from one of the capital's busiest downtown streets. In New York, the pedestrian has recently been encouraged by "instant pedi-malls" created on mile-long stretches of Fifth, Madison, and Lexington Avenues on weekends and week nights during parts of the summer, fall, and Christmas shopping season. The carbon dioxide count on some auto-less streets fell by as much as 90 percent, while the average noise level shrank from 78 decibels (shouting level) to 58 decibels (conversation level).

But while walking, use of bicycles, golf carts, and moving sidewalks ought to be encouraged alongside rail rapid transit, we still have to deal with realities. Those realities include a vast investment in highways and in the "automotive" vehicles that use them, roughly divisible into four categories—trucks, buses, taxis, and private autos. This investment has brought with it a commitment to continue the system's use unless the benefits of replacing it with a better transportation system can justify use of funds when weighed against other choices—education, welfare, corrections, or whatever. This means that it is very unlikely we will be able to make wholesale changes in our urban transportation system, and as I've noted before, it's probably undesirable anyway. So we have to resign ourselves to working with the "automotive" vehicle and the highways they use, trying to make changes on a piecemeal basis.

Recognizing one of our goals to be the development of close-grained, rich, diverse cities, it is better to bring about the attrition of private cars than it is trucks, buses, and taxicabs, because private cars are the heart of the problem. Other classes of vehicles—trucks, buses, and taxis—lend themselves to a desirable urban scale to a greater degree than do private autos. Since their numbers are less, they pollute less and cause fewer accidents on highways. They are not the cause of the erosion of cities in quite the same way as the private passenger vehicle. An important principle is that each of these vehicles competes with the other. If you favor buses or trucks or taxis, you work against the private auto. True, buses cannot bring about the attrition of the private car as effectively as rail rapid transit does. Buses, trucks, and taxis all use our highways. They all pollute, and they all add to safety problems on the highways. They aid and abet the oil industry, as well. But there are degrees of evil, and degrees can be important.

Too, those who favor mass transit must remember that over 70 percent of mass transit is now performed on highways, by buses.

But it is easy to make a case for buses. Fewer people understand the value of trucks. They crowd passenger vehicles off streets. And as Jane Jacobs says, "Trucks are vital to cities. They mean service. They mean jobs." Where trucks carry materials, men do not have to travel by passenger cars to get the materials. The inefficiency of trucks in cities is due in good measure to their being slowed down by competition with so many vehicles. "If the inefficiency becomes sufficiently great, the enterprises concerned may move or go out of business, which is another aspect of erosion. . . ."[10] says Jane Jacobs.

She suggests that we go about encouraging trucks, that we designate streets which only trucks can use (the reverse of common practice in most cities), and that we give trucks the fast lane of freeways. If we encourage trucks, she says, they will do their own self-sorting, in which long-haul vehicles would use fast arteries and short-haul trucks would use narrow, clogged streets only for pickup and delivery.

She also takes this theory one step further, by suggesting a "post-officing" system originally devised many years ago, she says, by Simon Breines, a New York architect. In this system all freight and deliveries into a central city are sorted, much like mail is sorted at a post office, with all the deliveries to one location being bunched for one trip. The distribution to points within the central city is thus "rationalized" and far fewer delivery trips are required. The reduced number of deliveries and dispatches can then also be made at night, when traffic is considerably less. The separation between trucks and passenger space thus becomes a separation in time, rather than in space.

Jane Jacobs makes the case for encouraging trucks and improving their efficiency. The case for buses hardly needs to be made beyond the case for transit that I have already tried to make. The question is, How do you encourage buses and bus systems to improve their efficiency? And the corollary to this question is, Why haven't the necessary and obvious changes been made before this?

There are three basic improvements that can be made in bus service. They are pricing, speed, and routing improvements. What rules have "free enterprise" bus systems discovered that apply to the economics of their business? If they have to make a profit, they have discovered that higher prices reduce ridership at a rate that often eventually eliminates profits from the price increases, but lower prices don't produce enough ridership to make up for the lost revenues, so lowering prices increases losses too. However, if bus companies could be looked at in terms of total public systems, it might quickly become clear that the losses absorbed by *publicly-owned* bus companies from lower fares would be meaningless. Higher ridership from lower fares would mean fewer people driving private passenger vehicles, and thus less need for expensive new highways. But privately-owned companies can't consider this fact. And publicly-owned companies have no political "reason" to consider the State Highway Department budget levels and how their bus operations can affect these. This is perhaps the strongest reason for unified departments of transportation that include common management of transit and highway funds. For the alternative is to have what we have now—both privately-held and publicly-held bus companies driving off riders by increasing fares. And the decision to increase fares being taken only in the light of the revenue needs of the bus operator, be it government or business.

Few bus companies have developed reasonable pricing systems. The main problem with the economics of the bus business is that ridership of buses occurs during peak hours, when people are going to and from work. This means that, in terms of both labor and equipment, there is no spread of use over time. Too many buses and too many drivers sit idle during off-peak hours. If buses would charge extremely low rates during off-peak hours, they could serve a valuable public function, and equipment and workers would not remain idle, collecting no revenues, during these hours. But there is seldom a difference in off-peak prices. There are many other ways to develop off-peak business. Bus trips to and from major evening sporting events are common in some cities, and weekend charter business is promoted. Also, *Esquire* magazine suggested in a recent issue[11] that, just as passenger planes can now be quickly and economically converted to freight planes for some flights by removing all the seats, buses, too, could be used for highly-profitable night-time freight deliveries. This idea seems to me to hold outstanding potential for failing bus systems. No longer would bus companies have to hire a work force for all day just to use them for two hours in the morning and two hours in the evening. Those two-hour-blocks of time could be at the beginning and end of nighttime freight delivery shifts.

The speed of buses is not important simply because passengers will use buses more readily if buses take less time. It is also an economic matter for the bus companies. Decreased bus speed increases operating costs. If buses are slow, fewer fares can be taken by the same driver and the same bus during the period of time the bus is in operation. Many times, increases in speed over a route will enable the same bus and driver to take on a second profitable route and reduce the equipment needs for a bus system—the number of buses it needs to serve its routes and passengers.

How do you increase bus speed? There are several obvious ways. The most obvious, and one that John F. Kennedy promoted in his transportation message of 1963, is the special bus lane on busy streets or freeways. On the San Francisco-Oakland Bay Bridge, for example, a test of a special bus lane found it cut the buses' time from 25 to 13 minutes crossing the bridge. On downtown Peachtree Street in Atlanta, Georgia, a special bus lane increased the speed of buses from 4.6 miles per hour to 5.8 (and the speed of private cars went from 6.3 to 10.5 miles per hour because stopped buses no longer stuck out into the middle lane.) But, if simply moving people is the objective, a highway engineer will argue, the *typical* bus lane on a high-speed expressway or freeway will not carry enough people faster by bus to make up for the longer time it takes people in

private passenger cars to cover the distance with the lane reserved only for buses not accessible to them. The answer, of
course, is that our objective is *not* solely to move people faster,
but to get them out of their private cars and to enable our bus
systems to operate economically. This may be more truly "economical" than moving people faster.

There are two adaptations of the exclusive bus lane approach.
One is the curbside special bus lane (often in peak hours only)
running *against* one-way traffic. Jane Jacobs has discovered that
when streets are made one-way in New York, bus ridership falls
off perceptibly, presumably because there are a certain number
of "marginal" riders who refuse to walk the extra block to the
bus stop. If bus lanes can run against one-way traffic, this
fall-off can be prevented. The second adaptation is the "bus-
way," or highway only for public transit, built because it is
both cheaper and more flexible than rail rapid transit. "Bus-
ways" would seem economical only where headways, the times
between buses, were particularly short, and ridership thus very
high.

Other special privileges can be provided for buses to speed
them up, as one E. Rockwell proposed in the *British Transport
Review* in August of 1962. Allowing buses to turn across traffic
where other vehicles can't, giving special treatment to buses at
police-controlled intersections, and extending "stop-lanes" for
buses into intersections (allowing a space for buses to accelerate
getting away from the traffic light and giving them the legal
right-of-way).

Many proposals for speeding up buses involve traffic lights.
Buses could be allowed to start on special amber signals that
preceded the green, Mr. Rockwell suggests. And Jane Jacobs
notes that William McGrath, traffic commissioner of New Hav-
en, Connecticut, deduced that buses would be speeded up by
regulating the traffic signals to short intervals and not staggering
them. As she says, "Owing to the corner pick-up stops required
in any case by buses, the short signal frequencies interfere with
bus travel time less than long signal frequencies. These same
shorter frequencies, unstaggered, constantly hold up and slow
down private transportation, which would thereby be discour-

aged from using these particular streets. In turn, this would mean still less interference and more speed for buses."[12]

Sumner Myers in an article in *The Architectural Forum*, January-February, 1968, proposes that traffic signals be equipped with special "transponders" and that buses carry equipment that matches these transponders and informs the transponders how many people they are carrying. The signals could then make adjustments to allow buses carrying more people right-of-way at the crossings. Such a system has already been experimented with in Los Angeles. It does make more sense to count "people" instead of "vehicles" when considering regulation of traffic speed, of course.

Besides developing more rational pricing systems and speeding up buses, the other area for major improvements is in routing. Indeed, ridership has been found to respond more dramatically to changes in either the location or frequency of routes than any other factor.

Far too little analysis and market research is done by bus companies. To make decisions about routes, zones, and charges, express versus milk-train runs, seats-for-all versus standee policies, the need for advertisement (such as mailing of schedules to potential customers in the service area), a great deal of information is required about demand for services, and about origins and destinations. The highway department in most states collects such information regularly, but it is seldom utilized by bus and transit companies. And what information a bus company collects about who currently rides its buses can tell it little about demand for new routes that might exist. A good market research program would provide data about car-ownership, income, place of employment, and number of persons employed per household, all of which would be extremely helpful in designing new bus and transit routes that would meet real community needs.

The newest innovations in bus routing or marketing are three: "driver-employed" non-profit transit, subscription bus, and demand-actuated bus systems (sometimes called dial-a-bus).

The "driver-employed" non-profit transit approach is being tried in Los Angeles where three small non-profit corporations established and controlled by neighborhood associations are being utilized. Their objective is to provide a sort of "bus pool" composed of a driver who works at a plant and others who want to travel a route somewhat similar to his. Each corporation also employs a local manager and part-time paid drivers to start routes and fill-in in emergencies. This approach has some of the same deficiencies of regularly scheduled bus routes to serve the ghetto, notably the fact that once residents find work they buy their own cars. But it is a way of dealing with the high labor costs involved in serving highly diverse route demands with small buses.

The "subscription bus" method was tried first in Peoria, Illinois, then in Flint, Michigan. The subscription approach provides guaranteed seats to monthly "subscribers" who are picked up right at their homes and carried either to work or to another bus stop that takes them to work.

In Peoria, the experiment was something of a success. Thomas H. Floyd, Jr., a Department of Transportation official, reports:

> Cost data from the Peoria project showed variable costs being covered by the end of the fourth to the sixth month, and total distributed costs by the end of the thirteenth month. Seat utilization went above 90 percent on some routes, at fares averaging $2.83 per month per mile for the average 7.0 round-trip miles per day (or under $20 per month, or under 50 cents per one-way trip).[13]

When the program really began to pay for itself in Peoria, the federal experiment was ended and local funds didn't pick it up and expand it.

The results in Flint resulted in quite a bit of bad publicity for the idea of a "subscriber bus." A story by Paul Ramirez in the *Wall Street Journal* was typical. It was headlined "Scorning the Bus. Luxury Transit Service Fails to Lure Commuters From Autos in Flint. Test is Flop Despite Comfort, Door-to-Door Runs..."[14] Mr. Ramirez describes the stereophonic music, air-conditioning, and the "Bus Bunnies" who sometimes rode the bus to take complaints. But, he says, "This city's 100,000 commuters have been offered bus service like that for the past year. And they've stayed away in droves." All the efforts, he reports, lured only 300 riders a day from their autos, and the 26 buses (dubbed maxicabs) used on the runs were losing $200 a day apiece.

The Flint experiment made two rather obvious mistakes, one of which Mr. Ramirez fails to point out, and the other which he leaves until the last two paragraphs of his story.

The first was setting its sights too high. The buses it used held 40 seats apiece. Why not mini-buses until the demand for the service was confirmed? Without the $1.9 million in federal grants the company received, this is the way any normal concern might start such an operation, with a reasonable chance for success.

Secondly, why Flint? The self-contradiction in this paragraph written by Mr. Ramirez is so apparent as to be ridiculous: "Such a dismal record is particularly puzzling in this town of 220,000, which would seem to be a natural for rapid transit. Of Flint's 100,000 commuters, 75,000 are auto workers who are employed at only eight different factories. With that concentration, the maxicabs can pick up passengers at their homes and deliver them right to the factory gates." In short, the people expected to shift from their autos live in a town, the economy of which is almost wholly dependent on the auto. Not only are most of them members of the working class, whom any sociological survey will confirm are most hung up on the status symbol, sex symbol, and power symbol of the auto, but they are also further brainwashed by being employees of the auto industry. Did the people who conceived this experiment expect this fact to have no effect at all? Is it with such minds that the future of transit innovation in the United States rests?

The third significant innovation—demand-actuated rapid transit, sometimes called dial-a-bus—has yet to be tried in any long-range experiment. But, to me, it appears to be the most attractive idea put forth to date, both in terms of what it can do, and how quickly and for what expense it could be implemented in our urban centers. Most importantly, *it would institutionalize a service which has the ability to respond readily to changes in travel demands.* It can also be easily hooked up as a feeder service to high-speed rail and express bus transit and, indeed, could be the key to loading these fixed-route services so they can attain their full potential as movers of many people. For example, one could, theoretically, direct a dial-a-bus to a continually changing rendezvous point with an express bus or rail car, thereby reducing waiting time and the inconvenience of transfers. It would also be quite easy to operate flexible fare policies for different classes of dial-a-bus customers, operating some low-cost subscription service, and other high-cost, taxi-like service.

In general, the ideal system might consist of a computer into which calls for service would be fed. It would know the location of each of the ten-to-fifteen-passenger vehicles and the destination of each of the passengers in the vehicles and the (corrected) schedules of all other transit in the area. The computer would figure which bus to assign to the new caller, and a communications center, which has an automatic vehicle locator and a two-way radio system, would relay the information to the driver.

The federal government has been busy designing dial-a-bus experiments, and General Motors Corp.'s research laboratories have been worried enough about the possibilities of competition from such a system (and the possibilities for sales of vehicles since GM sells about 85 percent of the country's buses) to make several extensive simulation studies of a dial-a-bus system and how it might work in a typical community. GM selected a case-study city with an area of about six square miles, a population of about 200,000, and population density of about 4,700 persons per square mile (not particularly dense). To get simulated ridership figures, it interviewed 1,000 people. The report, written by Herbert Bauer, says that a dial-a-bus system could be implemented if it had a 50-cent fare, fifteen minutes maximum waiting time, and a travel time no longer than twice that required to make the trip by automobile. Such a system would divert about 15 percent of the approximate 175,000 daily (weekday) trips to it and would result in a peak-hour ride demand of over 2,000 requests, requiring 178 vehicles, the study concludes. Mr. Bauer notes that the study was of a community where better than 90 percent are now using autos and are thus, he claims, the most difficult to divert.

The General Motors research labs study makes one other very important point besides the general conclusion that such a system is highly feasible. The profitability of such a system, if operated without public subsidy, would be highly dependent on wage rates. It is a highly labor-intensive system, requiring many drivers, and probably requiring them for split-shifts. Mr. Bauer says the wage rates used for the simulation in this case study were, however, as high as they would be anywhere in the country, and this, too, is a hopeful sign.

So, I have suggested a series of ways in which bus systems could be improved. To be locked in a cycle of higher prices and deteriorating service, both in terms of speed and routing, is inexcusable. Yet, in fiscal 1969 and 1970, 41 transit lines folded in cities of less than 100,000 population. In places like Joliet and Danville, Illinois; Owensboro, Kentucky; Evansville, Indiana; Saginaw, Michigan; and Albany, New York, the bus lines simply closed. Labor and equipment costs go up and so fares go up and so ridership declines. Suburban sprawl just accelerates the whole situation.

So, occasionally, does dishonesty. Consider the situation in Portland, Oregon, where the bus company for years cut back on routes and increased fares, until finally it was taken over by a special state agency formed specifically for that purpose. Portland Transit Inc., had two major subsidiaries. One of them, Rose City Transit Co., operated the buses and was regulated by Portland's city council. Another subsidiary, Landport Co., owned the buses and the real estate, and leased them to Rose City Transit, but was not regulated by the city council for some unknown reason. The council, while service declined and fares rose over a long period of time, never required Portland Transit to present a consolidated balance sheet. Yet a Portland State College professor, when interviewed by a local business editor, explained that while, "The holding company got the benefit of the accelerated depreciation (on the buses one of its subsidiaries owned) ... the operating company (regulated by the city) used a different rate of depreciation." The professor noted that the parent holding company was holding an enormous $2.5 million in cash on hand, although it was theoretically valued at only $3 million, and that it had been earning about 28.6 percent return on its investment, while the city had given a bus franchise to its subsidiary, allowing about 4.5 to 6.5 percent return on invest- ment. Such hanky-panky by private owners of bus companies to insure their return while the consumer of their service suffers has not been all that uncommon. But, on the other hand, the ineptitude of public agencies running bus companies has some- times been even more damaging.

One of the things that is clear from any study of buses is that it would not be too difficult to make significant improvements that could reverse the cycle of declining patronage and deterio- rating service. Another thing that is clear is that some of the changes suggested, notably going to smaller buses and making them demand-actuated, could make the bus systems more like taxi and jitney systems than bus systems. So, it is probably a good idea to take a close look, at this point, at our taxi and jitney systems in the United States. And closely related to taxis and jitneys are car pools.

In each case, the need for every person to drive his own private passenger vehicle is considerably reduced. Taxis, jitneys, and car pools decrease traffic by utilizing vehicles at a higher rate. Higher utilization of vehicles means lower over-all costs for society, and reduced traffic and reduced need for private cars is the objective I have tried to support throughout this book. Sarah Rosenbloom, of General Research Corporation, presented a paper on taxis, jitneys, and poverty at the Transportation and Poverty Conference of the American Academy of Arts and Sciences in June, 1968. She notes that in most American cities we have, by legislation, not by the free market, severely limited the operation of taxicabs and jitneys. For example, we fre- quently don't allow taxicabs to provide service in which they "share the ride" among several passengers who are strangers. And jitneys, traditionally holding 12 or 14 passengers and operating along fixed or semi-fixed routes with fares calculated at fixed rates per zone, aren't allowed anywhere to speak of in the United States. Too, all but three of our major cities severely restrict the number of taxicabs they allow to operate, limiting competition and holding cab fares at an artificially high level. In a study of 17 cities, Miss Rosenbloom notes that where *no* regulation of the number of taxicabs exists, the number of cabs per thousand people is significantly higher. In unregulated Atlanta, there were 2.7 cabs per thousand people, in Honolulu, 3.2, and in Washington, D.C., an amazing 13.3. No other city studied, and all of the rest were regulated, had more than two cabs per thousand people. More than half of the 17 had less than one cab per thousand people. Obviously, deregulation of taxicabs provides more cabs and better transportation, and, incidentally, lower prices. As a political matter, the companies would probably have to be compensated, at least in part, for the effects of deregulation, however.

Outside of the United States, she notes, jitney service has become quite important, even after the onset of the automobile era. Thus, in Caracas, Venezuela, jitneys carry 500,000 passengers per day, out of an estimated 2,700,000 travelers, while buses carry little more, 800,000 passengers per day. She suggests that other cities should adopt Washington, D.C.'s highly successful "Minibus" jitney approach, run by the D.C. Transit system, in which fares are low, the vehicles have wide doors and windows and hence "charm," and runs are frequent. A heavily-used business section that is spread over a wide area is probably a necessity for such a service to succeed without subsidy as Washington's does, she adds. But she notes that there would not necessarily have to be operation by public agencies. Instead, a simple "free market" could be set up and jitney operators could be private entrepreneurs, using their vehicles off-work as well.

An important side effect of allowing jitneys or deregulating taxicabs is providing hundreds of jobs in each city where this occurs. She estimates that an expansion of vehicles by 2½ times would be typical. Thus the driver force could be expected to expand at that rate, as well. She notes that in a city like Philadelphia this would mean an additional 7,400 jobs as drivers. The jobs pay only from $100 to $150 a week, but can carry with them the added benefit of an auto for private use.

Miss Rosenbloom says little about encouraging car pooling,

aside from taxis and jitneys, but it has equally beneficial possibilities. It remains a little more difficult to accomplish, however. There are two ways in which we might proceed to encourage car pools. One is through a small tax credit allowed larger corporations for workers who arrive regularly via car pool. It would be assumed that the companies would pass some of this tax credit along to their workers, and would encourage car pools, also, via sign-up sheets and studies of residence of their employees, etc.

Another opportunity for government encouragement of car pools exists when there are toll bridges. San Francisco is an excellent example. Currently, commuters coming into San Francisco by, say, the Golden Gate Bridge, can buy monthly tickets that reduce their fares, even though they come one person per car much more frequently than do non-regular users of the bridge. This, in effect, discourages car pools. If the bridge charged less for cars in which more than one person rides, down to nothing, for a full car or a bus, it would be in the business of encouraging car pools. (It should simultaneously double the cost of all of its fares and eliminate the toll booths on the side of the bridge in which the people are leaving San Francisco, as has been done on other California bridges and some in New York City. This would eliminate the labor costs of taking tolls both ways and would vastly speed up traffic going out of town. But the revenues from the bridge would remain about the same. Such logic, as I have been trying to point out, is beyond the ken of our modern highway-engineer-types, like those who run the Golden Gate Bridge.)

In discussing alternatives to the pure use of the private passenger vehicle, I am now down to two: adapting the private car (and bus) to dual-mode use and penalizing the private car. First, let's take a look at the possibilities of adapting the automobile. Essentially, there are two—dual-mode vehicles and pallet or ferry systems. Making autos dual-mode could take place in any one of a number of ways. Some designs simply see the freeways becoming automated, with overhead, electrically-run "guides," for example, that allow cars to go at speeds of up to 60 miles per hour, with very little space between, and a vastly more efficient use of space on the freeway. Other systems envision the construction of narrow "guideways" that contain the motivating power in, say, an electric third rail. Autos (and buses) would then simply be equipped with gadgets that allow them to be hooked onto the guideways. They could travel at high speed upon the guideways, and would not necessarily need such large, powerful, high-speed, polluting engines when off the guideways. In some dual-mode systems, the designers suggest that there would *not* be personal ownership of the vehicles, but that vehicles would be "turned in" at the end of some trips to be utilized by someone else instead of spending expensive idle time in a parking lot or garage.

While it is obviously less expensive to turn today's autos to dual-mode use than to build and establish an all-new system of vehicles and track, the pallet or ferry system goes the dual-mode concept one better: the vehicles wouldn't even have to be adapted, just loaded onto rail cars, for example. The typical design of a pallet system calls for rail lines that now exist between, say, the suburbs and downtown, to be supplied with special pallet cars that can be quickly loaded and unloaded with up to a dozen autos for rapid line-haul operation during the rush hour. The driver would simply stay in his car as it is transported downtown or home at high speed. Automated loading and unloading would obviously help.

In a take-off on the concept, McDonnell-Douglas Corp. designed a pallet system for St. Louis in which the pallets are levitated by air pads for frictionless support and run by a linear electric motor. After the driver drives onto a pallet and indicates his destination, he is shot down a ramp into a subway. The system uses the force of gravity to provide for acceleration of pallets to line speed of over 60 miles per hour. Upramps are used to decelerate the pallets. The system McDonnell-Douglas designed had a capacity of 9,000 cars per hour and would cost between $15 million and $21 million per mile, depending on the frequency and capacity of stations along the way. The company's study found the system to be more expensive than a subway, and with less capacity, but more flexible because people could drive their autos on and off it.

None of these dual-mode or pallet systems have actually been built yet, one should point out, but they do offer the potential of making auto travel faster and more efficient and requiring less space for roadways, as well as improving safety and reducing pollution.

Let us suppose, in our search for alternatives to the automobile, we find a community that is highly receptive to making changes. Let's imagine it would, in that community, be politically plausible to penalize use of the auto. Jane Jacobs has already suggested some ways we might go about it. Eliminating parking and standing on streets, adjusting the traffic signals to slow cars down instead of speed them up, widening sidewalks, and closing streets, are all ways she suggests that have been applied in recent years in U.S. cities. I haven't heard of cities developing dead-ends to thwart the use of certain streets as arterials, or actually creating mazes with traffic diverters to make it nearly impossible to drive through certain neighborhoods unless you know the way. But these ought to work too. Increased use of traffic bumps that require cars to slow down or else do damage to themselves are another tactic that is little-used. All of these tactics could be applied now in communities that want to get away from the auto and develop cities that are really cities. As Jane Jacobs points out, though, we must keep in mind that "the point is not attrition of automobiles *in* cities but rather the attrition of automobiles *by* cities." When something is taken away from the auto, a benefit of another sort should be provided to the community—a park, or a widened sidewalk, for instance.

But, hopefully, at some point enough political power will be generated against our automobile system to begin a rational discussion of flow-control or pricing systems on our roadways, whether or not such restrictions provide any benefit other than reducing traffic. Obviously, buses and trucks ought to be given preference in getting onto our freeways, for example, and flow control at access ramps would allow this. And, during peak hours flow control at access ramps could keep enough people off the freeway to make sure the freeways work as well as they are designed to work. Flow control would be even more efficient if combined with automation, of course.

What would be even better than flow control, however, would be a pricing system. In some cities, this might be achieved, in part, by taxes on all-day downtown parkers, for example. San Francisco has just initiated a tax on its downtown parking lots and structures.

But it would probably make more sense to place a toll on the facilities that are actually congested—the highways—to keep cars off them which don't absolutely have to be there during the congested hours, or aren't willing to pay to be there, because they can make the trip at another hour. A system has been designed that would place machines at access and egress points on major roadways and would take pictures of license plates of cars entering and leaving the freeway. Then, at the end of the month, a bill would be sent to the owner, with fees differentiated for use of the freeway during rush hours. There is quite a rational economical reason for making such charges. As I have noted before, when cars use a congested highway, they add to the congestion and slow down other cars, and if they are forced to pay for use during typically congested hours, they are paying for the congestion they cause by being there. The problem with a pricing system, of course, is that the very poor are hit hardest and such a system must be designed to provide for welfare considerations, too.

In this admittedly rather lengthy discussion of alternatives to and penalties on the automobile, I have mostly been discussing tactics in a vacuum. A cover article in *Newsweek* magazine on January 18, 1971, makes an indisputable factual point that I have passed over in discussing tactics—that commuter rail facilities in the East and Midwest have been deteriorating rapidly and are in desperate need of funds, and it therefore makes no sense to proceed elsewhere first. We must simply try to save the alternatives now in existence, because it is undoubtedly cheaper to do so than to make many of the changes I have suggested in this chapter.

But in applying the tactics I have suggested as alternatives to the auto it doesn't seem to me that the specifics of the situation will much alter the basic need for some variety of such tactics. John R. Meyer argues in *The Metropolitan Enigma*[15] that in newer and smaller, more auto-oriented cities of the West, for example, it doesn't make sense to try to do anything but make the automobile work. I would disagree with this radically. In every city in the United States, the auto needs to be discouraged and alternatives need to be encouraged. It is a matter of fitting the tactics, whether they be dial-a-bus, a network, grid system of personal transit, or a simple widening of a sidewalk, to the specifics of the situation, considering what is politically possible and what people can be mobilized to do. San Francisco might be able to pass a billion-dollar bond measure for transit, and surely not every city in the nation can do that. But San Francisco couldn't meter its freeways with a pricing system yet. And, on the other hand, there aren't many cities where simple improvements in bus efficiency, speed, pricing, and routing wouldn't be easy to achieve. What is important is that we force the political system to narrow the options, and not allow the technicians to continue to do the narrowing for the politicians. So let us proceed to discussion of politics.

NOTES

[1]Meyer, *The Metropolitan Enigma.*

[2]George Hilton, "Growth in the Metropolitan Region: Time, Space and Commuting in California," paper presented at the annual meeting of the California Chapter, American Institute of Planners (March 16, 1967).

[3]Karl Moskowitz, "Living and Travel Patterns in Automobile Oriented Cities," paper to Automobile Manufacturers Association Symposium, Detroit, Michigan (October 23-24, 1962).

[4]Edgar Z. Friedenberg, "In the Cage," *New York Review of Books* (September 3, 1970).

[5]Ronald A. Buel, "Some Farmers Strive to Curb Urbanization, Not Sell to Developers," *Wall Street Journal*, p. 1.

[6]Emil M. Mrak, "Food and Land: The Coming Shortage," *Cry California* (Summer 1966).

[7]Burton Wolfe, "Why BART Is Broke," *The San Francisco Bay Guardian* (August 30, 1968).

[8]John Burchard, written statement to the press (February 15, 1967).

[9]Robert E. Alexander, "Too Little, Too Late, Too Bad," *Cry California* (Spring 1968), pp. 7-13.

[10]Jane Jacobs, *The Death and Life of Great American Cities*, Vintage Books, Random House, p. 365.

[11]The Editors, "An Electric Solution to the Traffic Problem," *Esquire* (February 1969), pp. 63-67.

[12]Jacobs, p. 366.

[13]Thomas H. Floyd, "Urban Transportation to Alleviate Poverty," paper to Transportation and Poverty Conference, American Academy of Arts & Sciences (June 7, 1968).

[14]Raul Ramirez, "Luxury Transit Service Fails to Lure Commuters From Autos in Flint," *Wall Street Journal*, p. 1.

[15]Meyer, *The Metropolitan Enigma*.

CHAPTER 9 POLITICS

Faced with the problem of encouraging alternatives to the automobile, probably the most difficult step is the first and most necessary one—obtaining recognition of the problem. People are very slow to admit the nearly complete dominance of the automobile in the face of the serious difficulties it causes our society. For this is recognition, finally, that our corporate system and the institutions that support it are very resistant to change.

The size, the significance, the irreconcilability of the problems the automobile causes us is a very important point. Hardly anyone wants to admit the strength of the grip that the large institutions that constitute and support our corporate system have us in. Most of all, the people who control and operate and benefit from these institutions do not want to admit it.

As a result, much is made of exceptions. When the SST is stopped, when San Francisco stops a freeway, when Walter Hickel orders that an oil company pay for a spill, when Ralph Nader gets General Motors to modify their automobiles, there is much publicity. The media zero in to tell us all about it. The people who know the truth in their hearts and are compelled by their own personal interests to compromise with "the system" find emotional release in the "victory." But, more often than not, the "victory" is hollow and without real substance. Things

212

march on and those desiring change find that they are continually dealing with symptoms, and never getting close to a cure. They have to fight the same battle all over the next time.

Hopes for real change, for a more even distribution of wealth, for saving the environment, for creating cities in which people can live together, rest upon the ability to move the corporate system. The old ways of doing the changing—the liberal-labor-South coalition, for example—clearly are no longer working. A new coalition from entirely new sources is required. That coalition will not spring full-born from the way things are going now. It will be created only by education, by changing attitudes. It will require a new level of sophistication, if not commitment, from its members.

The problem is not just that people don't know how to change things. They don't know who has the power to change things. Furthermore, they don't know which action will achieve the goals they desire. Civil rights legislation didn't produce racial amity. The war on poverty didn't do anything but provide a few more jobs in the government bureaucracy. Welfare has hardly eliminated poverty.

If one wishes to stop a freeway, who can do it? The state legislature, the governor, the city council, your congressman? Or if one accepts the inevitability of the freeway, where does he go to make sure the expertise is provided to make it the best possible kind of freeway? More importantly, how do you get people to recognize that it may be both possible and proper to stop the freeway or keep it from destroying the communities it passes through.

The new level of political sophistication required by our technological revolution, our increasing size, and the vast increase in political alienation that has already occurred among a segment of our society, is frustrating.

For the means are not at hand to *rapidly* produce the political sophistication required by this complexity. To move the corporate system would require mobilizing government against it, producing a significant frontal attack from the scientific-educational-research segment within the coroporate system itself, reinvigorating the labor unions or reviving the democracy once inherent in our political party system and our electoral politics.

The only way one could mobilize government would be to produce a change of attitude among a vast segment of the populace, to make it a movement of people—from local government up. For power politics—the negotiation, compromise, wheel-and-deal politics that has become the rule—will not move the corporate system. The corporations, and only the corporations, have the means to play that game and win it. The vast shift in public opinon can come only from education—by our schools, by our communications media, by our political leaders, and participation in the political process itself.

Similarly, it is only through education, the media, or politics that the values of those in the scientific-education-research segment, or the values of our labor leaders and party functionaries, can be sufficiently altered to make a difference.

Let's briefly discuss the problems with our educational system, with our communications media, and finally with our political process that makes it difficult to use these as tools to get the political sophistication that would enable a new coalition to move the corporate system in new directions, or to completely fragment the corporate system as we know it, with its monolithic size and control.

Our schools and universities are sometimes thought to be our best hope for change, for shaping the kind of thinking individuals who not only desire a better society, but know where to start on it. There are two problems with the idea that our elementary and secondary schools are our hope for change. One is that, more often than not, they are dull, lifeless places, more concerned with discipline and control than teaching and learning. The teachers are required to take all sorts of useless "technique" classes in college and are seldom given any idea of what the life of the mind is about. When a teacher is good, it is unlikely that he will find himself in a school where the student-teacher ratio, the textbooks and other resources, or the attitude of the administration, is sufficient to the task. He is inhibited and beaten down. However, many schools are now adopting "open classrooms" where teachers allow students to progress at their own pace, investigate what interests them, and, in short, design their own educations in an individualized fashion, with the necessary minimum of guidance. Many schools are developing team teaching and volunteer, uncredentialed aides, both techniques to lower the student-teacher ratio. Modular scheduling has been widely adopted, making the allotment of time spent in classrooms flexible and elastic, instead of rigid and confining. Schools are being opened up to the outside world, made over as community centers, with adults encouraged to use the facilities. And many schools are increasingly using the "real world" as a classroom, getting students out of the school building and into real life situations.

But such changes as these, important as they may be to improving education, will not do the job, as far as providing the major impetus for societal change. One reason is that by the time six-year-olds get to school their personalities and psychological make-ups have already been established by their basic environment, their families and friends. The schools can seldom make truly basic changes in values, personalities, or psychological make-up of the students.

Schools must do their job within a context. At most, students spend little more than one third of their waking time (not considering summers) in school. The average American student, by the time he graduates from high school, has spent as much time in front of the television set as in the classroom, for example. The school that manages to develop a program that truly educates, that gives students an understanding of their society and themselves, does so *despite* the larger social context. Poor students still go home to split families. Middle-class students are still bombarded by consumerism. All are faced with the shortage of worthwhile work that is both useful and meaningful. Tom Wicker, columnist of *The New York Times*, says that when he was a boy he had to bring the coal in every night or his family would not be warm. His children have no such way to be "useful," he says. And many of our students leave high school to go to fight and die in a war.

The schools cannot end the war, feed the hungry, create useful work, or provide alternatives to the automobile. They can only begin to help shape people who will do this. And, meanwhile, they must exist in a country that is still fighting wars, failing to serve the hungry, and capitulating to the automobile.

Our universities and colleges are a second part of the story. More than the elementary and secondary schools, they have managed to step outside of society, to create their own campus worlds. As a result, they have long been the source of social innovation in our society, and they continue to be. This, of course, does not mean that the nearly half a million college and university teachers in the country have the *power* to innovate, to carry out their ideas, to substantially alter the larger structure of society. They *can* apply sanctions that affect the choices of career by their students. And, since, on the fringes, the members of the corporate technostructure melt into the scientific and educational estate that is centered in our institutions of higher education, the academicians can influence policy in other ways. The scientists who are at the forefront of technological change in the universities must, to operate there, be influenced by their colleagues in the humanities and classics, for example, and are liable to attempt to move the corporate structure, which needs their talents, in directions it doesn't want to go. So the power given by the creativity possessed by the scientific and educational estate does provide some leverage to change the society.

But the students who come to our colleges and universities are even more fully developed and less amenable to significant changes in values than those entering our elementary schools. And the ability to directly affect the corporate system has its drawbacks, too. Because "the system" supplies so much of the money for scientific research, and because it substantially controls the government from which higher education must also obtain funds, the corporate system has much influence on higher education. The corporations often dictate that their funds, or the funds supplied by the state, be used to supply talent that will respond to the goals of the corporation and participate with it and in it.

There is one further problem. The traditional operating style of higher education is inimicable to widespread social change. The "life of the mind" has traditionally been thought by educators to be the prerogative of a few. If higher education were really to begin to provide the means for implementing the innovative thought it produces, the ideas of narrow "disciplines," of undemocratic teacher tenure, of putting research and publication ahead of transmitting the knowledge and the desire to learn and grow to others, these ideas would have to be examined and altered on an extensive scale. It often seems to me that academicians find their work, and thus their lives, self-justifying. It is because of this that we, as a society, put more energy and effort and time and money into the study of how to destroy other human beings, for example, than into the study of how to limit that destruction. One is always just a little bit surprised to see Cal Tech and MIT among the largest recipients of "defense" contracts from the Pentagon. It is just as possible for a scholar to lead an unexamined life as it is for a plumber.

So if we are counting on education or higher education to change society, we had better stop.

One could hope that if education itself can't, then the communications media might contribute to the sort of broad-based sophistication that is required to move the corporate system. The problem is that the press, those involved in the mainstream of the communications media, have an unbreakable engagement with the society as it is. They may carp and nitpick within limits, questioning society's efficiency, but they do not question its values.

It is hardly a new idea to suggest that today's press does an inadequate job of examining society. Murray Kempton recently wrote in *Washington Monthly* that, with journalism as it is, "all the information seems to be misinformation." Norman Mailer said as early as 1962 in a *Playboy* interview that, "The mass media . . . give people an unreal view of life. They give people a notion that American life is easier than it really is, less complex, more rewarding." And Andrew Kopkind wrote in the *New York*

Review of Books that reporters "take on the ideological colora-
tion of their surroundings . . . Journalists . . . like the managers,
the union leaders, the foundation directors, the teachers and
students—are indoctrinated by the institutions they serve . . .
Dissent is allowed, even encouraged, as long as it is irrelevant to
change. Resistance is out of the question."[1]

Michael Arlen, in his fine book, *The Living Room War*, gives
us an excellent analogy:

> Father has left the house and the children have some new
> toys and are threatening to knock the house to pieces, and
> all that would be all right, it would be manageable, if we
> could somehow get inside the house and really find out
> what was going on, could sit down and try to understand
> the children, listen to them, at any rate if we could confront
> what it was that they were doing (let alone thinking about),
> but as things are, we make this big thing about how we
> know everything that's going on—*nothing* escapes us, be-
> cause we too have new toys, which tell us things—but what
> really happens is that we sit outside the house and every
> now and then a maid comes out onto the porch and stamps
> one foot lightly for attention and then reads us a brief
> announcement, and we sit there looking thoughtful or impa-
> tient and listening to the sounds of breaking furniture from
> somewhere on the second story. At a time when the ability
> of a people to order and enhance its existence depends
> increasingly on its ability to know what is really going on
> . . . we've given up the ideal of knowing first-hand about
> ourselves and the world in favor of receiving sometimes
> arbitrary and often nearly stenographic reports through a
> machine system we call "communications" which for the
> most part neither recognizes the element of chaos in the
> world for what it is nor is able to make contact with it
> except on a single narrow-beam wave-length.[2]

Journalism is inadequate to our needs because the corporate
system influences and controls the institutions reporters work
for and deal with. One need hardly dwell on the diverse corporate interests, of both a military and industrial nature, possessed
by the three companies who own the three major television

networks (and 15 of our largest television stations). Nor is it necessary to talk about the sources from which newspapers and magazines and television and radio derive their income. Neither is it necessary to explain at length the nearly total disinterest of government in trying to insure the independence of our communications media.

It is important, though, to be specific about how the press is influenced. The respectable establishment press makes a great deal out of how advertisers have no influence over editorial or news decisions. And it is, for the most part, true that a single advertiser has almost no power whatsoever. Thus, a newspaper finding crookedness in one of its large advertisers, might have no compunctions about detailing that crookedness. (Indeed, this is the kind of thing that, for a reporter, might produce journalism's highest rewards, right up to a Pulitzer Prize.) It is not simply that by writing a story about such crookedness, a story that usually defines such crookedness as a deviation from the normal way our society works, a newspaper would only be alienating a portion of its revenue support. The point must be made that the story doesn't endanger the status quo in any significant way. It doesn't generalize to the other advertisers, or to our society as a whole.

Someone had to decide, for example, that Thomas Dodd's personal use of money from testimonial dinners was a story about Dodd, not about the way the system works. When congressmen recently were forced to report some of their outside financial holdings, someone had to decide to report that story in terms that made it clear that Congress doesn't play by the rules of the rest of society, instead of demonstrating this is the way our society functions. And so it goes.

It is not that such handling of stories is clearly "dictated" from above. Just as decisions to purchase Brand X detergent are not "dictated," the reporter is not told how to report his story. Instead, there is a subtle indoctrination, an indoctrination that is reinforced by sanctions that the corporate system perpetuates in our media. Journalists who play by the rules get the pay raises, the promotions, the "choice" assignments. The illusory freedom of the reporter to report what he's interested in and write it in the way he sees fit, is seldom directly contradicted. The reporter's work is almost never censored directly or edited openly for its "slant." It doesn't have to be. For the reporter who wants to succeed is taught the traditional journalistic formula. He must keep himself out of the story, make it as impersonal as possible. He must work on the "cognitive" level of communication, rather than the "affective" level. That is, what is of interest is that x said y, not that x had a frown on his face when he said it, that the tone of voice of x seemed to convey that he didn't really believe what he was saying, or that y was an outright lie. And the reporter must, above all, be "objective." No matter that there are fifteen different sides to a question. The reporter must act as if there are only two sides and he is walking a path down the middle between the two. No matter that the myth of objectivity breaks down in each of the five different aspects of journalism—1. data assignment (Who decides what is worth covering and why?) 2. data collection (Who decides when enough information has been gathered?) 3. data evaluation (Who decides what is important enough to be put in a story?) 4. data writing (Who decides what words to use?) 5. data editing (Who decides which story gets a big headline and goes on the front page, which stories to leave out of the paper, which stories to cut, which stories to change?) Obviously, all the decisions are subjective. The reporter and the editor *ought* to strive for the sort of detachment necessary to put what they are doing in a larger context. But that is not "objectivity" as the editors now are encouraged to see it. The editors now worry about a reporter smuggling his opinion into a story and remain oblivious to the need for judgment.

There is the further problem that the traditional journalistic formula supports the notion that all news is of one substance, as Irving Kristol has pointed out. Only the magnitude of news differs. A one-alarm fire is reported in the same way as a revolution. Journalistic competency renders superfluous any true expert knowledge. One need only be a good reporter to do any story in any subject field, and so all journalists are generalists, and they should not specialize. This way, it hardly needs to be said, our complex society is seldom dealt with in its complexity.

There is still another problem. Since journalists do not have the reward of doing what they know to be a good job, they seek their satisfactions elsewhere—like the status value that derives from possessing inside information. Any reporter can normally tell you significantly more about a story than he has written. For the reporter soon finds that the "beat" system gives him a stake in his sources. As Kopkind says, "A reporter who must continue to cover the War on Poverty is not going to antagonize his best sources by exposing the frauds and futility of their programs. He will accept the top officials' perceptions of their work, and criticize only within narrow terms."[3] He will be rewarded by gaining membership in the inner circle of those who know what's happening and why.

Summing up, the communications media fail to educate people to how our society functions, to explain it in proper perspective and in its full context. It doesn't make sense of what happens and why. Instead, it adapts itself to the goals of the corporate system. The media give the illusion of dissent and controversy. But formula journalism disarms the critic. The reporter must be "impersonal" and "factual" and "objective." He must be a generalist and he must protect the sources on his "beat." If he doesn't he will not get the raise, the promotion, the choice assignment. Just like the members of the techno-structure, who adapt to the goals of the corporate system in order to increase their power by being part of the larger force of the organization, so, too, does the journalist adapt. And we are all losers for it.

If we cannot now look to our educational system or to our communications media for the impetus for social change, can we look to the political process, or to our political leaders?

Anyone who thinks that the political process, as it now exists, holds the seeds of our salvation, or that our current crop of politicians are our saviors, had better re-examine that situation, too.

One should start by looking at the obstacles to change that the corporate system has thrown up. The large sums of money spent on elections by the corporations, money spent to elect people who have internalized the goals of the corporate system —growth and progress. This amount of money simply can't be matched by those outside the corporate system. We should look at the extensive involvement of our current elected officials with the corporate system: the lawyers who still have companies as clients; the conflicts of interest that exist in the stock holdings or other types of business ownerships by politicians. Too, we should look at the huge lobbies that the corporate system finances, whether they are in front groups, such as the American Automobile Association, or whether they are the paid lobbyists of say, General Motors or Standard Oil.

Let me try to detail, speaking from situations that I know best, how the corporate system currently controls local, state, and federal governments, or at least controls the areas that it cares about.

The area of power reserved to local governments that probably matters most to the industrial sector is the power to control land use. Fremont, California, provides a classic case in point. Here was a "city" formed out of four small towns between Oakland and San Jose, California. Perhaps the sole purpose of the formation, in the eyes of those who carried it out, was to control the urban sprawl that was eating up the prime farmland and devouring the scenic hills surrounding the four small towns. The planners in Fremont hoped to keep development contiguous to existing development. The catch came when a local company wanted to develop a piece of land that wasn't contiguous, that didn't fit with the plan. The right to develop the land was worth quite a bit of money. The planners and the city council stood firm. When the next civic election neared, the company put up its own council candidates, backed them with money, won the election, and reversed the policy. There are few cities of any consequence in the entire country that have developed comprehensive land use plans. Those that have designed such plans usually cannot muster the support for principle necessary to carry the day against people who want to make money from a land use that doesn't correspond to the plan.

When I was a reporter in California, I became particularly interested in the battle between those trying to promote rapid transit and the auto-oil-highway interests. I was able to spend quite a bit of time at the state legislature and the way it functioned became increasingly clear. I was surprised, first of all, by the number of full-time lobbyists representing highway, oil, and auto interests—more than twenty altogether were registered. They included six representatives of California's mammoth oil industry. Al Shults, one of the six, was paid $53,411 for expenses and salary in six months of the previous session, according to the official state records. In a typical month, he was paid $4,500 salary, and $4,000 for expenses. That's for a *state* lobbyist.

I quickly discovered that such publicly-reported activities were only the exposed portion of the iceberg. Front groups were one example of the iceberg under water. The California State Chamber of Commerce normally wouldn't seem as if it should have an axe to grind for either freeways or rapid transit. But the state chamber had formed the California Freeway Support Committee and raised $200,000 for a public relations campaign to boost freeways, and oppose the application of gasoline taxes and auto registration revenues to rapid transit, bills that had been proposed in the legislature. The committee had hired the public relations firm of Spencer, Roberts & Associates which handled Governor Ronald Reagan's successful 1966 candidacy.

The committee's effort was tailored to look like a genuine display of popular opposition to rapid transit, complete with confirming "polls" with questions slanted to favor freeways, and with a number of citizen committees that magically sprang up throughout the state. But, if one inspected the committee closely, more than half of the sixteen appointed members, it became clear, had a direct business interest in the chamber of commerce's political activities. Among that majority were the president of Union Oil Co. of California, the chairman of Standard Oil Co. of California, the president of Western Transportation Co., a Los Angeles trucking firm, and the chairman of Consolidated Rock Products Co., a Los Angeles road materials producer. The $200,000 financing was raised primarily from the oil industry and the state's two auto clubs.

The two auto clubs turned out to be mostly front groups

themselves. Their lobbyists insisted to me that they represented the car owners who made up their membership (the Southern California Auto Association then had 850,000 family memberships, the northern club nearly 600,000). In this guise, they had strongly opposed the application of gas taxes and auto registration fees to rapid transit, not only through their four lobbyists, but through extensive newspaper advertising campaigns and their club publications. A former officer of the Southern California club explained to me that "For nearly 30 years Harry [Henry J.] Bauer, a major owner of Standard Oil of California, firmly ruled the association as president. When he died a few years ago, the orientation didn't change." Directors of both clubs, a working majority in each, had direct oil, auto, and highway business interests. The president of the Southern California club was then an oil company executive and the president of the Northern club was an officer of a roadbuilding machinery distributor.

There were some pretensions of democracy within the auto clubs. They did issue proxies so members could conceivably vote against directors who set the anti-transit policies. But the Southern California club's proxy, sought when one joined, wasn't offered to the member again for seven years, which means the member can't oppose directors or policies he didn't like during that period. The Northern club's proxy was buried on the inside of one of its publications every year. The club won't say how many are returned.

The lobbies and front groups have quite a bit going for them. They have access to money, to fight not only in elections, but ad hoc publicity battles on issues as they come up in the legislature, as the auto clubs did on gas taxes for mass transit. Their representatives are full-time at the legislature. They can "stay with" the things that they care about, get to know the legislators, follow the bills closely, ingratiate themselves with dinners, drinks, favors, and one suspects, a smidgeon of cold cash from time to time. And, as David Hapgood said in an article on "The Highwaymen" in *The Washington Monthly*, "There seemed to be a sociological difference between the highway establishment and its opponents. Those on the establishment side were all male, white, middle-aged, close-cropped. On the other side: the tweedy ladies who defend good causes, the black, the young, and the old (under 40 and over 60), the shaggy, the old-money oddball, the intellectual."

It's not that all lobbyists are crooked or even unethical. Many provide useful information, and never try to "buy" a vote. The problem is that the corporate interests can afford them and opposition to the corporate interests cannot, with the exception of the labor unions, who hardly oppose the corporate interests on every issue. On the matter of more money for highways, for example, the teamsters and the unions that include highway construction workers are definitely part of the highway establishment.

In California, the key man on matters of highways and rapid transit was (and still is at the time of this writing) the senior state senator and chairman of the Senate Transportation Committee, Randolph Collier. The Yreka, California democrat, whose campaign literature calls him "the father of California freeways," has fought rapid transit long and hard. His committee, which members say he runs with an iron hand, killed without hearings two rapid transit financing measures. One would have imposed a special sales tax on gasoline; the other would have increased auto registration fees. The next year his committee held hearings on a rapid transit bill, but it never made it out of committee anyway.

The effect of lobbyists, campaign contributions from private interests, and conflict of interest in private holdings, all rear their ugly heads in the case of Senator Collier. As for lobbyists, in 1962, for instance, he and his wife flew to an International Road Federation Conference in Madrid, Spain, accompanied by Bert Trask, chief California Trucking Association lobbyist and his wife. Mr. Trask also recalls that the couples ran across each other in London and Paris. Who paid for the trip? The Senate, says Mr. Trask. But the chief Senate accounting officer says that's not so. Senator Collier won't comment.

As for the Senator's campaigns, a program for a $100-a-plate testimonial dinner during his 1966 campaign (when his seat was uncontested, for all intents and purposes) sold advertising at

$1,000 a page. Among the advertisers: highway construction firms, the motor car dealers' associations of Northern and Southern California, and a lobbyist for cement and aggregate concerns. The dinner and program netted him over $35,000. He did not spend all the money in the campaign. When I was there it was still sitting in a fund in the bank, being used with some regularity for whatever purpose the Senator saw fit.

As if this weren't enough for a Senator from tiny Yreka, who, like all California legislators, gets paid over $19,000 plus expenses every year, Senator Collier also had another interest in highways. Over the past 30 years his title insurance business, Siskiyou County Title Co., had received considerable business from the State Division of Highways. In the 1964-66 period alone, the division says it gave Siskiyou County Title $28,604 worth of business. Since 1966, the title business was channeled to Senator Collier's company through another concern. In 1966, it seems, a new state code of ethics took effect. The obvious conflict of interest in the head of the committee which oversees the state department of highway budget receiving funds from that department is not all that unusual. In insurance, banking, and other fields, this sort of conflict of interest is found in our state legislatures all over the nation. Most legislatures do not require legislators to report outside financial interests. After all, how does the use of political power to obtain personal income differ substantially from the use of political power to obtain campaign contributions so one can achieve personal success in the political arena? This is how our system works. Randolph Collier is not an aberration.

Our federal Congress is hardly exempt. Everything is just on a bigger scale there. In an earlier chapter I detailed some of the highly profitable conflicts of interest our U.S. senators have maintained in the oil business. John W. Finney on May 14, 1969, detailed in a copyrighted news story in *The New York Times* some of the outside financial interests of members of the U.S. House of Representatives who were required under a new code to report interests in any concern doing substantial business with the government, or subject to federal regulation, if their holdings exceeded $500 or their incomes $1,000. Mr.

Finney reported that banking is the principal outside interest of 90 representatives, including twelve on the banking committee, and six on Ways and Means, both of which handle legislation affecting the banking industry.

He also reported that 77 members, including nineteen on the Judiciary Committee, maintain private law practices from which they receive at least $1,000 a year. Eight members of the Commerce Committee have financial interests in railroads, airlines, radio stations or moving companies, all of which are supervised by the committee. Forty-four members disclosed an interest in oil and gas companies. In short, conflict of interest is commonplace.

It is also certain that the lobbyists are hard at work in the U.S. Congress too. It was hardly surprising to read the United Press International story that appeared on August 3, 1970, reporting that key lawmakers were given "breaks" in the leasing of prestige automobiles, for example. The UPI story reported that Ford Motor Co. leases insured luxury Lincoln Continentals to at least nineteen House and Senate members for $750 a year. Ford said its offer was open only to committee chairmen and senior Republicans. Chrysler was also offering some senators similar cars at similar prices. And General Motors supplies to the government, at $1,000 a year, 33 of its top-line Cadillac limousines for use by key officials in both the executive and legislative branch.

As Rowland Evans and Robert Novak recently reported in one of their syndicated columns, when a strong anti-auto bill goes into committee, it really gets the treatment. When Muskie's clean air bill went into the Public Works committee, "Detroit's Big Four was well represented," Evans and Novak reported. "At one point, a quartet of automotive moguls—Edward Cole of General Motors, Lee Iacocco of Ford, Roy Chapin of American Motors, John Ricardo of Chrysler—were moving together from one senator's office to another pleading for delay."

"Also button-holing senators and staffers," Evans and Novak said, "were the auto industry's two prestigious lobbyists—Thomas Mann, former undersecretary of State, and Lloyd Cutler, a high-priced Washington lawyer. Other organizations represented on the fourth floor were the National Lead Association, the American Petroleum Institute, the Coal Policy Conference, the American Mining Congress, the Manufacturing Chemical Association, and elements of the aviation industry."

The American Trucking Association is another big Congressional lobbyist. It has ten registered lobbyists, including two former congressmen. But the truckers, like most successful lobbyists, don't stop at lobbying. In 1966 and 1968, the Truck Operators Non-Partisan Committee remembered thirteen members of the House Public Works Committee with contributions from $500 to $3,000, even though two had no opposition.

In 1968, the American Roadbuilders Association organized a $50-a-plate dinner for Rep. George L. Fallon of Baltimore, raising $13,000. This included $1,000 each from two Pennsylvania contractors, $500 from a California cement lobbyist, and $850 from thirteen South Dakota road builders.

The Presidential elections and the big Senatorial races are where the money really flows, of course. In 1968, the Republican National Committee and associated bodies spent over $17 million, while the Democratic National Committee spent about $3 million, according to *The Reader's Digest*. (The Nixon Administration's FCC says the figures were $12 million and $7.5 million, respectively.)

I have been talking as if the only effect of all this money is on legislation, but, of course, this is not true at all. Lowell Bridwell, former Federal Highway Administrator, in an interview in *Architectural Forum* said, "Every time I say no to a highway, you can bet there will be a governor, a senator, and some representative on the phone in 45 minutes."[4]

One way to negate the way the corporate system uses its power and money to influence government is to regulate lobbying; that is, to regulate the number of lobbyists per group, the salaries they can be paid, and the expenses that they can legally undertake in their positions. A second way is to regulate conflicts of interest. Pass laws in all states, and on a national level, that rigidly limit the outside holdings of all elected officials. A good start might be to raise all salaries and outlaw both outside legal practices and outside business and stock holding. Ethics committees should also become much more active in our legislative bodies. Finally, limits should be put on the amount of money that can be spent *for* (not by) a candidate on all of our media, and as a total amount in his campaign. When the Republicans spend millions more than the Democrats on national elections, it is hardly surprising that President Nixon would veto a bill to limit campaign expenditures on the electronics media, as he did. But it should not be politically profitable for him to do so, as it is.

With such laws, regulations, and limitations, we will not have changed human nature or the way the rest of our society operates. We will still have candidates who use the electoral process solely for their own personal ends. We will probably not get away from the "cosmetic" nature of our campaigns—the 30-second spot, the two-page information-less brochure, the over-generalized speech, the advertising emphasis on the politician who "cares" as portrayed by film of him listening to other people, as opposed to him stating public positions on issues that demonstrate that he "cares."

Nor will this set of laws and regulations get us away from the sort of government we have now when politicians can benefit by coming down on both sides of every issue, saying one thing one time and the opposite the next time. So as things work now, John A. Volpe, Secretary of Transportation under President Nixon, can get a story in the Monday, March 24, 1969, issue of *The New York Times*, the lead paragraph of which reads that he "is determined to speed up the pace of constructing inner-city expressways." Volpe is quoted in the interview with the *Times* as saying, "There are some people who feel if they object long enough, the problem will go away and the road will never be built. But you can't pour traffic off modern highways into nowhere."

Then, three days later, the St. Louis *Post Dispatch* can carry a United Press International dispatch out of Washington, the two lead paragraphs of which read that Volpe "says it may be necessary to curb the use of the automobile in the nation's cities unless a mass transit breakthrough is achieved within two years.

" 'Some type of mass transportation has got . . . to get into operation pretty rapidly or we do face the real possibility that either we have to shut off to rubber tires certain limited areas within a city or charge a fee to come in there,' Volpe said in an interview."

Take your pick. You can have today's politician on two sides of just about any question and that is not likely to change, either.

I agree with Tom Wicker when he says that the principal and most important aim of today's political leaders is to educate people. Our political leaders have a forum. But by being ambitious and safe they use that forum to misinform and to confuse, to oversimplify and to overgeneralize, to paint black-and-white instead of the necessary gray.

Mr. Wicker, in a recent speech reprinted in the *New York Review of Books*, also calls for a new political leader who is generous and magnanimous, who uses his energies and efforts to educate and to lead our nation into a new politics.

It is not that I disagree with Mr. Wicker that this is the sort of politician we need. Instead, I disagree with his starting point: national politics. Our President, indeed, even our senators or congressmen, are not going to solve our problems. The practices of Congress and the legislative process have become outdated, unable to deal with the complex problems of the day. The corporate pressures I have cited above are heaviest of all on the national level. Money is more important. The senators and congressmen are in Washington and the people are at home, far away. Most people don't even know who their congressman is. As we have grown, the method we use to elect a President has become less and less democratic. Hubert Humphrey could get nominated in 1968 without winning a primary.

What we need instead of Tom Wicker's *one* great, generous political figure, is a whole breed of them. A breed of them willing to spend their time in local politics, without higher ambition. A breed of them not looking for fast results, but willing to build the sort of political involvement and participation by all groups and types of people that insures that, at least at the local level, government will have to respond to people's needs and be financed at a level commensurate with the task. For local government is just that—local. If it does not do the job, people can find out in a hurry. If it does, attitudes will change. People will once again begin to regain their confidence in the ability of government to serve them, to deal with their problems, to bring about the required change. Political participation itself can do the educating that the schools and the media cannot. If that happens on the local level, where the problems are not quite as complex, the corporate influence less pervasive, the people easier to involve, it may some day give us the kind of coalition we need for national and state politics. But it must happen from the ground up. It must be a long, building process, a long period of laying of groundwork. I believe that it can happen. That we can once again have a government by, of, and for the people. That we can move the corporate system. That politics is the way it can happen. That, if the present generation of young people listen to Bob Dylan and "knows its song well before it starts singing," it can give us a New America.

That New America will be an America in which the automobile will play a much different role than it does today.

NOTES

[1] Andrew Kopkind, "Times' Square," *New York Review of Books* (May 4, 1967).

[2] Michael J. Arlen, *The Living Room War*, The Viking Press, pp. 106-107.

[3] Kopkind.

[4] Priscilla Dunhill, "The Freeway Versus the City," *Architectural Forum* (January-February 1968), p. 75.